*I think I could turn and live with animals, they are so
      placid and self-contain'd;
I stand and look at them long and long.
They do not sweat and whine about their condition,
They do not make me sick discussing their duty to God:
Not one is dissatisfied, not one is demented with the
      mania of owning things.
Not one kneels to another, nor to his kind that lived
      thousands of years ago,
Not one is respectable or unhappy over the whole earth.*

Walt Whitman, SONG OF MYSELF.

DELETED

Creature Comforts

JOAN
WARD-HARRIS

COLLINS and HARVILL PRESS
LONDON 1979

590 (HARR)
B10847
15·10·82

Unless otherwise credited, all photographs
are by E. D. Ward-Harris.

Printed in Canada
for Collins, St. James's Place,
and Harvill Press, 30A Pavilion Road,
London, S.W.1.

To
EDWARD
Who
Made It All Possible

And For
BERNARD AND AUDREY OUGH
Our Very Special Visitors

Contents

Acknowledgments

Most authors relegate their husbands or wives to the final paragraph of 'thank-yous' but I feel that my husband must take pride of place. He has not only had to live with the book, which has been bad enough considering that he is an author and literary critic; he has also accepted short shrift during the often difficult years when I have been intensively occupied with the animals in my story, and many others as well. Once the book reached the final draft stage he gave unstintingly of his time and invaluable critical help. Perhaps the greatest feat has been his willingness to subjugate his particular territorial imperative by offering suggestions and criticizing *my* writing objectively and without rancor. Anyone with a knowledge of the jealously guarded territory of animals will appreciate that this has entailed much understanding and patience. Without his help this book would never have seen the light of day.

I am also greatly indebted to Enid K. Lemon, who, when librarian to the British Columbia Forest Service, extended to me not only professional efficiency, interest and practical help, but who also generously lent me many valuable books on wildlife from her own collection.

The late Professor A. J. Wood of the Department of Bacteriology & Chemistry at the University of Victoria, spent many hours discussing nutrition with me. I am sad that I was not able to finish the manuscript and express my gratitude to him before his untimely death.

I am grateful to Dr. Peter Davies who came to help an animal and has remained our good friend.

My thanks are also due to Dr. N. J. Turner for reading the manuscript and making suggestions; and to the staffs of the Reference Sections of the Greater Victoria Public Library and that of the University of Victoria for their patient and courteous help in searching for information.

I wish to thank the editor of the International Zoo Year Book for permission to use material from an article by Dr. Miller Ben Shaul, Department of Physiology and Experimental Animal Unit, Hebrew University Hadassah Medical School, Jerusalem.

And I wish to convey my sincere thanks also to Keith Sacre of Collins Publishers for his many acts of kindness from start to finish of this project.

As I am indebted to many experts — with some of whom I have crossed swords — I wish to make clear that they are in no way responsible for any errors or omissions: these, together with opinions expressed (unless otherwise stated)— are my own.

Ravenshill,
Victoria, B.C.

Prologue

There is a story told in my family that when eighteen months old I disappeared one day and was found by a frantic nanny in an adjacent field happily crawling between the legs of an evil-tempered mare with a new foal. I played for minutes before horse and foal moved away and Nanny 'rescued' me — unscathed.

The story is remembered not because I trusted animals before I could walk or talk — many children do that — but because the unusually deep love and communication with creatures displayed as a child has remained all my life. Hence this book.

The experience with the mare was but one incident of many, and by the time I was about five I was bringing into the house a steady stream of small creatures: mice rescued from the jaws of cats; abandoned kittens; injured birds (which were the hardest to save). The mice climbed the hills and dales of my bedsheets; the kittens slept in my pyjama sleeves for warmth and were fed by doll's bottle. I tended these waifs with such patience and tenacity that my rather horrified mother had not the heart to forbid me to do so — she could see how thrilled I was when the animals lived and were well again. When they died I was devastated and accorded them elaborate burial services, attended in those more gracious, spacious days by whatever nanny or governess had been persuaded to reign over my small existence at the time; a gardner if one was not too busy; occasionally a maid; and always cook, dear warmhearted rock of ages who rejoiced in the name of Hepzibah, was possessed of an enormously ample bosom, and who was my best friend for many turbulent years. To unfailing sympathy she added practical solace from her marvellous sources of kitchen delights.

All these things are still with me in memory, with one especially vivid recollection of nursing and feeding a little brown owl until his broken wing mended and he was released. As I was only six, the splinting was done by my father, who loved animals.

The owl lived in the stables in a cage (which he hated) and the work of cleaning and feeding this brave bundle of soft feathers was left to me. I loved the feel of that little brown bird and waxed proud as he learned to trust my small hands.

That was the beginning — not only of a lifelong love of owls — but of a desire to see all wild things free ....

Chapter One

But there was . . . an Elephant's child — who was full of 'satiable curiosity, and that means he asked ever so many questions.

Kipling, THE ELEPHANT'S CHILD.

At the time this story begins I was living in Victoria, British Columbia, in a small house on a tiny city lot. In short order I converted the ugly rectangular apology for a garden into a blaze of flowers surrounded by tall fences covered by climbing plants to provide privacy. The loveliest feature was water in large free-form connecting pools, and a waterfall. Waterlilies and goldfish completed the transformation.

Ironically, it was here in a city that I saw my first wild raccoon. Equally ironical the fact that, having all my life craved the soft touch and closeness of furred animals, I found myself accidentally breeding slippery, untouchable fish.

It all came about through my " 'satiable curiosity".

A floating water hyacinth purchased from a grower in eastern Canada had interesting-looking roots, and they were being attacked by the goldfish. On lifting the plant to investigate I saw transparent blobs attached to the stiff purple root-hairs. They were goldfish eggs which my fish were frantically devouring.

In hopes of hatching them I transferred them to an aquarium.

Two days passed. The only change in the nursery tank was the cloudy appearance of a few eggs, which were either unfertilized or dead, so I removed them. The healthy ones were globes of clear jelly, about one thirty-second of an inch in diameter.

On the third day there was a dramatic change. Each egg developed a pair of bright golden eyes. The effect in the lighted tank was electrifying: hundreds of tiny eyes glistened among the floating roots.

Curiosity made me put one egg under the microscope, where to my delight it promptly hatched into a tiny fish, curled tail-in-mouth, golden orbs shining from the sides of its head. It straightened itself out in a quick, smooth movement to become a live, wriggling fish so thin and transparent it looked like a sliver of glass. Attached to its underside was the egg-yolk sac, which would nourish it for its first day or two of life.

I slid it into the tank, where it worked its way to the glass side, there to hang until it was strong enough to swim about in search of food.

1

Infusoria, microscopic animals upon which baby fish feed, had to be provided. I took some 'live' water from a ditch, floated a piece of lettuce leaf in it and left it to stand in the sun. After a day or two the water was charged with primitive forms of life. Under the microscope one drop contained innumerable green or colorless creatures of an infinite variety of beautiful shapes. They gyrated and multiplied as I watched — a marvellous, wholly unsuspected little world of living things.

While the infant goldfish were learning to swim after the infusoria, my kitchen became a hive of activity as I experimented with food preparations for when they would need something more solid. After a few messy failures, I succeeded in making a semi-liquid fish food that could be sun-dried on sheets of wax paper, sieved into various degrees of coarseness from a fine powder to the texture of granulated sugar, then bottled. I could have bought fish food, of course, but I have an aversion to commercial animal foods because of chemical additives.

My fish thrived. At first the colorless babies turned greyish, then darkened during the next month to a drab olive brown — the color young goldfish remain for some weeks or months until they begin to turn silver or gold or a mixture of the two, with an occasional jet-black moor or a handsome red-and-white. The darker colors are deceptive. Brown looks black, and the gold is really red when the fish is out of water.

After six weeks in the tank, the young fish were getting crowded and might develop all kinds of fungus diseases if they weren't given elbow room; so I put them into the pools.

Here was a dilemma in the making. Suddenly I was the possessor of some hundreds of goldfish. What to do with them all?

A few friends solved the problem by agreeing to add more fish to their large pools.

In catching the fish we were 'assisted' by Mr. Bentley, our middle-aged, much loved smooth red dachshund. Ever since the originals had arrived he had spent most of his waking hours trotting round the pools trying to catch them, but succeeded only in wearing a foot-path in the gravel and getting a mouthful of water whenever he snapped at a fish. Several times he fell into the deepest pool and had to be rescued, since the sides were too steep for him to climb out on his short legs. He never learned to leave the fish alone and I finally gave up trying to teach him.

My fish population now reduced to manageable proportions, both young and old cohabited amicably and thrived on solid fare: small bits

2

of chopped raw liver, chopped earthworms, hard-boiled egg-yolk, cooked fish, and — the greatest treat of all — daphnia.

A few of our fish were exotic fantails with short, compact bodies and long plume-like tails. Unhappily they swam slowly and rather awkwardly and soon fell prey to kingfishers, but the common variety throve mightily and grew fat.

Then one lovely day at dawn I looked out to see mayhem in the pools. To my astonishment there was a large raccoon sitting squarely on the waterfall. I had no idea they were to be found living freely in the city. He was a fat, full-grown male. One of my precious goldfish was disappearing down his throat. The waterlilies were decimated, flower heads torn off, leaves shredded, petals floating everywhere. He leaned over and pulled at the lily pads beneath which, presumably, he had first seen the fish. Then he slid silently into the water and swam around, feeling amongst the plants. Fortunately the pools had deep pockets where fish could safely hide; when they were built I had thought only of creating places where the fish would not freeze in winter.

I was torn between interest in seeing this new animal and outrage at what it was doing. The black-masked marauder returned many times on several successive days, but finally gave up when he realized that the remaining goldfish were too elusive for his questing hands.

That raccoon did more than tear up my lilies. He rekindled a dormant interest which was soon, and wholly unexpectedly, to create a new life for me.

Chapter Two

The labour we delight in
physics pain.

Shakespeare, MACBETH.

The paradox of having to move to the city in order to acquire an active interest in our local wildlife was only equalled by that of moving back to the country following surgery, when anyone in her right mind (and a permanent surgical collar) would have gone to live in an apartment.

The transition did not occur overnight, and may never have occurred at all had Mr. Bentley not slipped a disc. After an animal-loving chiropractor had successfully manipulated Mr. B's back, I happened to mention that I was losing speed and dexterity when playing the piano.

To cut a very long story short, he X-rayed my neck, didn't like what he saw, and advised me to see my doctor right away. After consulting umpteen specialists I entered hospital and underwent major spinal surgery — in the nick of time. If Mr. B hadn't slipped a disc I may have become a permanently city-bound quadraplegic.

Convalescence was hell. Inactivity was depressing. I couldn't paint. Gardening was out temporarily. Piano-playing was out permanently. I felt imprisoned, and couldn't even climb the walls of my cell.

The heaviest reading-matter I could manage was a newspaper. As the weary weeks of convalescence dragged by I began to look at real estate advertisements as a diversion from the news. Naturally, my eyes were drawn to country properties. I could imagine their scents and colors, the wind in the trees, rain pattering on water.

On impulse one day I rang an advertised number.

The agent mentioned a property he knew I would love — and its price. Far too expensive. I said no.

A month passed. He phoned again to say it was still on the market. Couldn't he drive me out to see it, just for fun?

Half-heartedly, on the strict understanding that it was indeed 'just for fun' and that there would be nothing in it for him but wasted time, I agreed to go. It was mid-November, dark and raining.

I could hardly believe what I saw that day. The triumphant agent showed me round a house that was immediately 'mine'; he led me, half carrying me at times, around a property that, even in pouring rain, seemed the living realization of all my dreams.

Once as a child, wandering solitary in a wood, I came upon an ancient shack beside a shimmering pond. Like an enchanting melody, the scene stayed to haunt my mind. Thenceforth I carried a vision that one day I would live in a house in the woods, beside a pool of water, with animals for friends. Since then my love of trees and water has drawn me to many places, always unconsciously seeking for that solitary hut hidden away in the woods of long ago. Woods, always woods — not sea, nor plains nor open fields, but woods — woods deep, mysterious and wonderful. I had lived in a cottage in England's New Forest, amidst beech trees glorious in antiquity and gold. In a small house lightly girdled by the pines of southern France. In a log cabin darkly immersed in the stupendous forests of Canada. But always these places were rented and therefore set apart from me. Never mine.

But here at last was the home of my dreams, and it was only twenty minutes drive from my husband's office.

The house was perched on ancient rock, surrounded by sweet-smelling cedars and firs. The rooms were spacious, with huge fireplaces; a dream kitchen; and the light pouring through floor-to-ceiling windows dissolved the barrier dividing indoors from out. Below the house lay a large sheet of shimmering water. And on the other side a swamp, ideal for the right kind of wildlife. At one end of it a spring-fed pool which would make an even better home for my goldfish than their present one.

The land could be allowed to remain in its natural state, wild and free. Even now, I felt certain, there were creatures lying hidden, watching us intrude upon their ancient domain.

There were plenty of places where they could be hiding. Beneath the high canopy of Douglas firs grew a tangled mass of salal — a tough, leather-leaved semi-shrub which is common everywhere in the forests of coastal British Columbia. It grows from a foot or so to head height and is important to animals for protection and food. Beneath the salal Oregon grape grew in profusion. There were many ferns, from the tall stately 'sword' to graceful little liquorice fern, sprouting from fissures in enormous grey rocks, rounded with antiquity. Upon them and the trees grew lichens — green, grey and even cerulean blue where they were wet. Cushions of moss a foot deep covered other rocky outcrops.

The entire picture was an intricate study in greens and greys. The tree-trunks' bark ranged from black through grey to brown. Their crowns of needle-like leaves, dark green and glossy, cast dappled grey shadows on the mosses below.

Beneath them, long-fallen trunks lay rotting, splendid habitats for beetles and the larvae of ants; for ground wasps in summer, and for innumerable other tiny scraps of life.

I have a passion for tiny things, and longed to make an intimate study of the miniature forest-within-a-forest provided by inch-high red-capped lichens, and of the host of mosses, themselves material for a lifetime study.

I leaned against a mossy rock, exhausted. The moment was pure magic.

Just then a small flock of ravens flew into the forest and dispersed among the bigger fir trees, cawing raucously. After owls and swallows, ravens are one of my favourite birds. England, legend has it, shall not fall so long as ravens live in the Tower of London. So ingrained is the belief that during World War II they were hastily replaced when the bombing drove them from the fortress.

The presence in my adopted land of these sable, deep-voiced birds seemed oddly reassuring. And suddenly, unsought, the name for 'my' house swam into consciousness.

"Ravenshill'.

The agent stood patiently, watching me. It was no use my pretending to be hard and businesslike; he knew from my face that I had to have this place. And so he drove me home again to face my husband, Edward, who, to humor me, agreed to look over Ravenshill. He inspected the house next day, while I gazed out at the lake below.

Later, in the car, I said simply "Well?"

Edward negotiated one of the many twists that made the narrow road so charming — and so dangerous. At last he replied gently: "You really want it, don't you?"

"But we can't possibly afford it. Anyway, we've already got a house."

"That's not what I asked. Do you really want it?"

"Mmmmm . . ." — and I burst into tears!

"Stop crying. I think the house is marvellous and you obviously love the whole place. I know you've tried to get used to the city but you aren't really alive there. We can't afford it, but we're going to buy it anyway. What was it Artemus Ward said? — 'Let us all be happy, and live within our means, even if we have to borrer the money to do it with!' "

*   *   *   *   *

To plant a tree and watch it grow gives one a sense of belonging, but I have moved so often I have never known the satisfaction of seeing my

6

gardens reach maturity. Perforce, since I can't stay with them, they go with me — at least as much of them as it is practical for me to take.

In many ways this move was different from its predecessors. Where I would once have undertaken it alone, now I required strong help to transplant partly established trees and shrubs.

Steve, our Hungarian gardener, thought I had blown my mind. ("Ve move dese trees in dis vedder?") But he set to in January rain, struggling against squelching mud which doubled the weight of every tree he dug up.

At last all that remained was to divide the water lilies and net the goldfish. Steve finished the job, bade us goodbye and departed, undoubtedly to take up an easier way of life. I can't say I blame him.

Some gardening friends came to my rescue and everything was transported successfully to Ravenshill, including the goldfish.

Mr. Bentley loathes wet weather but forgot about it in his excitement at watching the fish being transferred. He went slightly berserk, running in and out between our feet as we decanted more than a hundred fish into the big pool by the house. They had time to explore their new home before the ice covered it and then they sank to the muddy bottom, to stay there until spring.

Several wild ducks were swimming on the lake when we took possession and 'our' ravens flew overhead, as though to welcome us. A good omen.

We now had a big house but nowhere to put our books, so we called in a carpenter to build floor-to-ceiling shelves round the living-room. He refused to believe we would ever fill them. A year later he visited us and was dumbfounded to find them overflowing and that we needed more!

After weeks of camping out on garden chairs while the carpentry was in progress, we finally furnished the living-room, put Chinese grass matting on the floors and bamboo curtains at the windows that cast lovely shadows.

Meanwhile Edward had fallen in love with the place and was drawn into planning a garden of sorts, though less elaborate than the previous one had been.

With the help of Mr. Irving The Gardener, a gentle old man with one glass eye who once a week rode eight miles to Ravenshill on his antique lady's bicycle, we created a garden centred round a wide terrace overlooking the lake.

Outside the bedroom window we dug an ornamental pool to accommodate the best of our waterlilies. Later in the year I awoke to see a crowd of young ducks milling about on it, packed like sardines in a tin, doubtless to the dismay of several goldfish.

I had been right in thinking that wild creatures inhabited our woods. Deer came fearlessly to the lawn and ate leaves off our few fruit trees. We didn't care. The thrill of seeing five grown deer so close on my own land amply compensated for the loss of a few apples.

From the first day Ravenshill exerted a quiet and comforting spell. New life seemed to awaken in me, just from breathing in its atmosphere. I particularly loved the evening peace after the last car had passed on the winding road; the night sounds of owls and the morning splashings of ducks. These things filled a deep need in me for intimate association with the continuity of nature's ways, which can be neither rushed nor ordered.

Whilst on holiday in Paris at the tender age of fifteen my father lost everything in the 1929 stock market crash and I was stranded without funds. I remained in France, faked my age to obtain jobs first in Paris and later on the 'wicked' Riviera. My innocence protected me, but it was all pretty hair-raising. However, that's another story. The point is that from those early days in Paris I have led a varied existence, but it has been nomadic. Some missing element had always precluded absolute contentment — and I had to come to Ravenshill to find it.

Sitting on the rocks, soaking in the atmosphere around me, I suddenly realized that I had been a nomad by necessity and habit and not by inclination. At such a moment of revelation the normal thing to do is to up-stakes and rush back to the land of one's birth. But the urge to do so wasn't there. I had become a Canadian citizen and, what was more important, I felt Canadian and had no desire to live anywhere else, so choice of country was not the problem. The problem — the missing element — was the absence of roots and, in a flash of recognition, I knew that fate had brought me to the place where I could sink those roots and rest content; that for me Ravenshill was journey's end.

I thought of the raccoon I had seen in the city and was once more overcome with my old longing to touch soft, warm, living things. For the first time for months I dared to hope that I might yet confound my doctors to the point where I could again do hard physical work outdoors.

* * * * *

As the months passed and winter gave way to spring and summer I went daily to sit on the rocks beside my lake, to dream, to plan, and above all to strengthen body and soul by observing the magical scene around me.

It is not only sleep that 'knits up the ravell'd sleave of care', and I feel sorry for people who lack the inclination or opportunity to unwind beside some quiet pool. There is excitement in observing the reality of nature but somehow it is an integral part of the general peace. Rippling, sinuous curves of a swimming garter snake — through fluid, fluid motion. Polished brilliance of blue or scarlet — a damselfly poised lightly on a reed. Flashing wings stitched with sunlight — two zooming emperor dragonflies mating in mid-air. And best of all the breathtaking grace of that ballerina of the upper air, a violet-green swallow. Picking a feather from the lake's surface, she rises and allows it to fall so that she may dive to retrieve it before it touches the water. The grimmest cares evaporate while watching sweeping flight.

A muskrat swims swiftly, a smooth V-shaped ripple expanding behind his rudder-like tail. He dives beneath a patch of waterweed to emerge half a minute later with the roots still attached to long, straggling fronds of green. Trailing them behind him, swimming more slowly now because of the weight he is dragging, he makes his way to within a few feet of his den in the bank below me before diving again. He pulls the greenstuffs in after him. In his den the roots will stay fresh. The unwanted leafy stems are piled neatly on shore or left to drift in the wind. Often he feeds sitting on the bank or on a log. All his actions are neat and efficient. He looks as though he is doing some very urgent knitting, so rapid is the movement of his little paws as he nibbles the succulent rootstocks. Our three pairs of muskrat are modest little animals who go about their business quietly, bothering nobody. They are particularly welcome for their help in keeping our lake reasonably clear of weeds. They eat small numbers of water insects but are for the most part vegetarian. Little muskrats must make a life of their own at the age of one month, when the parents reject them. They have numerous enemies, which include mink and otter, who raid the dens for the young. Hawks near Ravenshill have learned to behave very much like seagulls following the plough. When our neighbor uses a big machine to deepen his lake and create islands for waterfowl, he disturbs the muskrats who emerge from their dens in dozens and many a hapless ball of soft brown fur loses its life to the sharp-eyed hawk.

On the shore a frog yawns (I saw it happen!). Taking an enormous leap into the water, he swims a few elegant breast strokes, at an angle, so that only his eyes and nostrils are visible. I once watched a large red-legged frog leap in terror from a snake which reared its flat head and several inches of body at right-angles to the ground, only to watch, rigid, as its prey escaped. Later this large snake struggled to swallow a whole young junco it had killed by suffocation. I saw it happen and am sure the little bird died of shock from the lightning strike of the snake's jaws. It did not struggle as the backward facing teeth began to inch the body into the throat.

On such occasions I keep very still, absorbing, observing and thinking; or sometimes just sitting. In the distance I hear a blue grouse courting — a series of strange, low hooting sounds like those one makes blowing across the top of an empty vessel — boom-boom-boom. It is a sound one feels rather than hears.

Exotic as a parrot, a western tanager flies through dark firs, flaunting his scarlet head and bright yellow body with its black back and white-barred wings. His mate, a study in dull green, follows unobtrusively.

Three great blue herons, unaware of my presence, alight in separate trees. Their clumsy landing is performed in slow motion. Six-foot wings flap awkwardly as they let down their long, spindly legs, pushing them forward to grasp a branch. Slow. Careful. If the bird missed its footing it might injure those precious legs which are an essential part of its fishing gear. It has to stand on them for hours, motionless in the water, waiting with eternal patience; then the deliberate stalk forward — one foot raised above the surface, carefully, carefully, with agonizing slowness. Not a drip, not a ripple as it slides in again to become one with underwater plant life. The long neck, until now folded down upon itself, stretches with infinite lack of haste as its owner peers into the depths. Suddenly the poignard beak shoots downwards, and a frog or fish is raised momentarily sideways in the bill before being tossed down the long gullet. At dusk the herons lift their slender grey-blue bodies gracefully and flap gravely to their roosting places, trailing their legs behind them.

On a summer's day these same herons stand on the raft in our duck pool, fishing for goldfish. Underneath the mallards the brilliant reds and orange of a hundred or more fish make an eye-catching sight. They mooch about in small groups just below the surface, diving deep when a duck comes too near. The centre of the pool is deep enough for them to elude most of their numerous predators but there is little likelihood of another population explosion.

Still, spawning time is always dramatic. It is then that Mr. Bentley's interest is reawakened.

On warm May days the primeval drive urges the fish to mate at the curiously specific hours of early morning until noon, but rarely later. Temperature seems to play an important part and one cold, wet summer our goldfish appeared not to spawn at all. The mating fish are oblivious

10

to danger and during their nuptial chases may injure themselves against the sides of a concrete pool.

At Ravenshill their pond is a natural one with plenty of trailing grass on which the females deposit hundreds of eggs. Even as she is in the act of spawning, other fish swarm to devour her eggs: usually more than one male is in attendance to fertilize them and enough survive to continue the race.

One of our fish, larger than the others, had a startlingly bright silver body with head, dorsal fin and tail of deep crimson. He was big, fat, greedy and lazy, and we named him Fred. He was so visible I feared for his life but he always managed to escape the razor bills of the herons to live and love another day. He had sired many a youngster, to judge by the color of some half-grown fish, though none was so red as Fred. He was not only bigger than the other fish, but friendly. He was always first to swim to the corner where I hand-fed him. Mr. Bentley had his eye on him.

He took up his position at the most likely spawning place where the grass was more lush, the bank less steep, the water shallower. Day after sunny day he sat watching the water. Being color-blind like all dogs he had probably singled Fred out because of his size. Time after time I had to fetch Mr. B. indoors when I saw the fish spawning. It was hardly fair to have a canine sword of Damocles poised over their unsuspecting heads.

The inevitable happened. Mr. B. saw his chance and took it. Fred must have been fertilizing eggs, unconscious of anything else. Mr. B. climbed down the bank. I looked out of the window just in time to see the unmistakable red and white of Fred's body disappearing head first down his throat. A few seconds later I would have missed this sight, and never known what happened to him.

I ran out, but it was too late. Mr. Bentley looked up at me, eyes limpid but head bowed in shame. He knew. I remonstrated half-heartedly. The poor old dog had toiled for years to catch himself a fish; I hadn't the heart to punish him. Let him have that much satisfaction. It was one of his few misdemeanors in a long and eventful life. I don't suppose Fred suffered. It was a quick end.

Here swam Fred, killed in action. R.I.P.

Fortunately Mr. Bentley caught only one fish in all his life.

*   *   *   *   *

If we have been blessed with a mild winter we hear the first frog croaking tentatively in the woods and the first one to make himself visible is a red-legged frog (*Rana aurora aurora*), about three inches long, dark brown and glistening as he sits on a comfortable cushion of emerald moss beside his pool outside our bedroom window, to which I had introduced him as a large tadpole.

The real frog chorus, however, starts in March and continues through the summer. The singers are the red-legs and Pacific tree frogs (*Hyla regilla*), who are so small one can sit on my thumbnail and still leave room. As soon as there is warmth in the sun they appear in pairs and trios, quartets, quintets, and still larger choirs. Each makes a sound like a creaking floor-board; once, then silence; then once again. They line up on leaves, on branches, on window-sills. Sometimes one climbs the window, obligingly allowing himself to be studied and sketched from underneath as he holds on to the glass with infinitesimal toes, three on each front foot, five on the hind, equipped with minute suction pads. Some of these frogs are bright green, others buff, or a mixture, and all have a black stripe on each side of the head. They have the chameleon quality of being able to change color to suit their background. One took up a position on the black iron balcony rail, under some overhanging leaves. It took him several days to change from green to almost black — a remarkable sight. These frogs return to the water to breed.

The males emerge to sing their first love songs following a winter-long semi-hibernation in holes in mudbanks or rotten logs. One starts, a single, rasping aaaaargh-aaaaargh; after a second's silence another replies and yet another, until the entire company of hundreds if not thousands are sounding a paean of desire to their ladies — who don't sing. On each succeeding night the chorus swells in volume as mating fervor grips these little creatures, until the din is so loud we cannot make tape recordings in the house, even with the windows shut, without picking up a background of guttural gaspings. Such attractive little creatures who look so oddly and disconcertingly human.

Frog choruses make me think of listening in general and I realize the word means different things to different people. There is hearing; and then there is listening. Listening involves an inner ear which gives depth and meaning to music, poetry, conversation — or a chorus of frogs.

One night as I lay in bed, I became aware of a rhythmic pattern in the chorus to which I had not listened before, although it had always been there. I sensed and felt and was thrilled by the universal pulse, which is apparent even at this humble level of artistry.

The rhythm of the human heart beats in two-time, luff-dub — strong-weak. This strong beat pulses through music and poetry (without it there is chaos) and we feel comfortable because of the responding rhythm in our blood. Until we are attuned to it, we don't feel comfortable with off-beat, polyrhythmic music; we feel tense, hectic, disturbed on hearing most 'rock' music because its beat runs counter to our heart's rhythm.

Sometimes I only hear our frogs. But when I take the trouble to listen to them I become aware of the throb of nature's pulse, made manifest by the duration and sheer monotony of their song. Hour after hour with hardly a pause — save in the presence of a predator, when there is instant silence — round and round goes the ceaseless rhythm: ONE, two, three four; ONE two three four.

Adding their deeper notes to those of the tree frogs, the red-legs sit crouched in their territories around the edge of the pond, where the goldfish live. I found them one by one with a flashlight, and marvelled at one of nature's more grotesque inventions: the monstrous air sac swelling balloon-like under the creature's chin as he sings — with his mouth shut. Frogs cry open-mouthed only when in distress. As long as the frog is singing he stays put. He is not bothered by footsteps reverberating on the ground, nor by having the greenery in which he is hiding disturbed, nor even by my light shining on him. But when he is quiescent his sense of danger seems to be more acute and the slightest movement in his protective covering sends him leaping into the water with a single sqwark.

Frogs are part of an eternal food-chain. Raccoons love them and spend hours feeling under the water for them. Snakes eat them. Owls and herons eat them. Given half a chance Mr. Bentley eats them. Mallards eat their tadpoles — and gourmets eat their legs. Yet still the frogs sing, their numbers apparently little diminished by predation — until the otters come.

I had been amazed to find that otter still live in a big lake not far from Ravenshill, despite speed boats and ruthless homeowners who don't like the messes they make on the rafts anchored at the end of their manicured lawns. But these beautiful, playful animals prefer either deep or running water, so I never expected to see one in our lake.

Every year during the month of July otters visit us. First the dog comes alone. Later his mate with one or two babies. They dive and roll and emerge from the water to amble about the woods, where I find their resting places, and their odiferous droppings. In the water they are the most graceful things imaginable as they quarter the bottom mud for frogs and other delicacies, alternately diving and swimming.

One day I managed to creep within a foot of one of the babies who lay asleep in the sun, to admire the thick, soft pelt, the round head with long whiskers on its snubby muzzle, the rounded feet and strong tail. Then

13

the baby woke up and looked at me out of soulful black eyes, large and round. I was granted a wide pink yawn before it slipped into the water and swam to rejoin mother and sibling.

Another morning a large, bewhiskered dog otter was standing in the water showing half his body; his powerful shoulders glistened. Presently he dived, swimming strongly towards the lakehead, cleaving the surface with a V-shaped ripple. He would find no fish in our lake, but the reason for his visit became clear when I went out to look at the pond. Out of scores of goldfish, only a few youngsters remained.

Poor fish. They had survived in their deep pool and learned to evade their 'normal' foes. But an otter in their midst, who could dive as deep as they, was too much for them. They were not replaced.

*   *   *   *   *

I did confound my doctors. Not only was I able to resume my professional career as an artist but the magic of Ravenshill began to repair me physically as it had already done spiritually. Within a few months of my arrival I felt ready and eager to tackle some new project and, in the odd way such things happen, a ready-made project presented itself without warning in the shape of a baby orphan creature in dire need of help.

Chapter Three

*Nonviolence is the first article
of my faith,
It is also the last article of
my creed.*

Mohandas Gandhi

She came in a carton, accompanied by two friends. By sheer coincidence she was a baby raccoon—one of a pair whose mother had been shot.

We had only been in the house a few months and I was totally unprepared. But improvisation in emergencies lends spice to life and soon I had constructed a large cage and an incubator. Excitement at being involved with an animal made the ensuing pain bearable.

I set this tiny bundle of brindled grey and black fur gently down into warm, reassuring darkness to give her time to recover from shock. Even now, after several days of being cared for by my friends, she was dreadfully thin and dehydrated. When I pinched a fold of her skin, it did not snap healthily back into place. Her fur was dull and she smelt vile from diarrhoea that was debilitating her.

After a long sleep she awoke, hungry and crying lustily. I lifted her to weigh her (she was less than a pound) and she sank a full set of needle-sharp teeth into my hand. She was about five or six weeks old and was to remain a biter for the rest of her life with me.

While she was sleeping I had prepared some slippery elm. This herbal food comes from the inner bark of the red elm tree (*Ulmus fulva*) and is a marvellous standby for humans and animals with stomach or intestinal disorders, especially diarrhoea (commonly called 'scours').

While I was mixing it and finding a bottle I tried to think of a name for this little orphan, whom I had already determined I was going to rear and release. I settled on Vixen — it seemed appropriate: her little masked face was foxy, as was her bushy tail, and she had a rather mean temper.

Vixen took the bottle but spat the contents out, never having tasted slippery elm. So I took her on my lap and gently inserted a finger into the side of her mouth, turning the skin of her jaw into a pocket into which I slowly dripped the mixture. This way there was little risk of being bitten. After an interval I offered her the bottle again and, to my surprise, she grasped it in her two little hands, lay on her back and drank lustily.

In a couple of days her skin became pliable again, and her coat looked less dull. Her scours improved and after three days on nothing but slippery elm, other herbs and boiled water, I gave her a milk formula.

Vixen was too young to climb in and out of the incubator without help, so I hung part of her blanket over the edge to the floor of the cage, which gave her something to clamber up and down by. She was a clean little soul. Whenever she needed to relieve herself, which was often at first, she climbed wobbily over the top and scrambled to the floor, hanging on to the blanket for dear life, and thence to the far end of the cage where I had put thick newspapers. She soiled her bed sometimes but even at that tender age was plainly distressed at doing so, making pathetic attempts to clean herself. I blessed the absorbency of paper towels, with which I had liberally lined her bed.

Her coat of short dark grey fur lengthened and grew silky. Her face lost its rounded, baby look, as her blunt muzzle became pointed. Her round, beady, jet-black eyes brightened, becoming alert for food and mischief. She began to play and I wished she could have had her brother for company. In his stead I played with her. I gave her a piece of knotted rag and she doubled herself in half trying to 'kill' it. She also bit me whenever she had a chance. It wasn't that she minded being stroked or handled, brushed or combed; she simply seemed to feel that since teeth were made for biting, therefore she should bite, no matter who or what was on the receiving end. It was painful but I understood.

After a week in the cage I opened the door to let her out into the room. At first she just peered down from the warm security of her incubator but her own " 'satiable curiosity" eventually got the better of her and she climbed over the side and down onto the table on which her cage stood. From there she tried to reach me, her back feet holding on to the table, front paws scrabbling at the back of my chair. Perilously stretched across the chasm, she let out a frightened howl, which stopped when I lifted her onto my lap. She sat and looked at me, at the room, at the huge expanse of floor.

Presently she climbed down my leg and started exploring, sniffing at furniture and feeling underneath it with her little hands, until, bored, she wailed plaintively to be picked up—yet bit me when I did so. I wondered if the hands which took her from her den had been heavy and hurtful, or whether she had undergone some experience when her mother was killed which had made her permanently suspicious and inclined to bite.

Yet one of her most endearing qualities was her total absence of fear. She had some charming habits, too. She slept either flat on her back with her forepaws clasped firmly over her eyes, or rolled into a ball with the top of her head on the floor, tucked between her forelegs, so that even her ears were invisible: a sphere of grey fur; you couldn't tell which end was which. She learned to roll a marble with great dexterity, chase a ping-pong ball, carry a small piece of paper, and to climb everywhere.

No wonder so many people have made pets of Vixen's relatives — indeed her own brother became one. The cruelty appalls me. They are kept in captivity in the full sense of the word — usually in strong wire enclosures, since they can dig or chew through almost anything. They are sometimes allowed in the house, when the owner is present. Being possessed of a distinct sense of mischief, they can be very trying if left alone to explore. Precisely because of their intelligence, curiosity and intensively active habits, it is dreadful to imprison them. The more active an animal is in its natural state, the crueller it is to cage it. 'Coons seem charming in captivity because they are playful. The reason is simple: their intelligence and desire to be active drives them to play to relieve boredom and frustration.

Therefore I do not believe in making domestic pets of any wild creature, bird or mammal, native or exotic. Even if they have the run of the whole house, they are still caged in spirit.

Vixen, I vowed, should have her freedom directly she was old enough to fend for herself; but without her mother to educate her, she would have to be reintroduced to the outdoors slowly and carefully, and this I started to do when she was about eight weeks old. Being a born climber, she might get into some impossible place and be too nervous to come down, so I casually slipped an old show leash of Mr. Bentley's over her head. She appeared not to notice it and wandered off, her rolling gait making her look like the proverbial drunken sailor. I picked up my end and the leash tightened against her neck — surely she would balk at this constriction? But instead she returned to me, climbed my leg and sat in my lap.

Vixen and Mr. Bentley had not yet met, so I decided to combine her first steps out of doors with a cautious introduction.

I tied Mr. B. to a small tree, then fetched Vixen on her leash.

Mr. Bentley sat erect, the tip of his tail wagging slightly. His whole being begged to be allowed to get at the newcomer. I spoke to him firmly, telling him this was a 'no' animal, that he must not touch her — ever. His tail stopped wagging; the eagerness went out of his eyes and he looked very crestfallen. He understood alright but he didn't approve.

Little Vixen, meanwhile, was perched on my shoulder, clutching with all her claws. She wasn't at all sure about this; her every instinct warned her against this strange animal.

I unhooked her claws and she bit me (after all, she was nervous). I put her down a long way from Mr. B. He stiffened, but remained sitting. Vixen immediately leapt up my leg to my shoulder, hissing. That was enough for the first time and I returned her to her cage and released Mr. B., who tore about sniffing her tracks.

The two were introduced like this on several consecutive days, until they had become accustomed to the sight and scent of one another. Eventually Mr. Bentley was unleashed. Once he has learned to respect a newcomer, he never forgets. He is a dear and remarkable old dog, willing to accept this discipline when I impose it on him, but equally eager to hunt any animal to whom he has not been formally presented.

Vixen, still on her leash, explored the edge of the pond, pawed at some small frogs, and made a start up a few trees, only to be removed before she climbed beyond my reach. Memories of kittens and cats stranded for days in high trees made me cautious.

A few days later I unleashed her. Directly she felt free she rushed across the lawn and straight up the nearest fir tree. The first branch was fifty feet up. She passed it and went on to the topmost branch. And there she sat.

I called, imitating her own shrill cry. From her precarious perch she looked down at me, but made no move to return. I decided to ignore her. There wasn't much else I could do and panic wouldn't help.

Making pretense of working in the garden within sight of her tree, I waited.

Soon she began to inch silently along her branch to the trunk, down which she made her way very gingerly, head first, in the approved raccoon manner. This was plainly instinct at work — the action was not learned from her mother, who died before her babies were ready to leave their den. Vixen took the last few feet too fast and lost her grip. She tumbled in a heap, but picked herself up unharmed and shook her supple body from nose to tail-tip, then scampered to me. She leapt for my arm and tore up it to my shoulder, where she sat panting, the tip of her tiny pink tongue protruding between her teeth.

After that I allowed her more and more freedom. She explored with me, but always returned willingly to the comfortable bed in her cage, which I had put out on the lawn. Eventually I locked her in only at night, when she might have been vulnerable to predators.

She ate the little frogs that at first she had only played with, gulping them without chewing; but she always ground fruit, nuts or cereals to a pulp before swallowing them.

By this time she had made friends with Mr. Bentley and played all over him while he lay in the sun. His tolerance was charming. When she bit the thick skin of his neck he merely bunted her away with his nose and removed himself to a more secluded spot. When she came into the house she curled up beside him in his basket.

Outside she rested curled on the smallest of forked branches, tail hanging, head aslant to watch what went on below. Her total relaxation was the envy of humans too prone to tension.

One day we took her to a swift-running stream. She played happily in it until she grew bored by her inability to catch anything more interesting that a floating stick.

And this is as good a place as any to dispose of the long-held notion that raccoons deliberately wash their food.

Raccoons do, indeed, search for food underwater — by touch. Given a bowl of water with a pebble in it, a 'coon will play happily, feeling it, turning it, pushing with front paws until, realizing it is inedible, the pebble is abandoned to search for food. A live crayfish is whipped out of the water so fast you can barely see it happen. It is devoured on the spot — raccoon squatting in the water. But it won't wash the food.

The idea may have arisen because food located under water has obviously been washed clean. People may therefore have argued that raccoons prefer their food wet and cleanly washed. This is not so. Although they will not under any circumstances take stale or rancid food, they have no objection to dirt in the form of mud or soil. Vixen dug up snails and ate them, shell and all, along with any adhering earth. Or a revoltingly juicy young giant slug (they grow to five or six slithery inches in our wet spring forests), which she ate slowly, first rolling it between her front paws until it shed its slime and her hands were thickly covered with it. And there, mixed with mud, the horrid slime remained until she either wore or washed it off. When her hands were really filthy, she looked for water and deliberately felt around in it. But I am sure washing was always secondary in her mind to her continual search for something to eat.

Even after I introduced Vixen to the outdoors, she continued to receive her milk formula from a bottle. This was gradually supplemented with cooked cereals, raw egg-yolks, and raw beef. She also adored peanuts and some fruit. Her forays into the garden with me accustomed her to look for small live prey and her bottle feeding was slowly tapered off to a small serving when she was put to bed. She informed me she was ready to stay out all night by chewing the floor and wire sides of her cage, and her instincts were far more wild than domestic. Nevertheless she had to find a place in our woods to call her own, where she could return and feel safe after a night's foraging.

Raccoons are extremely independent characters, travelling singly rather than in groups. Their protective coloring, noiseless progress and speed help to preserve them on the ground.

During her early explorations with me she had discovered a wonderful playground. A huge log lay partly submerged in the lake. It was a Douglas fir that had fallen, breaking its great back in the gale that brought it down. It became known as Vixen's Log. There was a fracture along its length which formed a gallery parallel with the water. Vixen established her headquarters in this convenient hideout, using the enormous trunk to run and play on, to sunbathe, feast and sit waiting for me.

It was to this tree that she ambled just before dark on the evening of her first night out. I returned to the house and put away her cage. That night I had difficulty sleeping.

But the following morning she appeared at the back door, demanding and getting a hearty breakfast. She was perpetually hungry, and being a nocturnal animal had undoubtedly already explored the lakeshore for an early breakfast of frogs and other delicacies.

From that time she never spent another night under our roof. Her natural diet of water snails, frogs, salamanders, leeches and a host of lesser creatures, was available in abundance in our pond, in the lake, and among the deep mosses on the rocks, which she soon learned to turn over in search of snails. She swam strongly but rather slowly, head and ringed tail held carefully above water. I frequently saw her on forays into the swamp beyond her log — a place almost impenetrable to humans, full of fallen trees sunk deeply into black, oozy mud. Spiraea and willow flourish on their rotted trunks and in summer become a jungle of tall canes topped by pink pyramids of flowers.

At dusk each evening I walked down the trail beside the lake to lean on Vixen's Log. I called to her in her own voice and she came silently through the swamp to greet me. The first sign of her presence was a faint splashing as she waded through the shallows. Then a scrabbling of claws and she appeared over the far side of her log, calling with her soft churring almost-a-purr. She climbed to my shoulder, clutching my hair to steady herself, or clung upside down to search my pockets for peanuts. She came to the house for an extra snack, a nap in Mr. Bentley's bed, and a parting gift of peanuts before going out for the night.

Normally raccoons begin their hunting as darkness falls. But circumstances alter cases and many are abroad during daylight hours, especially on fine early mornings. Vixen often explored the edge of the lake in full daylight, foot by foot. Raccoons who live near the seashore find quantities of food at the water's edge and in rocky pools at low tide, whatever the time of day.

Vixen was flexible about her hours. During babyhood she never let me out of her sight while I was working in the garden, running to feel in my pockets or climbing trees, coming down when I called. She was to become more and more nocturnal until eventually her daytime activities ceased altogether. But I am getting ahead of my story.

From the beginning her behavior was fascinating. When she was upset she laid her ears flat against her skull, which gave her a mean and angry look. If she saw something alive she was not sure about, she backed away, baring her formidable teeth, the hair bristling along her spine, at the same time raising her backside higher than her head. Her shoebutton eyes concentrated on the creature, which might be a large beetle. She planned her attack, then rushed in, mouth first, then forepaws, and in seconds her prey was reduced to pulp.

Like all raccoons she sometimes seemed to kill for the sheer hell of it. This is one of her species' less endearing characteristics. Chicken farmers get up in the morning to find their birds decimated but not eaten, their heads pulled through the wire and chewed off. The answer is to protect domestic birds with double fencing, but few farmers are willing to go to the trouble. Instead they ruthlessly hunt the predators.

'Coons have adapted to man's invasion of their territory. They are frequently enticed to back porches to feed and marshmallows and white bread are amongst the most common items offered to keep them coming. I do not believe in feeding artificial foods to animals, especially not candies or anything salted. Vixen's sweets were limited to fruit or honey; and salt is required only by herbiverous animals.

Here in the Pacific Northwest raccoons have difficulty satisfying their sweet tooth. The native fruits are mostly small and acid and the few sweet ones, like strawberries, must be sought in the face of fierce competition from squirrels and other animals.

Vixen's jet-black eyes didn't miss much. Most of the time they were looking at everything except what she was doing with her hands, which were so sensitive she only needed to feel with them while her eyes were directed elsewhere. The effect was to make her look like a thief playing innocent. The fact is that she was on the lookout for danger.

* * * * *

To people who only know a raccoon in a zoo, and to children everywhere, Vixen and her kin rank among the most interesting of creatures, and much of the information prevalent about them is erroneous. Dictionaries don't seem to agree on anything but their generic name, and the fact that they are native to North America. Apart from this, there are all sorts of discrepancies in descriptions of them, even in the spelling of their name. You can spell it with one 'c' or two; or avoid the problem by referring to them as 'coons. One claims that they are related to the bears; some sources say they are carnivorous; others that they are omnivorous.

Vixen's scientific name is *Procyon lotor vancouverensis*. On the face of it, not a bad effort on the part of whoever coined the title. *Procyon* is a Greek word — *pro*, before; and *kuon*, dog. It is the name of the brightest star in the constellation *Canis Minor* (younger dog). *Lotor* in New Latin means a washer, from the verb *lavere*, to wash or bathe. So far so good. It all looks very scientific and nobody questions it. The little animal does feel around in water and to the casual observer seems to be washing either itself or its food. Its rolling gait makes it look a little like a bear; yet its general appearance is more feline than canine. In fact bears are distant relatives, having the same kind of feet — plantigrade, which means that they walk on the whole sole of the foot (cats and dogs are digitigrade — they walk on their toes.) *Vancouverensis* means that this particular subspecies is native to Vancouver Island.

To add to the confusion about an animal unknown in Europe, the Germans call raccoons *washbär*, or "washing bear", which is wrong on both counts. In France they are called *ratons laveurs*, or "small washing rats": pretty wild, considering they are neither washers nor rodents.

The little 'masked bandits', as 'coons are frequently called, are actually omnivorous though referred to formally as carnivores. A carnivorous animal's teeth can deal with meat and quite a lot of vegetable matter. A ruminant's can't. The former tear and grind; the latter only grind. The omnivorous raccoon has carnivorous teeth — forty of them, which can bite clean through your hand. At the age of six months the milk teeth fall out, like a puppy's, and are supplanted by the adult teeth.

Therefore there is at least an element of accuracy in Vixen's Latin

name: raccoon teeth like dog teeth (minus four); raccoo
feet — flat on the ground.

The weight of a raccoon is difficult to pin-point; it dep
species is weighed and when. In the fall they put on fat
Records state that they weigh anywhere from four to thin
we'll let it go at that. Vixen weighed twelve pounds throughout the year
once she became adult.

The common name 'raccoon' derives from an American Indian word
'Arathkone', 'arakun', or 'aroughcun', depending on who was recording. It has a prominent place in the folklore of the United States. The
earliest reference is by a Captain John Smith who in 1612 described the
animals in Virginia: "There is a beast they call Aroughcun, much like a
badger" — (which it is, come to think of it). Linnaeus associated the
raccoon with a bear because of its similarity of form, and christened it
Ursus cauda elongata to distinguish it from the true bear, *Ursus cauda
abrupta*. He had a delightful sense of humor and his names are often apt
and pithy. Vixen, then, would be a 'bear with a long tail', to distinguish
her from her remote, tailless relatives, the real bears who 'end
abruptly.'

In 1718 a pioneer declared the raccoon is ". . . the drunkenest animal" if he can get hold of sweet liquor; he also found the fur made good
hats and linings and the dressed skin was used to make women's shoes.
Another, later account, mentions the 'coon as an item of food, and re-
lates that the "bone of its male parts is used for a pipe cleaner". All of
which goes to show that raccoons have always been hunted, by Indian
and white man, for both their meat and their fur. This is out of fashion
now, sartorially and gastronomically and raccoons have survived to
flourish in great numbers, to the delight of people like me.

Vixen often explored my face with her nose, getting quite excited as
she did so. She was not sniffing as a dog does, just touching like a blind
person who wishes to familiarize himself with one's features. If there
was a piece of some favorite food outside a door, she could locate it easily by scent, snuffling noisily at the bottom of the door and pushing her
hands under it as far as she could reach, tearing carpets in the process.
But when the door was open and I had a dish of food in my hands, she
looked rather than smelt for it. And she could locate a piece of dropped
meat half the size of a corn kernel purely from hearing it fall behind
her.

She had innumerable utterances which varied according to her mood;
some she used only when she was a baby. She could growl like a dog

and when hungry made a sound half-way between a whine and a purr. Short, sharp barks and snapping jaws denoted anger. She had a 'high C' like a soprano — a thin squeak at the top of her voice range which she emitted when alarmed or cornered.

Having handled Vixen a great deal I had been able to observe her 'furnishings' minutely. She had a double coat: the undercoat, grey and soft as silk, insulated her body against cold and wet; through it grew the hairs of her outer, or guard coat, grey or white with black-tips. Her tail was long and thick, with five black rings; it served as pillow, blanket and even mattress.

As she trundled about, pouring herself down steps or galloping across the lawn with her rear-end higher than her head, it seemed that she hadn't a bone in her body. Her forefeet resembled hands, with five long fingers capable at once of great strength and of incredible deftness and delicacy, as when she picked my pockets or pawed my hands to draw attention to herself. Their black skin was fine and soft, sometimes warm, sometimes cool. She could pick up a grape in one hand or hold a bunch in both, delicately removing them from their stalks with her front teeth. Very ladylike. Her hind feet were long and just as soft-skinned but their five toes are not so opposable as the fingers, which can fold towards one another. Her tracks looked like the imprints made by a tiny elf-child going barefoot.

Once past babyhood she played very little. I had done some reading on captive raccoons and her behavior was in complete contradiction to theirs. I find their invented antics pathetic and am glad Vixen never indulged in them: as a wildling she never had time.

On one point, however, captive and wild raccoons are much alike. However good natured the captured ones appear when young, their native ferocity flares up when they are about twelve weeks old. Tame ones become fierce if they are left without handling, even for a day or two. I can confirm this from experience with other raccoons — except Vixen, who did not quite fit into either category. She was gentle when I least expected it and dangerously fierce when I would have anticipated the opposite.

Part of her rather suspicious 'trust' was based on knowing her escape routes. I had to leave her familiar exits open at all times. If the door was inadvertently closed, she panicked, tearing at its base, then running up bookshelves, over chairs and round to all the other doors, squeezing out her high-pitched squeal of fear and frustration. At such times she was a truly wild thing and no human voice, however familiar and reassuring, was the slightest comfort. Once her line of retreat was reopened, she would first try it out, then settle down to whatever she had been doing before panic set in.

She was very sensitive to changes in my voice and although I did not try to train her in any way, there were times when a verbal reprimand was called for to save the furniture. A firm word was enough to dissuade her. But I think that if anyone had been foolish enough to punish her physically, she would never have forgiven them. Certainly they would have borne scars.

Adult raccoons are in little danger from predation except by man and his dogs. The young, however, are vulnerable when they first emerge from their den. Large owls can pick them off the trunk as they make their hesitant, wobbly descent; so can hawks. These birds are lightning fast and the mother raccoon has no time to help her baby back up the trunk to safety.

But Vixen survived and lived happily through the summer untouched, although I sometimes cast an eye skywards at a family of bald eagles who sailed regularly over Ravenshill. In theory they cannot lift more than a pound or two and I fervently hoped this was true. Vixen then weighed about six pounds.

September approached and warm days were drawing to a close. Vixen entered her second feeding phase. The first, from May to September, is a period of growth and summer moult, during which she required a light, nourishing diet with plenty of meat and vegetables. The second is the time of preparation for winter, marked by a considerable increase in feeding, especially cereals, as 'coons acquire a thick layer of fat to protect them against cold, particularly necessary in the more frigid areas of their wide range across North America. The third phase, beginning in February, is the breeding season, to which I will return.

Animal feeding is about thirty per cent science: the rest is art, intuition and a certain amount of artfulness. Domestic animals, if they are to be healthy and happy, rather than grossly fat, begging parodies (I am thinking of dogs and cats), need to be fed at regular hours. Once a day for adults. And nothing in between. No tid-bits. Wild animals are different.

I might have released Vixen straight from her cage and never fed her again. Having already interfered with nature by accepting her to rear instead of letting her die in her den after her mother was killed, I felt a responsibility to provide her with additional meals as long as she needed them.

All through September and October she devoured fattening cereals in the house together with whatever she found out of doors. When I put

25

suet out for the birds she stole it. I had to hang it on a string where she couldn't reach it. She was adept at making her needs understood and if her entrance to the house was barred, climbed the back steps to howl at the kitchen door until I let her in.

Since she elected to remain friendly I cut a small hole in the garage door and put a swinging screen on it so that she could come and go at will. Her little door made a noise on its metal rings so that I was able to hear her come in. If I didn't I might hear soft pattering as she came up the stairs, and if I missed that, too, I would be made aware of her presence by the lightest of touches on my leg. I would look down and there she was, sitting up on her fat little backside, pawing my leg and begging for a meal.

After eating she permitted me to handle her — with care. After she was about half-grown I was never allowed to place my hands round her body; if I tried she bit me viciously. But if I stroked her as she snoozed on my lap, then took her firmly by the skin at the nape of her neck, I could pick her up and she would remain relaxed while I groomed her with an old poodle brush and comb. Then roll her over and repeat — but never on her tummy.

She loved to curl up in a velvet-covered chair, her handsome coat contrasting artistically against its pale gold background. I think she knew how lovely she looked. Yawning her wide pink yawn, showing her snow-white teeth, she would stretch luxuriously, lying like a siren on her back. She bestirred herself only when Edward arrived home. As soon as he or anyone else entered the room she retreated beneath my chair where nobody would dare try reaching for her.

It was a sad fact that, much as Edward longed to touch her, she permitted no-one but me to do so — and then only when she was in the mood. She would sit on Edward's knee and accept peanuts from his hand; but he had only to extend a finger to stroke her and she would bite it before jumping away, and Edward prefers his hands unbloodied.

I should perhaps mention that while I naturally don't like being bitten or scratched, I don't attach too much importance to small wounds. I am one of those fortunate people who heal extremely fast and no wild creature's bite has ever turned septic. It is simply a minor hazard to be contended with if possible and put up with if there is no alternative.

* * * * *

Winter on Vancouver Island is not as severe as it is in the rest of Canada and unless the temperature drops below 28°F (−2°C), raccoons don't hibernate. When the temperature does fall that low, they den up

26

either singly or in twos or threes, in a hole in a tree or under an overhanging rock. On fine days and nights, when the weather is less cold, they emerge and wander about in search of food. At Christmastime, when Vixen was still very much in evidence, a drastic lesson was brought home to me.

We gave a party.

I thought she would stay away because of the cars parked near the house, but I was wrong. I heard her on the stairs and hurriedly went down to reassure her. She was quite calm.

I gave her a good grooming — she needed it, being soaking wet, her feet covered with mud and weed from the lake. When she was tidy she climbed onto my shoulder and held on to my hair.

Sudden pride made me want to show her to our friends.

Meantime Edward, realizing that she was downstairs, had told our guests, so there was an expectant hush in the room as I brought her in, cradled in my arms. A delighted murmur greeted us.

But instantly Vixen saw that the room was changed from her familiar safe, quiet place, where only Mr. Bentley and I kept her company. Here were potential enemies.

She bit me, long and hard, until blood ran down my hands and over my dress. Then she slid from my arms and disappeared downstairs and out into the night.

I don't think she ever fully forgave me.

I had, of course, broken the inviolable rule: always put animals' interests before your own. I had brought her into this alien atmosphere unprepared — indeed, how could she have been prepared? Naturally she was frightened, and I deserved her bites.

After this episode she treated me more distantly. I reflected sadly that through my own stupidity I had lost part of that trust which had taken so long to establish.

Chapter Four

In Nature there is nothing melancholy.

Coleridge, THE NIGHTINGALE.

The lake was the color of stainless steel — cold yet somehow soft. On its surface the light of approaching evening cast long pale reflections. No wind blew and the rain fell straight and steadily, producing myriads of concentric circles on the water.

Mesmerized, I stared down at the lake, my vacant mind wholly receptive to the dreams that such a day kindles. Not dull. Not the least depressing. Rather a moment of nothingness, when color takes a rest and nature turns from print to negative, all translucent greys. Grey the lichens on grey rocks; and grey the barks of trees. Grey the heron who stood, motionless as the landscape painted round him, contemplating the water. Grey the belted kingfisher, silent for once, perched on a dead branch, grey-black-white blending into the steel grey surfaces of trees and water.

Torrential rain falling straight down for days on end provides a pause — a breathing space. Birds not to water born take cover in sheltering trees. Four-footed animals lie still in the underbrush, rain running in rivulets from sleek flanks, the skin dry beneath streaming pelts, only their heads damp clear down to the skull. People can lift up their faces to let their hair stream in the rain, and not care about their looks for a spell. Grey is restful to tired eyes. Color will return, tomorrow or the next day.

I opened my window and went to bed, not because I was tired but because I wanted the experience of lying almost in the garden, able, simply by turning on one side, to watch the lily-pool and the semi-circle of big trees reflected coldly in the moonlit lake below.

Presently the rain ceased. The moon rose higher. The rising wind shoved a cloud across her face. Over the garden spread a great cold radiance. On the pool's surface lily pads glistened darkly; a frog, clearly visible, sat on one, enjoying the soft freshness of the new night. From the water the moon's shimmering reflections sent shafts of light into my eyes. Round the edge of the pool slabs of rock lay silver-grey and wetly shining. Everything — stone, pebble, branch, leaf — was sharply etched in black and silver. So much light shone upon the garden that every detail was lucently clear. And all was absolutely still.

Into this illumined little world a slight sound infiltrated. A dabbly, riffling-water sound. I propped myself on an elbow, the better to see the pool.

From the shadows a small form emerged. Grey and black fur intricately clothed it as though some master in the art of camouflage had designed it to blend into the night. Grey to the moon, black to the shadows.

Again the faint sound of movement of water which should be still. Another sound, a softly uttered churr with a little lilt at its end.

Water sounds ceased and were supplanted by a faint scratching on wood. The small form climbed through my window; soft feet padded across the polished floor. And Vixen climbed onto my bed to lick and groom herself.

Stretched to her full length, she took her wet ease against my covered legs. I reached down, holding out my hand. By and by, two silk-smooth paws found their way into my palm, gentle and warm, feeling to see if I was holding something to ease her voracious appetite. Finding nothing, the little hands ceased their wanderings, a cold wet nose sniffed briefly at my fingers; then a huge sigh. We slept.

In the morning she was gone. Only a damp patch on my bed and tracks across the floor showed that she had ever been there.

And in the morning I had time to realize how remarkable it was that Vixen had returned unbidden after an absence of months, for it was now early spring again and I had not touched her since the Christmas party — yet she had not bitten my hand when I lay in bed the previous night.

She had survived the winter, denned somewhere in the woods, emerging from time to time to forage. I used to see her tracks across the snow to the bird feeders. During the cold months I left food for her in the garage, where she could come and go at will, and she never failed to clean the plate of its last crumb — nor to leave a messy reminder of herself in a corner for me to clean up.

Vixen's year, like Gaul, was divided into three parts. She had now come to the third and most important, the breeding season. Female raccoons breed at ten months under favorable conditions of climate and available food, although twelve is more usual. Males mate when they are two years old.

One evening in March I set out to locate her by calling, not having seen her for over a week, and was startled by a strange guttural howl from the property adjacent to ours. I went towards it and soon saw Vixen. She was high up a fir tree, apparently wrestling with another raccoon. Both were making alarmingly aggressive noises, different from any in Vixen's earlier vocabulary.

During the winter I had released a live-trapped male. He had been after chickens close to town and someone had caught him and telephoned me to take him. I suspected he might be Vixen's sparring partner.

I walked quietly to the foot of the tree and called. Vixen turned from her companion, who promptly scrambled down the other side of the tree and ran off. I had expected her to ignore me: after all, at that season fun and games with another raccoon would be more interesting than responding to me. But she came down anyway, head-first as usual. I put my hand on the trunk and she walked across the bridge to my shoulder, where she sat churring softly in her best conversational manner. Butter wouldn't melt in her mouth. After a few minutes socializing and searching my pockets for the ever-present peanuts, she climbed down my front and loped off without a backward glance. I followed. But the thickly overgrown ground and large rocks made it difficult to keep up with her sinuous movements, which were deceptively fast, and I soon lost her. She was heading deep into vacant bushland, away from the house.

Raccoons don't make nests; they just take whatever convenient hole offers itself, from the ground up, and rely on their thick soft fur to cushion them and keep them warm. Holes in dead trees are favorite places.

I spent an hour looking for a likely den but although I found many dead trees with suitable holes, none of them bore the claw marks which would have indicated that she was a regular visitor.

Two nights later she made peremptory sounds to be admitted at the kitchen door.

After a meal and a long drink from Mr. Bentley's bowl, she climbed onto my lap and I turned her over to groom her. Suddenly she was transformed from a relaxed raccoon basking in the soft combing sensation, to an angry creature who doubled right over and snarled at me. I only just had time to snatch my hands away from her teeth.

Sitting, she began to lick her thighs, like a cat when it grooms its hind legs: first one stuck out in front, then the other. Then I saw two long gashes, one on each thigh. The wounds went down to the bone, which glistened in the light. They looked about two days old: she had cleaned them well and there was no blood.

Had she been wounded in sex-play? The two cuts puzzled me. They were exactly alike in position, shape and length, as though inflicted by a two-pronged instrument. Considering the depth of the wounds I was amazed at Vixen's continued agility; being directly over the joints, at the point where movement is greatest and therefore healing slowest, they must have been very painful.

Why two bites in such precise relation to each other? Why so long a cut? Why not a round hole? The questions niggled at me.

The next day I went to check on some of our nest boxes, including one designed for wood duck, high on a tree beside a big pool. The previous year it had contained a family of screech owls but this year there was no sign of life. I was about to leave when I glimpsed something in the reeds and was horrified to see a screech owl floating face down. She was dead, her eyes wide open. I picked up her body and swung it downwards several times to see if there was water in her lungs. There was: she must have drawn breath underwater.

Sadly I cradled her in my hands. Memories of the small brown owl I had cared for in childhood came back to me. Another time, another place, another owl. Only this one was dead, while the other had lived to fly again.

Here was a faithful little mother (they are said to mate for life, like geese), who must have died defending the nest she had made in the box. Owls are brave and will defend their young fiercely, even against humans, as many a nest-robber can testify.

I walked slowly back to the house, carrying her with me and wondering how she had died. My fingers played idly over her legs and feet without registering anything except the softness of the feathers, wet though they were.

Suddenly awareness flooded through me: the feel of her feet! I examined the bird in my hand. Her toes were spread wide and her 'ankle' joints (really part of her foot) were sharply bent. The curved talons, having been underwater for some time, were clean of any matter that might have indicated what they had grasped in those final moments.

The little owl had indeed died defending her nest. Her killer was Vixen.

It had to be true. The upturned talons, legs apart, frozen in death as they had been in life when they struck Vixen's thighs. She must have climbed the tree to the box, sat on the roof, and tried unsuccessfully to feel inside the deep box for eggs or nestlings. The mother owl was probably off hunting, returned to see the marauder, and instantly attacked. I looked carefully under her feathers and found two small punctures in her neck, clearly the work of Vixen's teeth.

Gallant bird. I mourned for her and for her young ones who would never grace our woods with their shadowy forms and soft whistles. A look into the box revealed four cold white eggs.

I cursed Vixen for a wicked murderess, knowing full well that it was her nature. Then I began to fear for all the other birds and small mammals who had found sanctuary at Ravenshill. Had I introduced one predator too many? Sober reflection told me no. I must not break my heart every time something was killed by something else: it was all part of the scheme of things. But I never get used to it; there is always a small heartbreak every time I hear a duck's cry of alarm in the still of the night, and know that something — raccoon or mink or barnyard cat — has taken one of her little ones.

During the next few days I was almost glad Vixen did not reappear. When she did her wounds had healed.

After that her visits became more and more erratic. Three days and nights would pass without a sign of her; then a demanding prrrup at ten o'clock in the evening. In for a meal and out again, rain or shine; no more lolling in armchairs by the fire. Often she was soaking wet and her belly fur covered with bits of duckweed from the lake. Sometimes her coat was matted with sticky resin. She must have been hunting over a wide territory.

She sometimes demanded — and got — three meals in an evening. Yet she remained thin. And she showed no sign of pregnancy.

Towards the middle of May her attitude underwent another change. Once more she began to come when I called and stayed longer in the house, eating until I thought she must surely burst. Peanuts were in short supply at the stores and had to be rationed, to her extreme annoyance. Her scrabblings up my legs to my pockets became increasingly frenzied; to compensate I provided her with everything a raccoon loves: bananas, apples, whole-wheat bread, raisins, grapes, thick porridge and even raw meat. Captive raccoons eat dead meat but wild ones refuse it, unless they are starving.

Raccoon kittens are born after a gestation of 63 to 69 days (the same as a dog), and their eyes open at about ten days. They remain hidden in the den until they are ten weeks old. Father has nothing to do with rearing his family. The kittens stay with their mother for ten months or even a year, by which time she is ready to mate again.

A second mating sometimes takes place if the first one did not bear fruit. Such second chances occur in late summer or early fall and, since they have been denied the benefit of the summer months when food is plentiful, such latecomers run greater risks in the struggle for survival.

Vixen again appeared regularly every night and was calmer and more tractable. On the assumption that she was nursing I gave her salad oil, raw egg yolks, milk and bone meal.

By mid-June I was certain. She stood on her hind legs to reach for yet more food and for the first time I could see she was lactating.

32

Where was her den? I quartered the woods like a hound, but there was no sign of occupation in any likely place and I never learned where she had made her home.

She seemed suddenly to have a lot of time on her hands and spent much of it with me, returning to her diurnal habits. But now she snarled at her old friend Mr. B, who took it philosophically. I wondered if she had lost her litter, to have so much spare time.

Meanwhile all manner of birds grew up around us. In April and May our population of wild mallard ducks had exploded to ten families each with up to ten ducklings. Ravenshill waters were alive with little balls of yellow fluff. They walked to the lawn and darted about, herded and guarded by their beady-eyed, watchful mothers. Of course I fed them, and some of them probably fed Vixen.

July came and went. The garden and surrounding woods were filled with hummingbirds, who visit us every summer.

And still Vixen kept her secret.

During these weeks we were busy preparing for the longed-for visit of my brother Bernard and his wife Audrey, from England. This would be their first visit to Canada and for the event we cleaned and polished the house until it sparkled inside and out.

They arrived one perfect day in August and we talked half the night and spent all next day showing off our dwelling place and its inhabitants. To give them a rest from this and other sightseeing, we arranged lazy days doing nothing in the garden.

It was on one of these that Vixen revealed her secret.

Chapter Five

Here is a green to ease the mind,
and recreate the will;
but shut your eyes, and you will find
its scent is greener still.

Piet Hein, GROOKS 4.

Under the big cascara tree the shade was deep and cool. Beyond it,
baked earth contracted under a scorching sun. The only sounds were
those of the flying insects beneath the forest canopy; a low droning that
enhanced the spell of summer's heat. No leaf stirred in the windless air;
nothing moved on or above the ground; even the hummingbirds were
resting from their bickering. The four of us lazed in luxurious idleness,
blissfully soaking up heat and long, ice-clinking drinks.

Into this somnolent scene erupted a caterwauling so raucous that in
one startled movement we all sat bolt upright.

Vixen was strolling down a mossy slope, followed by two kittens.

Every few seconds she stopped to look behind her to the base of a
tree, around which a third kitten, smaller and more timid than the other
two, was peering and howling his head off. She churred reassuringly
and presently number three joined the little troupe, running and tumbling across the lawn.

We could hardly contain our excitement, myself least of all. Here
was my Vixen, the scrawny little orphan of a year ago now grown beautiful, silk-coated and sleek, bringing her family to us.

Of all the stories in this book, this, I think, is the most remarkable because this was a wild-born, hand-raised animal who, released into her
native habitat, had mated with a wild one, raised her family alone in the
wild, yet retained enough trust in me deliberately to bring her babies to
me on their first outing.

She had made a den somewhere in our woods, conceived her litter
and carried it and given birth, quietly, efficiently and stealthily, as
though she had never known human contact. Was the father the young
male I had released?

I was deeply interested to see how Vixen would behave in this new
situation. She had already broken some of the 'rules' by consorting with
me after a long absence and now she approached humans once more
after another lapse of time.

I forced myself to get up slowly and walk to the house, when I

34

wanted to run, for cameras and plates of the choicest things I could find to celebrate this great day.

When I returned Vixen was rolling on the grass, the kittens playing round her, never more than a paw's length from their mother. Two babies were much bigger than the one who had lagged behind. These were females. Predominantly grey, with neat little black masks and pointed tails, they were miniature replicas of Vixen. The small male would eventually overtake his sisters' greater size.

I put down two plates of food. Vixen dived into hers as though famished. She had, of course, been nursing, hunting (or going to the garage) for herself late at night whilst the kittens slept in their snug hole. This was possibly her first daytime meal in a long time.

Now the babies experimented with this new food. Imitating his mother, the male noisily threatened his sisters with miniature snarls. Six little black hands felt around the plate while three pairs of eyes explored the heavens. They rolled grapes between their paws before popping them whole into their mouths. Some cottage cheese created a problem with messy fingers. Sliced banana rounds disappeared quickly, as did unsalted peanuts so beloved of Vixen.

The men took pictures while I sat on the grass near her, like a grandmother.

When the babies finished she led them to the large shallow pan of water we kept filled for thirsty creatures. She sat down in the middle of it and called. One of the females obeyed. The other two backed off and scrambled to the top of the winter wood-pile.

Things began to move fast. The baby would not step into the pan, so Vixen stood up and hauled her in by the scruff of her neck. She held the infant down with her front paws and, taking it in her mouth, literally swished her head about in the water. The little one sputtered as her nose went under, howled as she came up for air and was promptly dunked again. At last Vixen let go and baby scrambled out as fast as her little legs would carry her, up the nearest tree to a branch, on which she sat and shook water from her dripping coat over all and sundry below. Meanwhile Mr. Bentley lay placidly on the lawn watching the group with mild interest. Vixen didn't bat an eyelash.

She then summoned her second daughter and gave her the same treatment. Finally it was little brother's turn.

Nothing doing! He had witnessed his sisters' immersion and was not about to undergo the same thing if he could help it. But his mother was wise to all the tricks. She left the tub and firmly, efficiently, manhandled (or should I say 'coonhandled'?) him down his tree and into the water.

He put up a terrific fight, snarling, howling, biting, wriggling, resisting with every sinew in his small body. But to no avail. Vixen caught him after he had slipped out of her grasp for the third time and yanked him angrily into the water and dunked him until he had no breath left to yell.

When the bathing was finished Vixen lay down beside me to groom herself, rolling on her back, digging with teeth and tongue into her soft fur to unsnarl her matted coat. Then she climbed into my lap where she relaxed and closed her eyes: but not for long. Her parental duties would keep her alert for a long time and there was little leisure to lie around. It was time to go.

She called her family with a low maternal purring sound and set off towards another of her hiding places. This place we call Vixen's Drainpipe. It is a big iron culvert which serves as a run-off for the pond during heavy rains. In spring it channels a roaring torrent through the woods but in summer it is dry. It made a perfect hideout for Vixen midway along her route from the lake to the house. She could either disappear inside or peer out of the entrance, knowing there was safety at her back. The bottom of the pipe is covered in thick, black mud that stuck to her feet. She never bothered to remove it, so that it was apt to be tracked into my kitchen, into Mr. Bentley's drinking water and, of course, all over the floor. I became fed up with constantly cleaning up after her. But they were her feet and who was I to say she must wash them for my benefit?

This time, instead of leaving us, Vixen evidently decided to give her children one more lesson. They clustered round her and she took them into the pipe. I could just hear her calling from its depths, a strange, hollow sound which seemed to frighten the little male. The two sisters followed their mother into the dark interior of the drain, but he balked, meowling loudly, and Vixen had to fetch him.

Having taught them about this escape hole, she let them out again to play, herself sitting on the ground a few feet from us. While her babies gambolled she seemed to doze, though with one eye open for danger. Bernard and Edward took more photographs.

The little 'coons found a wide upended log. One climbed up and down the other side, watched by her two siblings. I could hear Edward muttering about getting a shot of three in a row. I thought 'What a hope!' and watched.

Suddenly one kitten was on top of the log, sitting bolt upright, eyes front, as if she was posing for the camera. The second climbed up and sat next to her, half a head shorter and in line. With baited breath we watched and waited.

The male clawed his way up. A head shorter than his sisters, he made the perfect third of a trio of little black and white notes in a downward scale. A camera clicked, and another; shot after frantic shot. Seconds later they broke, clambered down and galloped over to their indulgent mother who licked each one quickly and then, sinuous and silent, led them into the sunlit woods.

We did not anticipate that Vixen would bring her family again on their first day abroad, so we sat around and talked about the event. Bernard and Audrey felt vastly privileged to have seen a wild animal coming voluntarily with her young to visit humans. I started to assess the age of my four-footed 'grandchildren'.

Theoretically a wild raccoon baby does not descend from its birth den until it is ten weeks old. Then it ventures forth with mother, emerging in single file down the tree for first lessons in finding food. They return to the den to sleep. This pattern continues until they are too big for the den and are capable of hunting. The den itself is by then tenanted by thousands of fleas.

By working backwards I found the theories — based on captive animals — worked out, give or take a few days. Assuming Vixen had mated when I found her howling up a tree on March 20 and allowing a nine-week gestation, her kittens would have been born on or about May 22. When she brought them to visit us it was August 3 — almost certainly their first sortie, judging by their behavior — and as their subsequent growth in independence tended to confirm. On that momentous day, then, they were just ten weeks old.

Newborn raccoons could only be called pretty by their mothers and their voices are loud and raucous. They are born with a short-haired, velvet-textured dark grey coat, ears and eyes closed and sealed; the black mask that will become their most spectacular feature is a mere smudge across the forehead. By six weeks the exquisite upright ears outlined in soft white hair, are set well up on the broad head. By the time the coat has grown to a length of about two inches, the black and white mask is plainly defined; five black rings circle the black-pointed grey tail and the thick 'sideburns' have appeared which give the adult raccoon's face the appearance of being wider than it really is. Shorn of its coat, a raccoon's body is a thin little scrap. But the long hair, loose skin and striking patterns combine to make it a supple, seemingly fat, sleek and elegant animal.

Bernard asked me what I would call Vixen's babies? I turned to Edward, who has a gift for this sort of thing. And so our little wild raccoons became Eenie, Meenie and Mo, short for Minor. Two girls and a boy.

Vixen brought them daily to the back porch since they were frightened of the swing door into the garage. On the first day she climbed the steps alone whilst her nervous youngsters retreated up their fir tree.

Whilst she ate her fill her young kept howling like little banshees, watching their mother with hungry eyes. Eventually they climbed down and scattered on the ground. Vixen, whose back was turned, went on eating. Eventually she poured herself down the steps and instead of calling the babies as she had on the first day, tracked them silently by scent. When she found them she gathered them to her and groomed them, then settled down to let them play while she slept briefly. I was glad she did not try to bathe them again.

Eenie and Meenie decided to try the steps and started off across the grass. The lawn is large and wild animals have an instinctive fear of being caught out in the open. Raccoons are especially creatures of the woods and Vixen's babies, suddenly realizing the vast expanse of open space between them and their mother, decided that discretion was the better part of valor and rushed headlong back to her, climbing and tumbling over her in their anxiety for her warmth and reassurance.

Vixen rose, stretched, yawned and with what sounded like a resigned sigh, ambled to the steps followed, line astern, by her babies. She mounted two and sat down. Eenie and Meenie followed suit. Mo sat at the bottom and howled. Taking no notice of her wailing son, Vixen went to the porch and gave the dish (which I had meantime refilled), a shove with her nose. Her daughters climbed cautiously, their little hind legs barely able to negotiate the high steps. Once up they had to learn table manners. 'Mother feeds first'. She began to eat, growling at the kittens when they tried to follow her example. Mo was still yelling below but Vixen ignored him and I sympathized with her. If he wanted a meal he'd have to stop having tantrums.

Vixen's behavior was clearly just a demonstration, since she ate only a few token mouthfuls, then stepped aside to permit her daughters to feed. They dived in ravenously while mother sat down to watch. They snarled and barked at one another, scrambling their small black paws over one another's in their eagerness to get at the food. Meenie became so possessive she rounded on her sister with teeth bared, then climbed right into the dish and lay down there. Vixen looked on placidly.

Meantime, little Mo had climbed his tree and seated himself on a branch, his tail dangling like a drooping pennant. He never ceased yelling.

Eenie and Meenie finished their meal, then tumbled helter skelter down the steps and climbed to join Mo. In a few minutes all three were asleep while their mother sedately took her ease on the grass below them.

They came every afternoon, and each day seemed to grow more beautiful. Mo was so hungry he finally overcame his fear and climbed to the porch, but when he first caught sight of me he fell backwards with a loud shriek.

I almost choked with horror. Raccoons, like squirrels, can fall out of trees without suffering any harm, but ten feet below our porch is a concrete path. I had dreadful visions of a limp little body lying broken upon it.

I rushed to the rail, scattering Eenie and Meenie. Beneath me Mo stood up, breathless but intact, shook himself from nose to tail-tip, and ran back to the bottom step. Plucky little fellow. He climbed up once more, none the worse for his accident, and tucked straight into his food.

After lunch, when the children were safely asleep in their tree, Vixen decided to come into the house again. I sat down and she immediately climbed the back of my chair and down into my lap where she rummaged through my pockets as of old, her sensitive hands delicately feeling their way past a match, a Kleenex tissue, an odd button, until they found what they were seeking. She fished out the last nut, pulled everything out of my pockets to see if she had missed anything, then turned to my hand, which was hanging over the side of the chair. Clutching my sleeve in both hands she pulled until I relented and brought my hand into my lap. She dug her cold, wet nose between my fingers and prized them open so that she could seize the bunch of grapes she knew was there. Happily, she sat back, leaning against my chest, tail curled round her hind feet, and daintily picked each grape from the stem. Then she condescended to curl into a tight ball and slept for a while. I don't believe raccoons sleep for long, at least not when they have young. Before becoming pregnant, Vixen used to sleep on the bed with me for two hours or more at a time; but she never did so again.

After a brief nap she left the room to check on her babies. They had ventured as far as the open door, but to cross the step over the threshold demanded courage they did not yet possess. Until one day mother walked straight through the doorway. Before they realized what was happening, they had followed her into the living room. Vixen sat down on the sill and they scampered in all directions, looking wildly for the exit, which was right behind them. Their strange surroundings, the feel of Chinese matting instead of familiar earth under their feet, gave rise to shrieks and squeals, until it dawned on their little minds that mother wasn't panicking, was in fact regarding them calmly from the open doorway. Then they began to relax and play with her. They crawled over and round her, biting her tail, her ears, her face, but never her paws. The instinct for preservation of those vitally sensitive hands must be inculcated at birth, because I never saw them attempt to play with their mother's.

All through the summer the family came and went and I was able to sit and watch them or walk about the house without their trying to make a getaway. But I was never able to touch them. Vixen had done her job well. She had raised her babies to be wild raccoons, not tame ones, and I honored her decision.

Before dusk Vixen led her brood out of the house and on their way to wherever home was. Outside their drainpipe they all stopped and in one concerted movement reared up on their hind legs, front paws hanging loosely in front of their chests, stretching their necks to see what was going on above them. Three short and one tall, looking like little kangaroos. The slightest sound sent them scurrying into the pipe. Finally they ventured forth, little masks peering this way and that before trundling off into the shadowy woods through which they must pass to reach Vixen's Log, or points beyond.

Sometimes they crossed the dam I had built between the pool and the newly-excavated pond adjoining it. This is quite shallow, a lovely place for little 'coons to go fishing for frogs and salamanders. Beyond the dam is dense bush and more forest.

Then one day Vixen disappeared. A day passed; a night; two nights; a week. Although I had grown accustomed to her absences before her family had arrived, I could not reconcile myself to this one, burdened as she now was with the responsibility of three lively kittens. I began to worry when two more days passed with no sign of her.

I was realizing how fond I had grown of my vicious little raccoon and her rambunctious family. She was about sixteen months old. Although I was careful never to let her feel confined or trapped, I had come to regard her as one of the family — yes, let me say it who should not — as a pet, albeit an unusual one, since touching her was always a risky business.

Hope dwindled as I made the same note each day in my diary: 'No Vixen'. What disaster could have befallen them? If one or more had been killed, the others would surely have returned to Ravenshill, their home territory? Yet the idea of the entire family being wiped out was so monstrous . . .

Ironically, the weather was beautiful, ideally suited to food-hunting 'coons. The nights were lit by a brilliant moon. The trees were turning: a red-ozier dogwood by Vixen's Log flaunted leaves in rich reds, greens and purples. My Japanese maple was aflame with every shade of red in my temporarily stored paintbox.

Yet the joy I usually took in such things was dimmed. Vixen's food, left out for days, went bad; I threw it out and prepared fresh. When she still did not return it, too, was discarded and I put out no more. Each day I called and searched for her; and at its close hope died a little more.

And then, when I had completely given up, Vixen reappeared with little Mo. Just Mo. A Mo who was neither noisy nor querulous. Both mother and son looked thin and, I thought, harassed.

The next day they returned and both seemed especially nervous. They took their meal hurriedly, leaving it half eaten. Vixen did not touch me, nor look for nuts.

The following evening little Mo was howling pitifully. At the base of one ear a nasty gash showed through his luxurious fur. No wonder the poor mite was frightened and crying. But there was nothing I could do since he had never allowed me to touch him and I did not want to terrify him still further by trapping and handling him. He and Vixen ate a better meal, then left again. During the night I heard them under my bedroom window.

Each day they returned, each time a little less distracted. Mo became tamer and more inclined to come into the house with his mother. Slowly his wound healed. Once more Vixen began looking in my pockets for treats. Things seemed to have returned to normal.

Another winter was approaching, and Vixen and Mo would be beginning to feel sluggish. One morning the ground was white with frost and on that day I lost hope for Eenie and Meenie.

They were too young to survive alone. Had a pack of dogs attacked them? Had Vixen defended her family long enough to enable Mo to escape, but failed to save her daughters?

It is sad not to know. At least I would have liked the small comfort of knowing that they died quickly. They were so beautiful and snarly, so mischievous and so brave. Wherever they are, I wish them peace.

Vixen and Mo came regularly throughout the fall. He had many little habits that were different from hers. She used her hands to feed; he kept his feet on the floor and thrust his little pointed muzzle into the dish to guzzle. His feet were larger and squarer than his mother's, making track identification easy.

The two of them — Vixen partly tame and Mo wholly wild — continued to live within the sanctuary of Ravenshill. Throughout that winter her tracks were visible in the snow alongside those of her son.

* * * * *

Winter began to give way to spring, but the weather was still cold and wet. One evening in March Edward and I were sitting by a roaring wood fire when I heard a thud outside the back door and went to investigate.

The porch light revealed a bag of garbage half way down the steps, its contents strewn in all directions.

Standing on the top step was Vixen — alone.

I invited her in, and she came without hesitation. As she ate the food I had hastily prepared for her while she was feeling around in Mr. Bentley's bowl, I took stock of her condition. She was thin but wearing a hard, dense coat. She was nervous and repeatedly checked the open back door as she ate. As she had not felt my touch for a long time I refrained from trying to stroke her. Instead I offered nuts which she snatched from my hand with a snarl, and even felt in my pockets for more, just like old times.

When she had finished, she darted out and the last I saw of her was standing up on her hind legs, close to her drainpipe. Then she vanished into the night.

I wondered about little Mo. There had been no sounds to indicate he had accompanied his mother and I wondered if they had already split up. He would have been eight months old then and still in need of her. Had he come to grief during the winter? Had spring fever entered his little soul before he was experienced enough to live alone? I wished Vixen could have told me about her winter's experiences.

The time was ripe for her to be pregnant again and I had to be content that she, at least, could survive alone. I thought how remarkable it was that Vixen, reared by human hands, should have been able to teach her kittens so efficiently. She had had no mother to instruct her, yet gave clear demonstrations to Eenie, Meenie and Mo. Her instinctive behavior was passed on through her example, reinforcing her babies' instincts; the two females would not have been likely to forget the first washing lesson and would have done the same to their own kittens, if only in revenge! And Mo was clearly shown the difficult business of climbing steps for food.

Vixen was the first wild orphan to be brought to Ravenshill and through her I discovered that I wanted to devote myself to the care, nursing, or raising of others such as she. I determined to read and learn as much as possible about the needs of small native animals, readying myself in the event that others might need my help. My years of experience with domestic animals, of feeding and nursing with natural remedies, would be useful too.

Vixen brought new purpose to my life.

Chapter Six

Poor splendid wings so frayed
and soiled and torn!

Swinburne, *BALLAD OF FRANCOIS VILLON.*

I read widely but discovered very little practical information in books on wild pets. Turning to more technical literature I found some help, but the animals discussed had been raised experimentally and I felt there was a wide gap between these and animals taken from their natural habitat and destined for release as soon as possible.

Slowly a momentous decision took shape. I would create at Ravenshill a sanctuary for local birds and mammals where sick, injured, or orphaned creatures could be cared for, then released and given additional feeding if necessary.

I thought back to my earlier experiences with animal care and especially nutrition. Some years before a nestful of cedar waxwings provided me with interest and instruction under unusual conditions.

The nest had been built in a dense fir tree which was felled. Had I known it was there, the operation would naturally have been delayed until the babies were fledged. As it was the nest was cushioned by branches as the tree fell and the fledglings were unharmed. I took them, nest and all, into the house. After giving them a meal of berries and small insects (their natural food), I covered them with a dark cloth and left them for the night.

Next morning I fed them, cleaned up the nest and put it in a carton near a window. I noticed a pair of waxwings in an apple tree outside and thinking they might be the parents, took the boxful of infants out and secured it to a branch. Immediately I left the adults came to feed them, perching on the edge of the box and unconcernedly hopping down to the nest inside.

Thankful that these babies would be fed properly once more, but concerned that the parents might be unable to clean the nest, I checked it with a flashlight before going to bed. To my consternation the still-naked nestlings were alone and miserable in the chilly air. So they came indoors and were fed, cleaned and covered a second time.

The next day I put the box out again. The parents flew down at once and fed their young, but wasps were alighting on the nest, drawn by the

Ravenshill from the water.

Patient Mr. Bentley allows young Vixen to play jockey.

A lucky split second shot of Vixen's babies, unposed and wild.

Edgar, Allen, Poe with the author.

photo: Enid K. Ler

Cedar waxwings in their nest inside a carton, attached to a fir tree, where their parents fed them by day.

photo: Daily Colonist

Sos liked to be held almost upright to feed.

photo: Enid K. Lemon

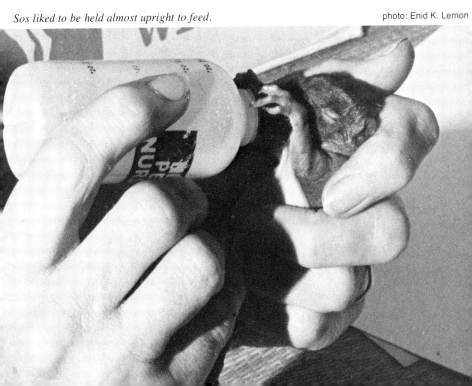

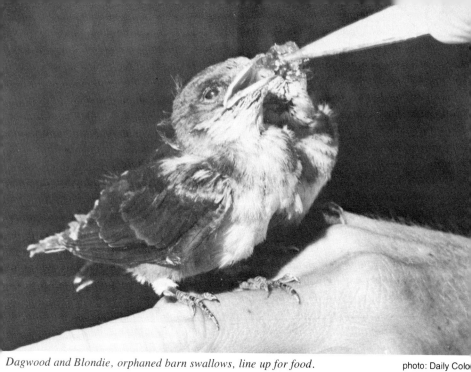

Dagwood and Blondie, orphaned barn swallows, line up for food.

photo: Daily Colo

Mr. Bentley tolerantly serves as perch for one of the crows.

photo: Enid K. Le

accumulated droppings and bits of food I had not been able to clean completely.

I transferred the babies to a new box and attached it to the sweeping branch of a fir tree, since the original site had been a fir. As soon as the parents discovered their much-travelled brood they fed them. But for some reason the mother bird would not cover her babies at night and I had to bring them indoors. The arrangement worked well and the nestlings began to sprout downy feathers. Using tweezers, I learned to pick up the smallest scraps of refuse and so thwarted the voracious wasps. Normally, of course, baby birds keep their nest clean by defecating over the rim or their parents remove the droppings.

In two weeks the small waxwings were identifiable and I judged them to be ready to leave their nest. Fearful of making a wrong move in this odd game, I waited to see what the parents would do.

They left the young after each feeding and slowly the intervals between meals increased. The little birds were restless, trying to hoist themselves to the edge of the nest. The weather was warm and they were crowded tightly in the small cup. Apparently their parents were not going to do anything about teaching them to fly.

I put a finger under one nestling and felt the grip of his feet. As I raised my hand the little wings flapped instinctively. I moved my hand up and down and his wings fanned strongly. At last, on an upward swing, the little bird took off with enough impetus to land him on a branch above the carton. He sat, teetering but safe, and looked about him. The three others achieved different branches by the same method.

Feeling rather smug, I sat on the ground and contemplated my handiwork. And then the parents appeared. They must have been watching because they took over from me, fed their dispersed family and flew off again, leaving me to babysit.

I had noticed that the smallest nestling fared badly when the parents did the feeding. I therefore paid particular attention to him. Without this he would probably have died and I was, of course, interfering; but in this novel situation my action seemed justified and once the nestlings were launched he received a full share of berries and insects when he sat on his branch — the competition being several feet away. The parents brought cropfuls of berries and 'shelled' them in a visible stream like peas from a pod down the babies' throats.

Not knowing what would be best for them in these unusual circumstances but fearing they were vulnerable in their present positions, I collected the fledglings one by one — they made no attempt to evade my hand — and reinstated them in their nest. Except that they wouldn't fit. Extraordinary how a mere hour or so could make so much difference to their size.

I wrapped a piece of cloth around a block of wood and placed them and it in a clean carton, first removing the nest. The block raised them and so kept their tail feathers clean.

After another night in the house I lined them up on one branch of 'their' tree, fed them and waited for the punctual parents to take over the day shift.

This time the parents did show their brood how to fly — by flying past them. The babies watched hopefully, with gaping beaks, but were not fed until several passes had been made. This was the only flying lesson they received.

That evening the whole brood left with their parents.

*   *   *   *   *

That was neither my first nor last experience as a volunteer bird-sitter. Take Dagwood and Blondie, for instance.

They were barn swallows. Dagwood looked like his comic strip cartoon namesake. They were both little at the time and had not attained the lovely royal blue livery of adulthood with white undervest and rusty throatpiece; their long, deeply forked tails had still to develop — barn swallows are the only members of the species to have this characteristic. In fact they were naked when I first made their acquaintance.

They were in a mud nest on a shelf under the porch where they were visible from indoors. I had watched their parents building, observed the laying and hatching of the eggs and could even see the tiny beak-pick the nestlings used to pierce the shell. This neat device, a little hook, is later absorbed into the beak as the bird grows.

The day after the first chick hatched in the batch of four eggs I noticed there was only one parent in attendance. Normally both work like slaves. I watched for three unbroken hours but only the female made the countless journeys to and from the nest with beakfuls of insects. She was growing tired and sat forlornly on a telephone wire after each feeding. At times she clung to the nest with drooping head. I timed her visits at an average of ten-minute intervals, which left me enough time to step in and lend a hand.

A mixture of small flies caught at the window, scraped raw beef and hardboiled egg yolk (eternal standby) made a reasonable ration, to which I added a minute quantity of powdered vitamin-mineral supplement. I fed the first and finally four babies during their mother's absence. By the time she returned I was safely indoors.

She survived heat and exhaustion for two days after the last chick hatched but on the evening of the second day she did not return. Perhaps, worn out by her almost continuous flight in search of food, she was caught in the down-draft of a car on the nearby highway, and killed. Her mate may have suffered the same fate.

Once more I became a parent substitute.

One baby had died. Another died that night, leaving me with Dagwood and Blondie who had sproutings of fluff on top of their heads.

I fed and watched over my little orphans, taking the nest with them in it wherever I went, even to an art show. They stayed in the car and I visited them every half hour. At the end of a week they were covered with soft down. When I fed them they pushed one another around in their eagerness, beaks gaping so wide their little heads seemed to be split in half. After each mouthful they stared solemnly at me from eyes disconcertingly devoid of expression.

Feather quills began to show through the down and presently they began to perch on the edge of the nest to flex their wing muscles as flight feathers grew in. And I thought I would never be able to keep up with their demands for food.

Swallows are almost impossible to nurture on natural food. I had never been so tired in my life! They were too small for mealworms, even had I known at that time of their usefulness as bird food. I caught insects and flies in nets; I caught them on meat put out in the sun; I caught them on windows; on melon skins; and still there were not enough. The egg-meat-vitamin supplement was necessary and the babies miraculously grew.

At the proper time their parents would have coaxed them out of the nest by flying past instead of feeding the ever-gaping mouths, in much the same way as the parent cedar waxwings of the previous story would have done had I not intervened.

Determined to do my best as a parent swallow I perched a baby on a finger of each hand, took them outside and unhanded them onto the laundry line. Then I uncorked a bottle of pre-caught flies under their noses.

The result was to galvanize them into flight to chase their first meal-on-the-wing. Would they return or fly to the roof out of my reach?

They returned.

For three days the two flew on practice flights near the house, were fed regularly on the line and at dusk stepped confidently backwards onto my fingers and were caged for the night.

In a week they were finding all their own food and I left them out at night. Unlike the cliff swallow I was to raise some years later, who flew off when released and was not seen again, Dagwood and Blondie stayed nearby for several weeks, wheeling about us in the air or sitting on the roof resting. Then migrating flocks started to congregate on the telephone wires and I knew their time had come. Would they be strong enough to survive their long flight south to California? As I watched them soaring gracefully above me for the last time, I remembered Whyte-Melville's lines:

> *The swallows are making them ready to fly*
> *Wheeling out on a windy sky:*
> *Goodbye Summer, goodbye, goodbye.*

*   *   *   *   *

Armed with such experiences I felt I might reasonably undertake to care for small wild animals. So I made it known through friends, veterinarians and humane societies and soon all kinds of animals began to arrive. Creatures injured by cars; birds with broken wings; nestlings found by children who did not know how to rear them. In fact creatures in every kind of distress. I obtained government permits to look after those animals which require official authorisation before they can be held captive, even for a temporary period prior to rehabilitation.

Spring and summer are the busiest times but winter storms cause casualties, particularly among birds. Life is always busy, often exciting and sometimes tragic, for naturally some patients die or are too severely injured to treat. These are given a quick and painless death.

I also quickly learned to discriminate between suitable and unsuitable animals. It is so easy to say Yes and then find the animal you have accepted is impossible to cope with. For instance, there was a black brant who had been shot. Could I look after it? I hesitated. It was a sea goose and, living too far from the ocean I knew I could not feed it the specialized diet it would need. For the bird's sake I advised that it be taken to a marine garden where it was nursed and successfully released.

Sometimes I am asked whether I feel lonely or bored since I do not have the 'benefit' of television and for years not even a radio, and no near neighbors.

With so much to do it is impossible to be lonely and how can one be bored when there are live animals to watch over — be they wild and free or temporarily in my care?

I feel deeply that one must see the animal's point of view when it is brought for care. Creatures in captivity are often considered to be 'lower forms of life' and little if any understanding is given them. Appreciating the desire of a captive wildling to be free can hardly be termed anthropomorphic. To identify with the pain of the wounded, the terror of the hunted and the loneliness of a creature deprived of its mate, should not be cause for derision. I go cold when I think of the killing of a goose's mate who has been chosen for life; or hear someone actually laugh while relating that they have a baby animal because the mother was shot. I believe that some at least of my small successes have been partly due to this feeling of sympathy, allied to a gentle voice and even gentler handling. It seems to communicate.

$$* \qquad * \qquad * \qquad * \qquad *$$

One morning the telephone rang at some ungodly hour. The voice at the other end of the line asked if I would take a nestful of crows. Half asleep, I brewed tea and awaited their arrival. The thought crossed my mind that I would have liked them to be ravens as it would have been fitting to rear living emblems of Ravenshill.

Three little crows arrived in a carton and the lady who brought them explained that they had been blown out of a tree, still in their nest. The nest had cushioned the fall and the birds were unharmed but very hungry. I fed them by hand five times a day, and being of a scavenger species they took just about anything I offered them from worms, raw meat and vitamins, to chopped egg and whatever other live food I could catch.

They were solemn birds who regarded me collectively with soft, violet-blue eyes which turned black later. One was well feathered, aggressive and nearly ready to fly; the next, hatched a day or two later, was naturally smaller; the last hatched was still fluffy. All had the attractive yellow 'smile' denoting their youth. This soft yellow extension on each side of the beak grows out until the bill is hard and black.

They lived in an aviary cage until they were strong enough to fly, by which time they had inevitably become tame, as crows do. They then bathed in the pan in which Vixen had washed her kittens, and sat on the edge to drink, dipping their beaks into the water then raising their heads politely to swallow, which looked like saying thank you.

Knowing I would have liked them to be ravens, Edward christened them Edgar, Allen and Poe as a gesture!

A week after their final release Poe II arrived.

Edgar, Allen and Poe stayed around for weeks before eventually tak-

49

ing off to look for more suitable territory. But Poe II was different. She had been in the care of a boy who discovered he did not know how to look after her and she was weak and undersized; although about the same age as the other three who were flying strongly, her feathers were only half developed, she was lame, and her naked neck was plainly and pinkly visible. From a short distance it disappeared so that her feathered head looked disembodied.

Even on a good diet Poe took a long time to recover and one wing drooped obstinately from lack of muscle. It was months before she could fly properly and she had to be caged at night. She too became very tame and was a most endearing bird with quite a sense of fun. Her balance was poor and she often landed clumsily on the slippery iron hand-rail of the balcony steps, losing her footing and sliding ignominiously down, wings flailing. At first I felt sorry for her but after watching her repeat the performance again and again I came to the conclusion it was fun. She put in an appearance whenever I went out and often marched into the living room. She accompanied me on walks in the woods, sometimes perched on my arm, shoulder or head, sometimes flying from tree to tree with frequent walks on the ground almost under my feet. She talked directly into my ear, gently, with little rusty noises ending with a 'pee-eep'? question mark. When she had had enough she flew to the roof and from inside we could hear her gallumphing about up there, pecking at the metal ventilators, which made a frightful noise at our end. She also made friends with Mr. Bentley who allowed her to ride piggy-back for short distances.

Let no-one say that animals have no sense of humor. Poe's was often exasperating. She had a habit of landing on the balcony with a raucous, hungry caw, and performing what looked like a curtsey. I wanted to draw her but as soon as I sat down with pad and pencil she flew to my shoulder, walked down my arm and stole the pencil. Eventually I gave up but the trees at Ravenshill must be rich in pencils.

She dug up plants and tried to ride Vixen, who disappeared into the woods with frantic snarls. She was a destructive bird, like all her kind, but I wouldn't have missed having her.

As she grew independent Poe absented herself for days but came home irregularly for meals. I was not alarmed, therefore, when she was gone a week since she was capable of finding her own food by this time. After ten days I became anxious and after a month gave her up as lost — to me, at any rate.

Once freed, a bird cannot be controlled or watched unless it chooses to stay with us. Our days were sadly empty as we watched and listened in vain for Poe's familiar noisy arrival.

An almost insoluble question arises when such an animal is to be raised. Crows are devils at nesting time (so are ravens), taking baby birds to feed their own young. We have a large bird population at Ravenshill and many nests I would hate to see robbed. Yet I cannot refuse to succor an animal unless, like the brant, I have no means of feeding it. Edgar, Allen and Poe left of their own accord for more suitable country and Poe II was certainly strong enough to survive alone. But if any more crows arrive I will probably release them in a public park where they can join up with their relations.

Does one have the moral right to save one creature at the expense of others? This question comes up again and again.

*　　*　　*　　*　　*

One day a beautiful male varied thrush arrived in the inevitable carton. His orange breast, banded with a wide necklet of deep slate-grey, was soiled with mud. Blood oozed from a bone-deep gash beneath one wing and from a long wound on his thigh. He was aggressive, like all his kind, and pecked at my hands when I began to dress his wounds.

He arrived just before Christmas, which is not the best time to look for worms, insects or fresh fruit. His crop was empty and food had to be provided quickly. At first he was in shock and would not eat but after an hour in a warm dark cage he pecked hungrily at a piece of apple.

The problem with feeding some wild birds in captivity is that although you can approximate their natural diet through a knowledge of their requirements, the result is not always palatable to the bird. When this happens you have to resort to force-feeding while mixing batch after batch of varying content in an effort to please the bird. I taste what I produce, although I draw the line at raw worms, and although it seems alright to me, I am not a bird, and it's his palate that matters.

I made many mixtures based on egg-for-protein and even, at somebody's suggestion, purchased dog meal which the thrush refused as I expected. It is best kept for larger, scavenger-type birds like crows. As my thrush was aggressive he opened his beak whenever I went near him and it was easy to give him vitamin drops, which he would otherwise have refused. But live protein was needed if he was to build new tissues. Meat, no matter how disguised, was refused. He ate the meagre supply of earthworms I managed to dig out of the compost heap but they were not enough. Other insects had gone to ground and none flew.

The answer lay in meal worms, which start life as eggs laid by a small, dark brown beetle (*Tenebrio molitor*). They hatch into minute worms which pupate after they have grown to about an inch in length and in turn become beetles, which lay eggs . . . and so on. The worms (larvae) are relished by insect-eating birds and by my goldfish. They are dry, scaly, and move fast on mere dots of legs on either side of the head. They live on bran and wheat germ with half a raw potato for moisture and on this monotonous fare reproduce in large numbers throughout the summer and fall.

I located some larvae in a pet shop at a penny each. This sounds reasonable until you realize that a bird the size of my thrush requires at least fifty a day. The problem was less one of price than of acquiring them in sufficient numbers.

I sent out an SOS to bird-lovers and donations began to arrive. Kind people rallied to the cause and for several days all was well. The thrush ate all the worms I offered him and began to preen his feathers wherever he could reach round his bandages. He continued to attack my hands — a good sign, it meant he was not going downhill.

People arrived with bags of worms. Others went to Edward's newspaper office. The switchboard operator took the little bags in all innocence and handed them to Edward, who kept quiet about the contents. But one night a torn bag was given her and she peeped inside. Not being an ardent bird feeder, she was horrified by what she saw.

One absent-minded bird-lover rang up to say he had two hundred mealworms for me but unfortunately had left them in a store and couldn't remember where. It took him two days to trace them. Happily an assistant had looked in the bag and run screaming to the manager who, with great presence of mind, put it in his desk and locked it. Lesser men would have consigned package and contents to the garbage can.

Meantime I had begun to breed the worms to guarantee a continuing supply of live protein. In a short time I was able to let my thrush out for short periods of exercise in the utility room. At first his wing was stiff and awkward and he could only hop about fluttering the good one. I gave him my large jade tree and introduced into its pot as many earthworms as I could find. They buried themselves in the soil and my thrush soon discovered the natural food.

From time to time I damped his feathers with a very fine mist of plain water to counteract the dry artificial indoor atmosphere, but as soon as he began to practice flying I gave him a roasting pan of tepid water. He hopped to the edge and had a look, then a drink. I retired behind the door to see what he would do.

He jumped into the water and hesitated. Then the urge to preen must have taken hold because he began to dip his chest and belly and flutter his half-open wings, throwing water over his back, waggling his tail and twisting his neck, the better to soak himself. He made a frightful mess of the walls and floor, but it was a joyous sight. After his bath he flew to the top of his cage and spent an hour tidying himself until he looked like a proper thrush once more, each feather smoothed and neat. From that time he had a daily bath and grew so eager for it that he flew to it before I had time to put it down.

Convalescence is a time I can enjoy. My patient is no longer a constant source of worry; has become accustomed to my presence, and I find it immensely rewarding to participate in the process of healing.

The thrush's wounds, which I had dressed with a smelly but effective mixture of cod liver oil and sulphanilamide powder, had healed cleanly. It was time to release him, but the weather was abominably cold and he would probably have perished since shock and captivity had brought on a premature moult of the feathers on his neck. So he remained in the house a further three weeks, flying round the room by day, perching and roosting on or under the jade tree.

At last a day came when the sun shone and the temperature rose to about ten degrees above freezing. I placed a net over the thrush to catch him and took him to the terrace, where he promptly ate some meal worms I put down for him.

He hopped about and seemed in no hurry to go anywhere. A chickadee flew to a feeder above him. This startled him and he jumped into the air and flew to a tree. Thanks to weeks of practice his flight was strong.

The following day he was standing where I had put his food the day before. He ran a few yards when I went out but directly I left he hopped over and gobbled the meal I left for him. Thrushes eat on the ground, so it was no use putting food in one of the feeders. This necessitated watching Mr. Bentley, who discovered the food and ate it before the thrush had a chance to reach it. For the next few weeks it was a case of Mr. Bentley-in-thrush-out.

One day my thrush was missing from his place on the terrace and I never saw him again.

＊　　＊　　＊　　＊　　＊

Owls are not always as wise as they look. I switched on a floodlight one summer night, intending to take a stroll in the woods before going to bed. As the light came on a young screech owl tried to land on the trunk of a big cedar a few feet from where I stood. He flapped wildly until he gained purchase with his feet, righted himself, then flew to a low branch.

Screech owls are ineptly named since their voices are low-pitched, tremulous and gentle. The woods surrounding Ravenshill are often filled with their lovely small whoooo-ing. The grey-feathered, round-headed, solemn babies, looking old before their time, sit at the entrance to their nest-hole staring unblinkingly down out of round yellow eyes with enormous black pupils. When the parents go hunting at dusk they crowd the entrance, making little clicking noises with their beaks like some elfin typewriter.

This one was a mere fledgling. I crept to a position beneath him and addressed him more or less in his own language — well enough to cause him to reply with a wavering three-note downward phrase. I made a small mouse-like sound and the little bird became vibrantly alert, turning his head sideways and down, staring intently at me. I wished I had something for him to eat but was unprepared for this surprise visit. Thinking only to keep him on his branch so that I could enjoy him a little longer, I made more small sounds and stepped back to see him from an easier angle.

Swiftly and silently the little owl glided to within a pencil's length of my feet. I was so thrilled I must have drawn an audible breath; perhaps it sounded like the squeak of a frightened mouse. The baby owl tilted his head down and hopped one hop, looking for the mouse that wasn't there.

Finally he drifted quietly away to join his brother who was whistling softly from a group of firs. In due course I watched their mother feed them, side by side on a branch. She, of course, being an experienced owl, would not have behaved as her offspring did. But he was only a little owl, at the beginning of his career, and he had to learn by his mistakes.

I have mentioned how I nursed one as a child. Since then I have always cherished the hope that if some unlucky chance should cause one to be injured, whoever rescued it would bring it to me. Accidents happen all too frequently: cars hit owls as they fly low at night across busy roads. Sometimes they fly into high tension wires or against buildings. That is what happened to Mr. A. Dooley.

Mr. Archimedes Dooley (Archie, informally), is a tiny saw-whet owl. He was found with a broken shoulder blade and brought to Ravenshill. He is a little under seven inches tall, smaller than a screech owl and without the ear tufts worn by that species. Saw-whet owls are thought to be fairly common, but are rarely seen because of their small size and a habit of perching close to the ground in dense thickets.

The incredible thing about Archie's species is lack of fear. Wild ones can be watched from within a foot or two of their perch and Archie made himself at home within a few days of his arrival by appropriating the back of an armchair: I know of few things more charming than sitting three inches from a tiny brown owl who looks down at you from enormous eyes. He grasps his perch with three-toed feet. White trousers of fine, short feathers extend over his yellow toes (one back and two front), each of which ends in a wickedly curved, needle-sharp black talon. He is softly brown over his back and stumpy tail. His creamy breast is streaked with light brown, vertical, broken stripes, and a little heartshaped face completes the picture. White, sharply-defined 'eyebrows' rise at a steep angle above his round eyes, from which radiate buff-colored feathers raised slightly from the 'ground' feathering. Slender black feathers extend down his cheeks from the inner corners of his eyes. His wing feathers are softly frayed at the edges to make his flight silent by cutting down the sound of air whistling through them. His prey receives no warning of his approach.

In spite of his 'tameness' Archie is an aggressive little owl who attacks anyone foolish enough to try to touch him. He launches himself feet first, wings half-open, feathers puffed until he is quite round, and drives his talons into your hand. Then he pecks and one is dumbfounded by the amount of flesh so small a bird can remove.

This angry attitude made him difficult to handle when I had to put a dressing on his injured wing. Since a glove made my hand insensitive, I fitted an 'Elizabethan collar' round his neck whenever I had to pick him up with my bare hand. Unfortunately Archie was not brought to Ravenshill immediately he was discovered and the broken bone had already formed a callous which would distort the angle of his wing for perfect flight later.

The poor little chap had to learn how to balance with his body encased in a tubular stocking which kept the taped wing in place, whilst leaving the good wing free. At first he fell over repeatedly until he taught himself to jump to a low perch where he sat regarding the world with a wise if baleful stare, frequently interrupted by slow blinkings of exquisite eyelids which are covered with horizontal rows of tiny white feathers, like frilly lace. Fascinating.

Once I was dressing near the bedroom window, which is set at right-angles to one of the living room windows, through which Archie was watching me. I became aware of his gaze as one does when being stared at, and turned to look at him. With great solemnity he closed one eye in a worldly wink that was irresistibly funny.

Feeding Archie presented a mammoth problem. He refused raw meat which he regurgitated no matter how it was fed to him — even in a gelatin capsule. His principal food consists of mice, occasionally supplemented with small birds and a few insects such as beetles — in fact more or less what comes to hand — saw-whet owls are opportunists.

I put out another SOS, this time for trapped mice to be frozen and given to me rather than thrown out. Laboratory mice that had been killed by chemicals — often chloroform, which reeked — were no use. The supply was sporadic and I had no alternative but to breed them.

I obtained several healthy pairs from one of the university laboratories and made some cages from plastic dishwashing bowls (the oblong kind). Fine wire mesh framed in lightweight wood fitted neatly over the top of each, through which I pushed special water bottles with ballbearings that prevented drips. A pair of mice to each cage. To give them some privacy I bought a dozen coconuts, sawed them in halves and removed the flesh, cut a hole in the edge and upended each half in a cage. The mice loved their little wooden igloos. For bedding and cleanliness I gave them sweet smelling shavings.

Feeding the mice was in itself interesting. Once again I declined to use commercial feed, partly because it only came in fifty pound bags and was used so slowly it became infested with mites. With a little ingenuity and some technical reading I soon had a first-class diet, especially for pregnant and lactating females who required a lot of fat. Once a female has mated I remove the male to a separate cage and this, too, presented another problem. Male mice fight viciously among themselves and had to be kept one to a cage. Now I make sure that I never have more than two or three adult males at a time. I enjoy my mice — the babies are exquisite little creatures when they grow hair — and incidentally they provide me with the opportunity to do some very interesting experiments in color breeding.

But I do not enjoy having to kill them for Archie, who is too incapacitated to deal with them live. Mice are beautiful little animals. Why should I kill dozens of them to feed one small owl? After all, birds die in the wild — should not Archie have been left to die? But he injured himself against a man-made building and the woman who found him was obliged to rescue him.

56

I debated the ethics of the case. Owls, I reasoned, are valuable rodent controllers. Without them the rat and mouse populations would soar to unmanageable proportions. Owls breed but once or twice a year in small numbers (two to four eggs). Mice, on the other hand, can bear litters every three weeks, as they come in heat within twenty-four hours of giving birth. Archie won.

And so I have to steel myself to feed him a freshly-killed mouse every night. I assure my readers that the mice do not suffer — I do. But natural food can mean the difference between life and death, especially over a protracted period. Sick birds do not live long.

When Archie receives his mouse he grasps it in his talons and opens the skull to extract the brain. He then severs the head and swallows it whole. An hour or two later he coughs up a neat, hard, oval pellet of bone, hair and teeth — roughage that has served its digestive purpose. Pellets from immature owls contain hair — bones are absorbed for their calcium. Archie is then ready for the rest of the mouse. He carefully removes the stomach and intestines and deposits them some distance away before swallowing the rest of the carcass. The tail hangs from his beak as he gulps his prey. An amazing capacity for so small a jaw. A pellet is regurgitated about eight hours later. Oddly, although water is always available for him, Archie never seems to drink or bathe.

Any animal unable to make his own way in the wild after treatment at Ravenshill is given a home for life. Archie's injury healed but predictably left him with a malfunctioning wing. To release him would be sending him to death. Saw-whet owls are vulnerable to predation due to their small size and they require one hundred per cent physical fitness and a lot of luck to survive.

He is the only wildling in residence and is a delightful bird although he causes no end of small problems. When I nursed the little brown owl during my childhood, I was not concerned with things like furniture and owl droppings. Now it is different. Archie has the freedom of the house and I keep up with him as best I can with a damp cloth. He dozes most of the day, coming awake at dusk. He has established habits and is quite conservative, like insisting on eating in precisely the same spot on one particular chair, which now has a washable cover for his benefit. When we go to bed I cover all the furniture and the place looks as though we are away; every morning it all has to be removed again. Sometimes Archie gets a cover off and picks a neat little fringe on a cushion or chair cover.

He climbs chairs — even people — to reach his favorite perch on the log pile beside the hearth. There he sits all day, unmoving, alternately

57

dozing and watching out of his benign, wise-looking eyes. Visitors cannot believe their eyes at first when they see that the wee bird by the fireplace is not stuffed.

Archie seems to accept his restricted life with equanimity. He has established a territory in my studio and the living room. He never tries to go through the windows but walks sedately across the floor to sit on the sill and look out, tapping the glass gently from time to time with his beak. I frequently change the branches of the 'tree' I have made for him beside the fire logs, so that he can perch on live wood, and I give him as many insects as possible to vary his regular diet of mice. Like the varied thrush he receives a fine misting from time to time, since he doesn't bathe himself. He is healthy and a great joy to us — we think of him as part of the family. His contribution is to act as an effective deterrent to house-mice!

*　　*　　*　　*　　*

Growing time at Ravenshill is so exciting I spend a great deal of time running from window to window to see what's going on. The earliest happenings are baby mallards. Their mating 'practice-runs' start in October but there are no results until April when breeding begins in earnest. The broods appear in May. One year we had ten, each family averaging eight ducklings so that the water of our ponds seemed to be covered with little balls of brown and yellow fluff.

There is no cradle-rocking, bottle-sucking comfort on a duck pond. Danger is ever-present, even from members of the same species. Lessons begin the instant the babies have pecked their way out of the egg, and the first is in obedience. I watched a proud mother sail from the protection of the swamp brush with her brood clustered closely round her. A jealous duck with another brood joined her and promptly attacked her rival's babies, doing her best to drown them if they strayed into what she considered to be her territory. A third family emerged and all hell broke loose. Thirty-odd ducklings and three furious females. Until the winning duck finally gained ascendancy the mixed-up babies skittered over the surface, peeping frantically, tiny wings flailing, while angry mothers chased them, pecked at them, sat on them, biffed and buffeted them with hard-boned wings. At last, admitting defeat, two families scrambled ashore. Under their mothers' beady eyes the little ones formed single file and trooped across the lawn, the columns separated by several yards, each mother stretched tall with dignity and indignation. They threaded their flat-footed way down the gulley past Vixen's Drainpipe, through the shadowy woods, atoms dwarfed to nothingness by the giant trees. Under some of last year's brown bracken and so to the lake, where there was room for dozens of families.

The newly hatched babies arrived from some very curious places. Mallards are waterfowl. Why, therefore, in the name of all that's wonderful, does the mother choose to nest anywhere up to four hundred feet from the nearest water? Having built her nest on the ground, laid a large clutch of eggs, sat on them for twenty-six days and finally brought forth her numerous progeny, her babies have to start walking almost as soon as their down has dried, all the way to the water, where they are expected immediately to start earning a living. We all know the cute newspaper pictures of mother mallard, followed by a string of ducklings, crossing some busy city street, holding up the traffic. Wouldn't you think there could be a more efficient arrangement, such as building a nest near the water in the first place?

Ducklings quickly learn to feed on land and water. Before they are allowed ashore to eat the finely cracked grain I put out for them, their mother inspects the area from the water, the family clustered beside her. You have to be very close to hear her call, so soft it is; the merest whisper of a quack.

Given the all-clear the babies rush ashore, peeping, and dart hither and yon, little bills vacuuming grain at tremendous speed. Then back to the lake to practice jumping for midges a few inches above the surface. Duckling catches sight of midge and jumps — a whole inch, maybe, falling back with a small plop; then he runs along the surface with wildly paddling webbed feet, downy wing stumps flapping, until the next insect attracts his attention.

All this is tiring for small ducks. Soon mother calls them and takes them to a sunny spot on shore where they cuddle under her soft feathers or lie beside her and try to imitate her by tucking their heads under non-existent wings.

Two weeks after hatching, ducklings are more than twice the size they were at birth. They have already lost a little of the exquisite charm of tiny animated powder-puffs. Their bodies have grown longer and their down thicker, necessitating a lesson in preening. Mother's every action has been unconsciously observed and copied, and it is endlessly amusing to watch tiny bills trying to straighten fluff instead of proper feathers. But the action is there.

As feathers develop, each barb will be drawn through the bill to 'zip up' the tiny hooked barbules, rendering a feather smooth enough to lie tightly over or underneath its fellows. A preen gland near the tail — the well-known 'parson's nose' — supplies oil to be spread on the feathers both by the bill and the top of the head. But it is the arrangement of feathers rather than the oil which makes them waterproof. Even if natural oil is removed with solvents, it has been found that the feathers remain waterproof *providing they are unruffled*. Which is why one should not touch a water bird unless it is really necessary.

Nature's classroom is well organized. Having learned the elements of keeping themselves tidy the ducklings must learn to keep clean.

Mother duck goes through her washing routine for the babies' benefit. She dips her head and throws water over her back, doing a half-roll to wet her sides, opening her wings to wash underneath, preening with her short, flat bill as she does so. Then she shakes her body from billtip to tail in a beautiful shimmy, ending with a tail-wag.

The babies earnestly do their small best to imitate her but sometimes duck disastrously deep, surfacing beneath one of their siblings, to the consternation of both. One lags behind and panics when it sees mother is a long way off. Peeping frantically it half runs, half flies over the water to join the brood. Sheer panic propels the little bird over the surface.

All too soon comes the gangling teen-age stage and with it the instability common to all growing things facing new decisions. One minute the little ones cluster round mother in a tight, security-seeking bunch; the next, they are off in little groups or daringly alone on a gnat-chase or for a nibble at a succulent skunk-cabbage leaf. Danger is always just round the corner: otter, mink and raccoon are good swimmers; overhead, hawks keep watch on the broods. At such times mother utters a loud warning quack and her children rush obediently to her.

Whenever I watch ducklings or chicks I am reminded of that marvellous musical sequence in Mussorgsky's *Pictures at an Exhibition* in which the whole story of baby chicks pecking their way out of their eggs and eventually running about is graphically 'told', so that audiences nearly always break into smiles as they listen.

But life for the wild ones is far removed from the comparative security of the barnyard, and tragedy is never far away. Now and then I am lucky enough to prevent it.

Wandering through the woods one evening I heard a mallard's alarm note coming from the middle of the swamp where some spiraea canes were waving about. Fearing that Vixen might be looking for ducklings to eat, I went to investigate. The sound had changed in the meantime from a loud quack to a strangled cry.

I was wearing shoes and slacks instead of boots and jeans, which made it difficult to penetrate the tall growth which obscured much of the swampy water. When I was at last able to peer through the bushes I saw a mallard in deep trouble. She was not warning her family but desperately crying for herself. She had caught her neck in a forked branch just above water-level; the more she struggled the more firmly the whipping cane held her.

She was at her last gasp. She had ceased to cry out and just hung there, twitching feebly.

I waded into the muddy water, which rose chillingly to my thighs. Parting the bush, I reached for the strangling duck and lifted her clear of the death-trap with one hand while balancing myself with the other.

Back on shore I sat on a log and gently massaged her neck. She lay quietly with closed eyes, barely breathing.

Suddenly she opened her beady little eyes. Her neck writhed under my hand. She began to breathe rapidly, breast feathers heaving. I removed my hands and let her lie in my lap, where she remained for a couple of seconds. Then she heaved herself to her feet and flopped to the ground. She took a few steps, shaking her head, her neck feathers all awry. Then she jumped into the air and flew off, apparently none the worse for wear. I heard her splash down on the lake and imagined the intensive preening she would have to do to restore her wearing apparel to its original tidy state.

I, too, was in a sorry state and needed a bath and change of clothes. But I blessed the happy coincidence which had made me take that route for my day's-end stroll. I shuddered to think of the duck's fate if Vixen had come upon her in her plight.

Not that our ducks are entirely helpless in the face of predators, as I have already mentioned. In the fall I had an opportunity to witness evasion of a different kind from that of a mother duck warning her young by voice.

A mixed bunch of ducks swam rapidly to one end of our lake and took up positions close together, with their heads all turned towards a bush at the edge. Three mallard drakes stationed themselves some distance away, apparently as sentinels, floating several feet apart from each other and facing the main group. The whole manoeuvre was made all the more curious by the mixing of species: mallard, American widgeon and tiny green-winged teal. During the fall they fraternize but not so closely as they were grouped at that moment.

I became aware of sinuous movement under the bush at which all were gazing and a dark brown wild mink appeared at the water's edge. He ran about for a moment or two before disappearing into the bush.

Immediately the ducks dispersed to resume their normal activities, each species again separated from the others by a reasonable amount of water space.

I had witnessed a demonstration of waterfowl tactics. The mink was a serious menace to the ducks and they temporarily abandoned territorial rivalries to group in unaccustomed cooperation in order to create confusion in its mind. There were no alarm sounds. Each duck seemed to know exactly where to position itself.

* * * * *

'Is it weakness of intellect,
* birdie?'*
I cried, . . .

W. S. Gilbert, THE MIKADO

Ravenshill, because it is a rehabilitation centre, experiences more than its share of sadness and suffering but there are lighter moments and one of these was supplied by a common house sparrow we named Alfie. There was nothing wrong with him physically but he was in sore need of a psychiatrist's couch.

To begin with, Alfie differed from his kind by being meek and mild. He was adult, yet apparently retarded. He should have been looking for a mate but was usually to be seen on the ground beneath a feeder, fluttering his wings submissively, beak agape, like a baby bird asking to be fed.

A female began to feed this curiously infantile bird, flying to him with morsels of grain or crumbs which she shoved into his beak. His babyish gestures evidently fooled her into thinking he needed mothering.

When she flew off to feed herself Alfie investigated a nest box under the eaves of the house. English sparrows are notorious thieves of nest boxes and some people go to a lot of trouble to keep them out by means of various ingenious devices. Not being particularly bothered by the species, I took no steps to prevent such habits and in any case I was intrigued.

He collected bits of straw, dried grass, string and wool. A blade of grass, too long to fit the entrance, defeated him. He struggled this way and that, yanking at it from the roof of the box or fluttering directly at the hole, which, of course, was barred by the grass crosswise in his beak. He looked hot and bothered and from time to time entered the box and stuck his head out, chirping loudly.

Morning and evening this crazy bird kept up the nest-building routine, attended now by two hens. Each was kept busy filling his insatiable maw from the feeders. If they were too slow, he fluttered his wings and opened wide his bill. While one hen went for replenishments the other remained as a sort of nursemaid.

The farcical performance, which lasted uninterruptedly for about two weeks, indicated that both foster-mothers, as well as Alfie, needed counselling in the worst way.

Needless to say, psychotic Alfie never succeeded in constructing a nest — which is the female's prerogative in any case — and, as far as we could determine, he remained a bachelor. Had he tried any funny business he would have risked forfeiting the attention he received, but as he obviously hadn't the wit to realize that, we presume he was simply ignorant regarding the mating game. If ignorance is bliss then bliss is relative.

Freud held neurosis to be an exclusively human attribute. It would appear that he was as wrong about this as he was about several other things.

Chapter Seven

When Keats wrote of swallows twittering in the skies he wasn't referring to distress, but when swallows twitter at Ravenshill that's what it means and the cause is invariably a squirrel.

Our nest boxes are built to precise specifications: some for tree-nesting ducks like hooded merganzers or wood duck; some are for owls, flickers and violet-green swallows, all of whom like dark cavities in which to rear their young. Each box has an entrance cut exactly to the size most suitable for the bird-tenant.

But you cannot be certain what will happen when you try to encourage wildlings.

Two swallow boxes were taken over by a clever, agile, bushy-tailed red tree squirrel (*Tamiasciurius hudsonicus lanuginosus*). She enlarged the one-and-a-half-inch hole to about two inches, evicted the swallow and moved in, first into one box, then the other.

For three successive days she gathered long strips of cedar bark from trees or from the wood pile. These she chewed roughly into portable lengths, stuffing them into her mouth. But pieces stuck out on either side of her face and her attempts to force the mass through the small opening in the box ended in failure, reminding us of Alfie. Frustrated, the small, slim squirrel scuttled to a branch to paw at the unwieldy pieces, frantically trying to cram them in further with quick, irritable gestures. With perseverance and much rearranging she succeeded in pushing her first bundle through the entrance and followed it inside to pack it down. She made twenty journeys — quite an undertaking for a small animal who had to run up and down forty feet of trunk, fetch the bark from up to a hundred feet away, chew it into manageable lengths and arrange it all in the box. Finally she retired inside to shred the bits into a fine, silky mattress and to await the birth of her litter.

Native west coast Indians use the soft fibres of cedar bark to make clothes, blankets and even diapers; and baby squirrels burrow in it as soon as they are born. Mother squirrel, making allowances for changes in the weather, regulates the temperature inside the nest box by constantly adjusting the depth of bedding across the hole. Sometimes it is pushed out like a bow window, thick and warm. On fine days, if there is no wind, she opens the entrance; but on chilly, windy or rainy days she draws her 'curtains' half-way or completely across, from whichever side she deems necessary to maintain an even temperature within. When she is away the babies lie snugly in air-pocketed, loosely-knit fibres.

After forty days the babies are born naked, blind and pink like Archie's mice, squirrels being rodents. Litters range from two to seven (mice have up to fourteen babies). I would have given a lot to know how many squirrels were squeezed into the small swallow box.

The second box contained a similar nest; a sort of second bedroom where mother squirrel could retire when she felt like getting away from her babies. These periods gradually increased to the point where she visited them only for short feeding spells.

About a month after I thought the litter had arrived I was watching the box through binoculars and saw movement inside: a tiny head showed momentarily against the opening. The mother was out at the time. Then a sudden flash of movement — and a little shape hurtled downwards. My imagination pictured a broken, lifeless body lying at the foot of the tree — forgetting the earlier experience of little Mo. I rushed down to the lake shore as fast as the steep rocks would allow and searched for the corpse but found instead a very much alive baby squirrel who was extremely angry. It was sitting up under the tree, chattering shrilly.

Mr. Bentley arrived. Hurriedly I cautioned him and he obediently sat down to watch.

I approached the little thing slowly and picked it up. Four of the sharpest teeth it has ever been my misfortune to feel sank into my fingers. I glanced over at Mr. B. His obedience was wearing thin. Were it not for his presence I might have dropped the squirrel; but his eyes were alight with anticipation, so I held on and climbed up the rocks. The little animal in my hands calmed down. Now I had to decide what to do.

The nest box was out of reach except with a ladder which was too heavy for me and anyway I had the infant to cope with. Furthermore, I didn't know what sort of reception it might get if it was returned to the bosom of its family by a human hand.

A baby squirrel's eyes open on or after its twenty-sixth day and as those of the one in my hand were wide and bright and it had a fine bushy tail as long as its body, I assumed it to be five or six weeks old and not yet weaned. It proved to be a female.

I wanted to raise a squirrel and this one seemed to have fallen literally into my hands. I decided to rear her on natural foods. When released she would continue on her normal diet while I would have gained valuable knowledge about food and behavior which would otherwise have been unobtainable. In particular I would discover a formula against the time when somebody might bring an orphan to me. There is nothing published about squirrel milk and so mine would have to be a pioneering effort. I had no intention of keeping anything as agile in captivity for long. The sheer boredom of caged life for such an active creature must be a living death.

The little blob of soft fur remained quietly in the warmth of my hand until I moved a finger, when I was bitten again, so I put her into an old sock while I fetched Vixen's incubator. The baby squirrel used the sock much as she must have used her nest, rushing down to the toe to hide but learning quickly to come to the entrance for food. Squirrel, sock and incubator went temporarily into a bathroom. Mr. Bentley hopefully guarded the door while I went to the kitchen to concoct a meal for the newcomer.

I thought about the life-style of squirrels. They spend much of their lives chewing things and would have high calcium requirements when young to build strong teeth. They eat quantities of greenstuff and fruit which indicates a need for vitamin C. I managed to create a formula suitable for this particular baby. Later, with much younger orphans, I was to encounter difficulties; but more of this in due course.

The mother squirrel's nipples are tiny and comparatively very elongated and there is no rubber equivalent small enough to duplicate the natural version. Nevertheless my new baby managed to suckle lustily from a small puppy-rearing bottle and fell contentedly asleep while I went to devise a house for her.

A baby animal, bereft of its mother, needs warmth even before food and is happier when given a warm, dark place, small enough not to be frightening, but big enough to move around in. If it is fitted with soft bedding, a draft-free box to which additional heat can be supplied if necessary, one's worries are reduced by fifty per cent. Vixen's incubator was not suitable for a protracted stay.

Squirrel nests are often made of moss, alone or mixed with cedar bark, as I have described. Since I was unlikely to be as adept as mother squirrel at reducing the latter to fibres fine enough to be soft as silk, I settled for moss, of which there are acres in our woods. Taking only the dry green tips, I filled a small wooden nest box where the little squirrel could delve and burrow as she had in her birthplace.

The keynote to my animal activities is improvisation allied to an enthusiastic, if inexpert fondness for carpentry, which enables me to construct houses for a wide variety of creatures. The results are not beautiful but they work.

After several abortive sketches I finally devised a sort of three-storeyed house consisting of the nest box, a run and a climbing tower — each unit complete in itself but locking onto the others at will. For drinking I attached a bottle-and-tube hamster feeder. In the wild, one is rarely lucky enough to see a squirrel drink and I was fascinated to watch the baby lapping with her minute pink tongue.

Mr. Bentley was still hovering round the bathroom door as I set up the new squirrel complex on a table by a sunny window. He was disappointed when I corralled him before opening the door but it was a wise precaution. As soon as I opened the incubator lid my new baby escaped in a flash.

She couldn't get out of the bathroom but stupidly I had not thought to bring something to retrieve her with and now I, too, was trapped. She skittered about on the cold linoleum making angry clicking noises. I hurriedly closed the toilet seat in case she should jump.

She finally came to rest behind the toilet where she was nearly inaccessible (one can't even clean behind the damn things). I managed to cup one hand over her, got bitten several times and started to bleed all over the floor. But at least she was safe, if frightened. Transferred to her new quarters she immediately saw the two-inch entrance to the nest box and climbed in without a glance at the rest of my creation. I left her to recover.

This squirrel would never, of course, be imprinted on me; she would never enjoy being handled even if she came to tolerate it. She took her bottle at the entrance to her nest whenever a tap on the box informed her that her meal was ready. The moss, being absorbent, took care of her toilet facilities and there were no odors; I renewed it weekly. The little animal always slept at the back, near the bottom, with all her bedclothes on top of her.

To me, squirrels are almost fairy people. They are so marvellously round: roundly curved body, curved shell-like ears, curved haunches, tail either S-curved over the back like a mantle, or flying straight out behind the long slender body; sometimes proudly swept round the feet as a peeress gathers her train and swirls it round her before sitting down. The large dark eyes are set half-way between the base of the ears and the nostrils and are outlined by a neat pair of pale tan brackets, like this:⊂

The family name for squirrels and their relatives the chipmunks and marmots is *sciuridae*, which comes from *skiouros*, a Greek word meaning 'shadow tail' (*skia*, a shadow; *oura* a tail).

Pictures can give you some idea of the beauty of a squirrel's body but the camera doesn't do justice to their feet which in the wild, no matter how good your binoculars, are always moving too fast to see.

The forefeet each have four fingers and look like long, slender hands. The hind feet have five toes. Each bears a sharp, curved nail, which is non-retractable and greatly facilitates climbing. A squirrel holds its food by pressing its wrists together to use a fifth, rudimentary digit, an oblong cushion of firm pink flesh without nail or joint. Mice and other rodents also have this curious 'thumb-ball'. The fingers, held in-curved to the palms whilst eating, are at other times used for grasping. The effect when a squirrel is having a meal is like an elderly person with arthritis — all you see are knobby knuckles. Baby squirrels, however, use their fingers to help them turn what they are eating, until they have grown strong and experienced enough to use the extra thumb only.

To prevent squirrels and other climbers from reaching the seed, my bird feeders are set on long thin metal poles. The books say this is a reliable method. Our squirrels climb happily up them, negotiate the considerable overhang and sit in the trays eating sunflower seeds. They have to squeeze through the wire mesh which is designed to keep large, aggressive birds away from the small birds' feed. Amazed visitors see a squirrel sitting behind the wire and ask why I keep it caged? Until the culprit climbs out, slithers down the pole and bounds off.

The newcomer had to be named, of course. Edward decided that her constant scolding chatter earned her the name of Higi, short for Higgins, or Mrs. Higgins to be precise — a little person who used to help me in the city house, after my spinal operation. Mrs. Higgins, known as Higi, occasionally as Higlet, was a mere five-foot-nothing of energy with an infectious laugh and an awesome propensity for work. When we left town she couldn't follow us in person, being permanently domiciled in town, so she followed by phone. Every so often I received a scolding from her for overdoing things and not looking after my health. Secretly she longed for the countryside where she was born and her love of animals communicated itself down the wire when she asked avidly for news of the latest denizens of our woods. So she is with us still in spirit, as is her namesake, a pert, agile bundle of mischief. You pronounce her name "Higgy" but Higi looks better in print.

However I pronounced it my four-footed Higi failed to respond; she preferred a sound like a whirring egg whisk. When I fed her she came to her nest-opening like a bullet from a gun: she never in her life did anything slowly. She banged on the door until it rattled, grabbed the bottle, drained it in a few energetic mouthfuls, then shot back into her tunnel until next feeding time.

A week after she arrived Higi became impatient with her bottle, chewing on the nipple as well as sucking it, making generally clear that she wanted something more solid. Her thin yellow teeth — two upper and two lower — were growing long so I gave her a sunflower seed. She took it into her run, nibbled it, played with it, then discarded it. I gave her some juicy stonecrop leaves which she ate at once, followed by a single green fir-cone scale.

Seeds from the Douglas fir cone (*Pseudotsuga menziesii*) are the staple diet of red tree squirrels. They are required in huge quantities, since only the seed is eaten and it is exceedingly small. Two seeds lie at the base of each scale, which must first be deftly chewed to free it. Directly this is done both seeds are bitten off without dropping the cone; the empty scale is then discarded. In time a little pile grows — and grows. The next time you walk through a forest of evergreens and see piles of browning scales against a tree or rock, you will know a squirrel has eaten many meals, over many seasons, enough to make a heap so deep that fresh cones can be stored in it for winter use.

I was hard put during Higi's first summer to keep her supplied with cones. They grow high up and are mostly out of reach unless one uses climbing spurs or tall ladders. Sometimes I was lucky enough to find firs with low-sweeping branches from which the green, excruciatingly sticky cones could be cut.

Fortunately a large flock of crossbills visited our tree-tops. They obligingly cut the cones free, extracted a few seeds and dropped the half-eaten fruit to the ground. Thousands upon thousands of cones lay in the road, the hedgerows and in the woods, so that I and anyone I could induce to help, had merely to gather them into plastic bags and store them in the refrigerator.

No wonder nature is so lavish! Competition for the seeds is fierce. First come the squirrels, who eat them on the spot or cut them off neatly at the stem for winter caching; then the crossbills with their odd parrot-like beaks (although they are finches) — the shape of the bill is adapted to prize open the hard scales so that the birds can extract the seeds with their tongues; then come chickadees and nuthatches who hang upside down to work at the cones. Last come the juncos and other ground-feeding seed-eaters for the seeds when they reach the final stage of their journey towards germination, spiralling down from the few cones still left in the trees. All in all, it is little wonder that so few mature and from those that drop their seeds where they can germinate, how many seedlings survive? On a rotting stump in our woods, two future giants of the forest have started their climb towards the light — two years old and now all of one-and-a-half inches tall. A few yards from them, throwing its colossal shadow as if in protection of the small-fry, stands one of our proud ancients. Two — three — four hundred years old?

Occasionally the fir crop fails and squirrels have to rely on cedar cones. Higi found them good until they matured, when she refused them. The sap may be bitter then, and may contain some of the poisonous qualities of this tree which is inimical to squirrels.

Higi spent most of her days on top of the 'tree' in her climbing tower. I made this by stripping bark from a cedar log, soaking it until it was pliable, then shaping it into a circle secured with wire. A hole where a branch once grew served as a small cache. To prevent everything Higi discarded from falling inside I jammed a piece of bark across it just below the hole. A wide strip of bark attached to the top made a platform, where she spent hours lying in the sun watching life outside the window.

She clearly was not pining away in captivity since she ate voraciously, and played and exercised round and round her house, upside down, right way up — any which way. When she was tired she flattened out on her platform, her feet extended like a bearskin rug, head on forepaws, nose twitching in dreams.

Squirrels have fleas — very small, thin, dark brown ones. I doubted they would bother us or Mr. Bentley, but didn't want them irritating Higi or multiplying indoors. So I occasionally dusted her and her nest with rotenone powder. This is a natural insecticide, harmless to warm-blooded animals (excepting hogs), though it is fatal to fish.

A varied diet makes for a healthy animal and while it is possible for a dog to be kept well on a monotonous but balanced diet, a wild animal has to forage for a variety of foods to achieve it.

The natural food supply for Higi is strictly seasonal and the work of picking and storing goes on ceaselessly all summer and fall. In addition, of course, squirrels must eat to keep alive and store up body fat for the winter. Cones must be buried and, where the climate is dry enough, mushrooms stuck into tree-holes or forked branches. On the coast the Douglas fir cone is the main item stored but in other areas other species of fir or pine are used. When spring returns, birds' eggs and even nestlings form part of the menu, for squirrels are omnivorous.

An unbalanced diet will always show somewhere, sometime. In Higi it became evident in the form of a tiny bald patch on each cheek, barely visible; but you need eyes like a lynx if you're raising animals.

My first thoughts were not dietetic. I checked her for parasites under the skin by taking a very small scraping from the bare spots. Nothing showed under my microscope, so I turned my thoughts to those unsaturated fatty acids that play such an important part in maintaining the health of skin and hair. I added a few drops of soya bean oil and vitamin E to Higi's formula and took to offering her peanuts, rich in oil although not one of her native foods.

A week later the bald patches improved and in two weeks were gone.

I wondered about Higi's emotional state. This baby squirrel had lost mother and siblings. Yet she was unwilling to accept my touch. A pity, since I enjoy touching animals and far from making them afraid, have often been able to calm them by touch alone.

I tried and tried again. Yet the most I achieved was to have Higi come to my hand for food. Even the lightest touch sent her tearing up her tree. I decided to bide my time. Had she fallen into my hands before her eyes had opened I would have had no problem — or so I thought at the time. Later experience showed that squirrels dislike any kind of handling at any age. Meanwhile, with Higi my decision to wait turned out to be a wise one.

Chapter Eight

I once had a sparrow alight upon my shoulder for a moment . . . and I felt that I was more distinguished by that circumstance than I should have been by any epaulet I could have worn.

Thoreau, WALDEN (WINTER VISITORS)

While Higi was living in the house, her mother was providing us with another drama outdoors.

On the evening of the day Higi fell out of the nest we saw more movements at the entrance to her birthplace.

The next day things began to happen.

Watching from the window, I saw a baby peering out at the world beyond its nest. Then the tiny head withdrew hurriedly. Mother returned from an expedition to stay a few minutes with her family. By now she was feeding her infants about three times daily and as far as I could see they received an average of only twenty-five minutes of her time in the entire day. She was absent for a long time during the afternoons, spending some of it peacefully in her second nest.

The June sun was very warm; it must have been crowded and hot in the small nest box. I wondered if squirrels perspired. Most animals have sweat glands in the pads of their feet but are unable to exude moisture from their bodies apart from their tongues; they rely on the insulation of their coats to protect them from heat and cold. Higi's feet sweated a waxy substance which built up into a tough layer on her platform; once it had hardened I could only remove it with a knife.

Anyway, suddenly the head which had reappeared when mother left, leaned far out from the entrance, followed by a tiny body. Half-way out then panic at the enormous void beneath and a hasty retreat. Five minutes later the baby tried to climb out. I thought this might be its first venture into the world beyond the nest and, if so, wondered how it would manage to negotiate the steep overhang to the roof of the nest box. To go down would surely be to fall. To go up meant first attaining the rooftop.

The infant was too small to manage alone and mother was away. The clawing nails found no foothold. It fell. The second baby to tumble forty awesome feet to the unyielding rocks below.

Once more I scrambled to the beach and found a baby squirrel sitting beneath its nest tree, apparently as unharmed as Higi had been. When it saw me, this one scolded in a high-pitched voice and ran up a nearby stump. We examined one another eyeball to eyeball. Instinctively I put out my hand, slowly, aching to touch this exquisite little bundle of shiny brown fur.

The little one was brave; although it urinated in fear it stood its ground until my hand was almost touching its soft body. Suddenly it leapt onto my arm and the next few seconds were a bewildering kaleidoscope of agility, lightning speed and accurate judgment. This four-inch atom, full of fear-generated energy, scrambled up the claw-tangling wool of my sweater, up my arm then round my neck to the top of my head. There it paused. I could feel the clawed toes taking a grip on my scalp in preparation for a prodigious leap to the mother tree. Then up its trunk, chittering in anger and fear, to the lowest branch, some fifty feet above me. All in a matter of seconds.

He (or she for all I knew) sat looking down at me, at the lake, at a whole new world.

I returned to the house and my binoculars.

Soon mother returned in quick, tentative jerks across the ground. She had probably been watching from the woods nearby, but that she did not know exactly what had happened became clear as I watched her searching the ground in ever-widening circles, looking for her infant. Failing, she ran up the tree and found him, whereupon she seized him by the scruff of his neck and a struggle ensued. Plainly she was trying to get junior onto his back. Squirrels carry their young belly up, with tail curved round mother's neck. But could she succeed with a youngster so independent that he had already been on the ground and climbed back unaided? Furthermore, he was almost as big as his mother.

This was the first squirrel family I had been able to observe closely and I was unaware at the time that such behavior is normal: the unusual aspect of this little drama was not that the baby was out of the nest but that he had fallen out. Possibly the artificial nest box with its slippery sides was to blame. Possibly the mother was young and inexperienced.

After several abortive attempts to get her baby onto his back, she finally threw her body across him, pinning him down with her feet on either side of him. With her teeth she got a firm hold on his soft underbelly and in one supple movement heaved him out from under her. She raced head first down the tree, baby's tail wound round her neck in the approved fashion.

She tore into the woods and remained hidden for some time. Meanwhile I trained my glasses on the nest box. There were two more heads at the entrance. One baby in our house, one in mother's mouth, and two more in the nest. Total four. No wonder they were warm. At that time I had no idea what the temperature inside the nest might be, but subsequently discovered it varies from 70°F to 85°F (21°C to 30°C), according to season, time of day and the way the nest is constructed.

Soon mother squirrel returned and enticed two more babies from the nest. It took a long time. Once they had negotiated the overhang of the roof they were able to swing themselves on top of it. There mother mauled each one around until she had a good mouthful of underbelly, then ran down the tree, across the lake shore and into the woods. One baby was prettier than the others, its fur redder, its tail fuller; otherwise they all looked alike.

Yet another head appeared, smaller than the rest. The runt, perhaps? Mother was still away and the baby made valiant efforts to get out of the box, failing dismally. Each time the smooth wood proved too much and after slithering about ineffectually it withdrew inside. Finally the tiny creature emerged again and by reaching above its head and hauling prodigiously on its forefeet, heaved itself at last around the overhang and so to the roof.

Still no sign of mother.

What was she up to? Had my presence beneath her tree frightened her? Was she encouraging her family to leave because she wished to move them to a safer place?

During her absence her baby climbed back inside the nest.

Eventually mother rushed up her tree once more and with soft appeasing grunts tried to induce this last infant to follow her. He wouldn't, so she climbed in and stayed for ten minutes, presumably suckling. That her babies were still being breast-fed was easy to deduce from her swollen nipples.

For four days we were treated to the incredible spectacle of a mother squirrel running two homes. Three youngsters were stowed in some new nest but the last remained in its birthplace. Edward and I took turns watching as mother squeezed through the entrance hole to feed her lone baby, then rushed off again to take care of the rest of the family. We wondered how long she could keep up this intensive double housekeeping.

On the fifth day the single baby tried to climb out again and for once mother was there when she was needed. She sat on the roof making small encouraging movements of her head and body but no sound. Her infant made it to the top and was carried down like the others.

The next we saw of them was a month later. The young had taken over a nest box by the pool — the same that, although intended for wood duck, had housed the screech owl who fell victim to Vixen and which was to serve its original purpose another year.

I never discovered where the mother had hidden her babies. For all I know she might have used the wood duck box — I had not thought to look there. At any rate, when I saw them playing on its roof, Higi, still indoors, was ceasing to be bottle-fed. The two parts of the family were weaned at the same time.

Meanwhile Higi sat in the sun on her platform, completely at home. She chattered at us and at Mr. Bentley; seemed not to mind the noise of the vacuum cleaner and was vitally interested in everything that went on indoors and out.

She relished various young leaves and grasses, particularly catkins from a weeping birch. As the season progressed she ate wild strawberries, tearing at the cage as soon as she saw them and devouring them in preference to all other food; young maple seeds, an occasional small piece of sweet corn, ripe apple, or raw carrot; and always the irresistible Douglas fir cones, green and sticky. Her fur never became soiled, no matter what she ate and she taught herself deftly to shove cones through the two-inch tunnel connecting her run to her climbing tower.

She began to take food from my fingers through the wire. This was a wary process of circling round and round her tower past my hand, nearer and nearer to the tid-bit. A quick sniff, then on and round again. As though she sensed that I was about to give up, she suddenly spun round the wire at lightning speed, snatched the nut and dashed to the platform at the top of her tree to eat it at leisure (if a squirrel is ever at leisure).

A month after her arrival I stopped her formula. Once off the bottle — she was about sixty-five days old — she devoured wild plants in greater and greater quantities. I was intensely interested to learn precisely what she found acceptable.

Indian plum, for instance (*Osmaronia cerasiformis*). I thought she would like the flesh of the fruit, rich in vitamin C. Not so. She tore it off and ate only the kernel inside its woody seed-coat. Undoubtedly a source of vegetable protein and oil. Cascara berries (*Rhamnus purshiana*), devoured by band-tail pigeons, she disdained. She ignored plantain seed-heads but loved wild wheat and barley, first snipping off the dangerously barbed barley-awns. Grass seed-heads formed a minor part of her diet. When I offered her salmonberry (*Rubus spectabilis*) or thimbleberry (*Rubus parviflorus*) she went wild with delight. Although wild squirrels leave rose hips alone, probably because of their uncomfortably spiky stems, Higi in captivity ate all I brought her, notably the tiny, brilliant fruit of *Rosa gymnocarpa,* which, like all rose hips, is very rich in vitamin C.

And so by trial and error I found the right plant foods for my small charge and in addition, since she was in no position to rob birds' nests, I gave her raw egg yolk and small pieces of raw chicken.

One day a deer and two mallards appeared beneath Higi's window. She crouched low on her platform and barked at them! Suddenly she gave out a soft, melodious whistle. The tone was round and sweet. Three notes, repeated twice, then silence. I couldn't believe my ears. A squirrel whistling! I had heard them chattering from the woods in many voices: angry calls of aggression at intruders into their territories; appeasing calls to their babies or to each other; short barks; prolonged rattling trills. But never this beautiful whistle. I interpret it as meaning frustration or anger. I have since heard and recognized it in the wild but had Higi not provided me with incontrovertible proof of its source, which I tape-recorded, I would have sworn that this lovely sound was made by a bird. In all the literature on squirrels that I have read there has been no mention of whistling.

*   *   *   *   *

Higi was not quite ready to return to the wild. First she must be introduced to a wider variety of food and I had to learn more about her habits.

During the following weeks she either ate or ignored the various wild foods I brought her twice a day. She did not eat during the hot afternoons, preferring early morning and evening, like all wild things. On sunny days she flattened herself on her platform and slept spreadeagled, head on forepaws. If it was shady she curled into a tight ball, nose in tail, like Vixen.

Stale food was never touched, nor did she ever retrieve anything she dropped. In a land of plenty, why be economical? She kept her teeth filed by enlarging the hole in her tree and gnawing raw bones.

Her coat was glossy and silky, a beautiful warm brown with black guard hairs; a black line divided her pale grey-white underbelly from the rest of her body fur, and the hair on her legs was a brighter shade of cinnamon. Her ears were covered in fine red hair, but had not yet developed the charming little tufts or tassels that characterize the ears of her species in winter.

She was thriving but never very tame. She would come down from her tree to my hand, nip it, take the proffered food and then return home at the double.

At the end of July there was a marked change in her behavior. Whereas previously she had looked out of the window with interested detachment, now she grew restless. Whenever a bird or other animal appeared in her line of vision she ran up and down her tree, scolding. Or was she expressing a longing to be free?

During the second week in August I decided to release her. The cone crop was good and her siblings had established territories away from the house. Only her mother remained in the area.

Would Higi take to the wild immediately, or would she need time to adjust, and perhaps need help from me? Squirrels receive no parental guidance after weaning. While the mother is using her spare nest to get away from the kids, she also establishes a new territory from which her young are excluded even before they are weaned; or sometimes she moves the whole litter to a new nest near the edge of her original territory. If there is enough food available she may designate a portion of her holding to her offspring, who in turn spread out and find their own. Once weaned they never return to their birthplace nor to their mother — in fact they may even fight with her.

I wondered what Higi would do when her turn came. She had missed her mother's donation of a portion of territory and so would have to stake out her own piece of real estate. In this she could meet with opposition from other members of her species.

Not having the detachment of the pure scientist, I dreaded losing this exquisite little creature who had brightened my days. She was a living, breathing being, full of mischief, resentment, fear, and quite a lot of what looked like pure fun. In short, I had become very fond of Higi. Would I lose her altogether or would she return to me of her own free will as Vixen had? Not being imprinted on me, Higi would retain wild memories. There was nothing to do but take the plunge and find out.

*   *   *   *   *

I prepared for Higi's release by constructing a food tray, nailing it to a tall fir within sight but not reach of the balcony. It was placed below her mother's original nest box, which we hoped Higi would use. I designed a tool to avoid using a ladder. It consisted of a plastic bottle with its top removed through which I stuck a long bamboo rod: nuts in bottle — reach over and tip into tray.

Edward put a ladder against the tree and did a 'dry run' to make sure we could reach the box. The idea was that Higi would be transferred in her nest box to the one on the tree. But it didn't work out that way.

I coaxed her into her box and confined her with a sliding wire door. This made her angry and she began to shake it with hands and teeth.

It was a glorious day. The rocks were redolent with a "stream of rich distill'd perfumes", flowers bloomed, the lake was warm. Perfect for Higi's return to her own world.

We stood on the balcony to watch Bernard, who had undertaken to perform the transfer so that Edward could photograph the act. Audrey and I had nothing to do for once.

Bernard climbed the ladder, carefully carrying Higi in her box. He arrived at the one on the tree and raised Higi's to it, holding the boxes entrance-to-entrance. Perfect. But he needed three hands. One to raise the little door, one to hold the box steady and one to hold onto the ladder. Something had to give. Inevitably the gap between the boxes widened and when he finally opened Higi's door a space separated them.

Higi needed no invitation. She was out — whoooosssh! In one breathtaking movement she leapt from box to tree to the top of the second box to a branch to the end of the branch to the ground — all in a series of lightning bounds. We clutched the balcony rail in an agony of alarm lest this time she might be injured, although by that time we should have known better. We must have presented a curious sight: Bernard rooted in astonishment to his ladder; the rest of us just gaping. Edward looked helplessly at his camera. There would be no pictures of Higi's release for posterity.

Higi sat up on the ground and after a second tore off across the rocks to the woods, where she remained for the rest of the day. And the next. And the next.

Sadly I dismantled her old home and disinfected it, ready for who-knows-what future occupant. Sadly I sat outside calling her. Sadly I retired to bed that night and subsequent nights, afraid I would never again see her at close quarters.

Three days passed. We enjoyed them because we were on holiday. Yet in each of us there was a small inner question-mark: would Higi return? Nothing was said. But I think we all had what Audrey described as 'a small cold tear trickling down inside'. Releasing a wild creature who has been cherished inevitably leaves one with a sense of loss — and responsibility.

We were resigned to Higi's absence until one evening about two weeks later when all the doors and windows were open to the summer air. Our desultory conversation had lapsed into silence and I became aware of a small sound behind my chair, the tiniest scratching on the grass matting.

Higi was standing just inside the door. Alert, stretched full length, on tiptoe for retreat, curiosity visible in twitching whiskers and side-to-side motion of her head as she peered nervously about her. She moved across the floor in rapid jerks, pausing after each step.

Silently I signalled the family. Somebody coughed. Higi shot up the bamboo curtain to the valance rail, where she sat studying us, muttering.

After a time she climbed down head first and resumed exploring the room. She carefully examined a vacant chair, then suddenly leapt from it to another — which had me in it. Startled, she perched on the arm, her raised forepaws in the air, teetering slightly on her haunches.

With great caution she inched towards the hand lying in my lap. Sniffed it. Put two cool little forefeet onto the back of it and looked me in the eye. I spoke her name softly, moved my hand a fraction. She did not jump away. And miraculously she did not bite.

There were no tid-bits in the room to tempt her. Had she returned to our habitation because it was familiar? There was plenty of food outside, so she must not be returning from necessity.

Eventually she leapt down and ran out, but not in panic; she had simply finished her exploration for the time being. When I went onto the balcony she was sitting on her fat little bottom in her tray, eating a sunflower seed. I resolved to have nuts handy indoors at all times.

Slowly a pattern established itself. Higi disappeared in the woods all day, but in the evening would rush into the living room if the door was open. If it was not, she would return later and scratch at it. The sound was so faint that, fearful of disappointing her (and us) by not hearing it, I generally left the door open.

Mr. Bentley had to be shown anew that this was Higi, who was not to be touched. The old fellow never tried to chase her, but sat quietly whenever she was in the room. Having seen much of him during her stay in the house, she soon became accustomed to his presence and often passed close to him without flinching, although she never became familiar with him as Vixen had.

I set out some nuts in an ashtray. She climbed the curtains and dropped to the table, where she ate them at leisure, front paws rotating each nut as she peeled it. It was messy, but worth the vacuuming just to watch her adroitness. I moved the ashtray to other places. She always found it. One day she took one of her unerring leaps from the floor to a table three feet above her and skidded across its slippery surface. Undaunted, she began to cache nuts around the room: on the valance rail, in the soil of a potted plant on the dining room table, and above all, behind books. We have so many books I felt she would need a card-index to find her nuts again.

Her confidence in us was flattering. She did not show fear even when the doors were inadvertently closed one evening by someone who thought she had left. Shut in, she merely inspected all her caches and ate some nuts while she waited for the door to be opened again; then made a leisurely exit.

One day while she was sitting eating nuts on the curtain valance, Vixen and her babies strolled through the open door. With an air of fascinated concentration, Higi stared down at the rolling, tumbling, snarling little raccoons below her. It must have been an alarming sight. Each was three times her size, but none so fast as she. She remained silent until they departed and then left herself by way of the nut dish. None of the raccoons had noticed her presence above them. I found it interesting that she had kept silent. The creatures she had scolded from her cage in the house had not been predators. I wondered whether she would have kept quiet had a raccoon passed under her window.

Eventually she came to eat from my hand, rewarding my patience. In time she became tame enough to sit in the palm of one hand eating the nuts I fed her with the other, even letting me stroke her with one finger. But she never went to anyone else.

She developed the habit of rushing outside to bury whole nuts in their shells, while eating all broken or shelled ones on the spot. These would not keep in the warm soil and so were to be eaten at once. She increased her waistline, became very bold, and even insisted on thrusting her head into the jar if I wasn't quick enough with the nuts, a habit that was to prove immensely important later. She drank from the pool on the terrace, or from puddles in the rocks, for about half a minute at a time, lapping rapidly with her tiny pink tongue.

I wondered whether she would know how to establish a territory. She did. In time I determined its boundaries and a rough calculation showed she had staked out a normal squirrel area of a little over two acres. It contained one magnificent fir tree as a rich source of cones, also several smaller ones and a wide variety of shrubs, ground-hugging plants, mushrooms, mosses and fruits. If a food-tree forms part of a common boundary between squirrel territories both neighbors recognize that discretion is the better part of valor and respect each other's right to eat from it. Which is more than can be said of some human neighbors.

There are differences of opinion about squirrel memory. Some say it is good and that the females know if they have sufficient cached food in the spring to support a spring litter. My own observations show that about fifty per cent of their stored food is forgotten and wasted, as testified by bird boxes filled to the roof with moldy peanuts, cached and forgotten, while newly buried ones are constantly being dug up. Higi screamed at the window for nuts in spite of all the hoards she ought to have remembered. Since buried food must be located by smell, birds could not have stolen her supplies as they have a poor sense of smell, if any. The only bird to steal cached nuts is the Steller's jay who does it by accident. He picks up large pieces of bark or small stones, looking for insects beneath them, and if he finds a peanut instead of a bug, eats it.

One day in November Higi dug frantically under a group of deep-branched cedars. She unearthed something round and black and shiny, which she began eating on the spot, glancing round from time to time as if on the watch for competition.

I was intrigued, and when she scampered away went out to see what had made her work so furiously. She had dug up half a dozen fungi I had never seen before. Unable to identify them from my books, I elicited the help of one knowledgeable in mycology.

She looked at the specimens with a glint in her eye.

"Where did you say you found them?"

"In my garden, under some cedars — that is, Higi, my squirrel, found them and dug them up."

"So. The squirrel. Yes. Now I am sure and I wish I had found them myself. Only one member of this species has ever been found in this vicinity. You have the rare *Mycenastrum corium*. It is a relative of the puffballs, which are beloved of squirrels."

I asked if it was edible, since I am interested in wild edible fungi and gather many for our table. She told me its edibility was not known, and advised me to leave it off my menus.

I went so far as to cook a tiny piece and Edward watched fascinated as I ate it straight out of the frying-pan. I think he thought I would foam at the mouth and drop dead on the spot. Instead I reported a mild, dull flavor and a leathery texture. *Mycenastrum corium* was memorable only for its scarcity. It has appeared again at intervals and I have collected a few of the truffle-like growths, about the size of a golf ball, black-skinned, with dull greyish tan within, but generally I leave them for Higi and her relatives, who obviously enjoy them more than I do.

*　　*　　*　　*　　*

Higi herself grew in beauty and in grace and her stay in captivity had not done her any harm as far as I could see, nor dimmed any of her natural instincts.

As the weather grew colder it became too drafty to leave the big door always open for Higi's convenience. She had to learn to come in by a narrow glass door beside the living room windows. I shut 'her' door and opened the other just wide enough to allow her passage. Under it I fixed a sturdy log up which she could run to the sill. She quickly understood that the way to food was just round the corner. She never forgot that, whatever else slipped her mind.

Cold winds blew; snow and ice covered the land. For two and a half months our ponds were frozen solid. The ducks left for the open water of bigger lakes than ours. Birds fed ravenously from the feeders. The quiet in the woods was palpable. Everything slowed down or slept, including Higi. There were no more squirrel barkings or scoldings from the trees; neither she nor her mother nor her siblings gave any sign of life.

Her next big adventure would be the coming of spring and the finding of a mate. In the meantime she would be dozing in some tree, perhaps in an old woodpecker hole. Squirrels make nests almost anywhere from ground level in a half-rotten log, up to sixty feet above ground. If they cannot find a ready-made hole they construct a nest on a branch, away from the trunk.

Would Higi survive?

Chapter Nine

If you look anew
with every new day's dawning,
as aware as though
the world had just begun,
you will fill your life
with meaning every morning,
but apart from that
get very little done.

Piet Hein, GROOKS 4.

Worry is surely one of life's more futile activities, yet each time one of my animals is absent for longer than I think it should be, I worry like a mother whose daughter is travelling abroad alone. She knows the girl can take care of herself but she worries about predators. So do I. When I reach the stage of becoming really alarmed, the animal usually returns, healthy, unhurt and in perfect control of itself.

Higi was missing for months. Since we had one of the wettest springs on record, with rain pouring everlastingly and everything flooded, I thought she would stay sensibly warm and dry wherever she had denned up the previous winter. It was idiotic to worry. But I did.

A torrent of spume-flecked water poured through the woods from the pond overflow, coursing through Vixen's Drainpipe and eroding precious soil. The lake turned muddy with silt. By March we despaired of ever seeing the sun again. Early aconite and snowdrop were bashed down by the rain; when the time came for the crocuses to bloom, they wilted in bud and drooped, sodden and sorry-looking. A few brave bees tried to gather pollen but were frustrated by permanently closed petals. The flowers which I was waiting to paint could not be pollinated and I marvelled at and blessed nature's forethought in providing a second means of propagation for this species, from an underground 'flower' which shed its seeds without benefit of insect.

Perched on our rocks, surrounded by water, we waited anxiously to see how our creatures had fared in the flood — unlike Noah, who knew.

On the last day of that desolate March our depression was lifted when the first male hummingbird arrived, dazzling us with his gorgeous coloring.

Higi's mating season was almost over and I had neither seen nor heard her. There was no sign of squirrel activity in our woods and I wondered if they had all moved to other locations.

There was still no sign of her through May. In June a second batch of screech owls was reared in the wood duck box. By the end of the month the garden was alive with hordes of buzzing hummingbird babies. But still no sign of Higi.

In July violet-green swallows taught their second-brood offspring to fly and feed on the wing, diving and swooping over the lake with infinite grace. And at last, after an absence lasting longer than any other I had ever had to endure on the part of a wildling I had reared, I heard Higi whistling from her tree near the house.

Blissfully unaware of the alarm she had caused, she took up her life where she had left off months before, straightway demanding nuts. But on the day of her return she was palpably angry at something.

The object of her ire was a small, young female squirrel at the foot of her tree. The newcomer began to climb in quick jerks as squirrels do when unsure of themselves. Higi, who had been sitting on a branch with her back comfortably against the trunk, stood up and stamped her hind feet. She peered down at the intruder, whiskers akimbo, throat taut with the intensity of her open-mouthed, staccato machine-gun scolding. Her body vibrated with fury.

In spite of Higi's warnings the new squirrel continued to climb and disappeared inside the box I had nailed to the tree in the hope that Higi might nest in it. (She didn't, but it was useful to her as a dry place for storing nuts.) This was more than Higi could bear and she lost her temper. Tearing down the trunk she spreadeagled herself on the face of the box. Holding on for dear life with two hind feet and one forefoot, she boxed the ears of the other squirrel who was looking out. With swift jabbing movements of her doubled fist, Higi drove at her enemy's face until the beleaguered little animal shot out of the hole, down the tree, and away over the rocks to a group of cedars on the other side of the house.

As is often the case with humans, Higi when extremely angry looked quite ugly. The beautiful, soft contours of head and body hardened into rat-like meanness (after all, she is a rodent). Directly her peace of mind was restored she reverted to a charming, gentle-looking bundle of fur and went back to living as she had always lived, vastly busy and always in a hurry.

The hummingbirds left us in August and migrated south. By September Higi and the newcomer were still sparring over the nuts I put in the box. Repeatedly she tried to enter Higi's preserve, only to be violently repulsed with shrieks of rage which sent her scurrying back to the cedars that appeared to be part of her territory.

This group of trees had once been part of Higi's domain, so my conclusion was that the new squirrel must be one of her babies to whom she had given the territory. Higi had become a mother and we had never even known she had mated, let alone where she had made her nest. The phenomenally wet spring must have kept all our squirrels continually running for shelter, and their mating probably took place at times when I, too, was under cover from the elements.

Higlet, as Higi's daughter was immediately christened, established one of her boundaries precisely in the centre of our living room window. Peace reigned as long as each remained in her own domain, but if either crossed the invisible dividing line there was mayhem. They gave chase with fine disregard for maternal love on one side or filial duty on the other. They chased each other from the nut supply, appearing to fight madly on the ground, or on stumps on one side or other of the boundary. It looked quite vicious, yet I never observed them make more than fleeting contact. The chase seemed to be more a matter of speed and bluster, calculated to rout the rival without dealing out any physical damage. The invaded squirrel proclaimed her ownership of territory in vituperous trills, high-pitched barks and the 'egg-whisk' rattle. As the intruder drew nearer and nearer her goal — the other's nuts — in a series of tentative jerks, tail twitching, the owner let out a shriek and rushed down her tree to drive the thief off by sheer noise and force of personality. The invader always turned tail and fled. It wouldn't do for animals to fight each other to the death whenever they are upset.

During one of her raids on her daughter's precincts, Higi, stolen nut in mouth and with Higlet in hot pursuit, missed her footing on a slippery rock and fell into the little pool on the terrace, losing her peanut in the process. She swam easily, as animals do when they must, and soon scrambled out, dripping and undignified, forgetting the nut in her haste. She shook herself briskly and in seconds was dry again, her fine straight hair shedding moisture easily. Later in the day I watched her with amusement when she returned stealthily and leaned precariously over the edge of the pool in an effort to retrieve her peanut. It floated away, driven by her paws riffling the water. She sat back on her haunches, as though working out the next move. Then she scampered round the edge to a point near the nut, took a firm grip with her hind feet and leaned far out, grasped it in both forepaws and transferred it quickly to her mouth. Hauling herself in by sheer hind-quarter muscle-power, she rushed off, for once unchallenged.

This rivalry for peanuts between mother and daughter became serious when for the first time in years the fir cone crop failed. To tide them over, I decided to buy a supply of their favorite nuts, but found that, as it was not yet Christmas, the stores were not selling raw peanuts in the shell. I had to buy them shelled (and unsalted) at health food stores, an expensive and luxurious treat for a couple of wild squirrels. In addition, birds like juncos, towhees and even tiny chickadees, stole the nuts as fast as I put them out. Higi and Higlet were so busy hiding them they hardly had time to eat any.

Higi usually ate shelled nuts and stored only those with intact husks. Whether the natural food shortage altered a pattern of behavior, or whether the effortless ease of collecting piles of readily available food triggered a frenetic urge to store, I do not know. The fact remained that neither squirrel stopped to eat more than the barest minimum of shelled peanuts. Most were buried: a small hole hurriedly dug, the nut shoved in, the soil pulled or pushed back at frantic speed by the forefeet. Nuts were hidden in bird boxes or holes in trees, even in flower pots and a bag of peatmoss. Many were subsequently dug up and eaten by deermice. No doubt Vixen helped herself whenever possible.

When the stores again sold peanuts in their shells, I bought a large supply to keep the squirrels fed until winter's cold sent them into hibernation. Two little squirrels, weighing about eight ounces each, accounted for more than ten pounds of light-as-feathers peanuts.

* * * * *

Another winter settled in. Higi spent the cold months in a tree box with a hinged lid, made for Vixen, who never used it. When I occasionally looked in, Higi's nest of moss was always untidily strewn with empty peanut shells, proving that she remembered where she had hidden some of them at least. Higlet denned up in a woodpecker hole.

Suddenly, in the last days of the dying year, our squirrel population doubled overnight.

Two muscular, bushy-tailed males erupted onto the scene and began to chase Higi and Higlet, who were up and about that mild morning. Round and round, up and over and round again, little pattering feet skittering unerringly along the highways and byways of the treetops, making prodigious leaps, running to the extreme tips of slender cedar boughs, leaping to the next tree just when it seemed they must catapult into space — they seemed like circus acrobats on the high wire, their tails the parasols. They gave me the impression that they were socializing rather than sparring.

In Higi's species, territories are occupied and defended by single

86

squirrels, whatever their sex. When the females are in heat they allow the males to enter their terrain. They may become involved with as many as ten different partners during the mating season in March. This was December.

I rang up several naturalists to see if any of them had experienced such unusual behavior. None had. All agreed that this was a phenomenon, out of season, out of pattern, to be noted and written up, which is what I am doing now.

From time to time Higi and Higlet advertised their territory by calling, but the males were silent. Had it been the mating season they would have uttered appeasing calls before crossing territorial boundaries. As it wasn't, the females should have chased them off.

The males found the nut supply and we were treated to the sight of four squirrels climbing to our window every day.

After a week, as suddenly and unpredictably as they had come, the two newcomers vanished, leaving Higi and her daughter once more in sole possession and no more friendly to one another than before.

I wondered if the invasion was due to the food shortage. But I cannot explain why, if they were not playing the mating game — and I am sure they were not — Higi and Higlet permitted the males' intrusion without protest.

In due time at least one male reappeared. I spent hours in the woods watching Higi near the centre of her territory, playing with him and mating, both chattering their soft, grunting love-calls, occasionally rattling out a not-too-serious aggressive call, but never a whistle.

And there Higi's story might have ended had I not taken a particular trail one evening.

I was looking at a sunlit cobweb stretched between two leaves when I noticed some fine grey, brown-tipped hairs caught in it. Closer inspection showed that they were squirrel hairs. I was standing beside Vixen's Log and on raising my eyes saw a mass of the same hair spread on the bark. I gathered some of it and found it dry, proving it had been shed that morning, it had rained the night before, which would have soaked it.

Despite the fact that this was probably outside her territory, fear for Higi swept over me. I began to search for clues. Had she invaded another squirrel's territory and fought with it? Having watched many squirrel fights, I felt this explanation did not fit, since their normal behavior was to frighten but not wound.

I climbed Vixen's Log to inspect the tufts of hair lying there and almost plunged my hand into some sloppy fresh raccoon droppings; an experience, as my grandmother might have said, from which I hastily withdrew!

Vixen must have caught the squirrel unawares — something I would have thought impossible. There was no blood, no body or part of one to show whether there had in fact been a death at this spot; nor was there anything significant in the surrounding bush. I could only surmise that the squirrel had been unable to escape the strong hands and stronger jaws of the predator and had, I hoped, died quickly. If it escaped, there would be a squirrel around with a great deal of fur missing.

I returned to the house not much wiser but determined to continue my detective work next day. The thought of Higi mangled and dead haunted me.

As if to confirm the nightmare, she was still missing in the morning. Nor did her daughter appear for her usual hand-out.

The following day my systematic search for clues produced nothing new. 'Reading the landscape' is part of the fascination of living in the country. So much is revealed by close observation of small things. A chewed leaf here, a torn cobweb there, a footprint in the mud. In this case a few tiny hairs caught on a spider's thread were the central point in an ever-widening search for the secret of how a squirrel had met disaster.

So far I had looked at ground level and just above it, without result. So I began to look higher and discovered a newly-built squirrel's nest in a cedar tree, an untidy rectangle of moss with an entrance facing south, perched cunningly on the outspread, brittle twigs of a dead branch which had fallen and become firmly wedged. No raccoon could reach it without crashing down under its own weight.

This would account for the squirrel's presence and I sat down on a stump to observe the nest overhead until I became damp, cramped and weary. Just as I was about to leave, a squirrel materialized a few feet away. For a few seconds we stared at one another in silence. Then it leapt into the tree beside me and ran up to sit on a high branch, scolding me or announcing its territory or both. Its coat was sleek and smooth all over, not a hair missing.

I forgot my discomfort in the desire to see whether this animal would enter the nest. It ran round the tree, skirted the nest by a foot or two, then disappeared. Exasperated but patient, I sat on. After a time the squirrel reappeared and again we looked at one another. Again it skittered about near the nest without entering. Four times it came and went.

By which time the light had gone and I had to return indoors, still no wiser.

The next day I returned to my post. A squirrel appeared and two more burst on the scene a few yards away, chasing each other wildly. The resident began calling, making it plain to all of us that this was his or her territory. I had a fleeting glimpse of the two newcomers before they took off, enough to show that they, too, had unblemished coats.

In this species, male heads generally appear to be slightly broader, their tails a little longer and their eye brackets darker than the female's. In the absence of more positive signs these small differences were all I had to go on. In any case it was too dark under the evergreens to be certain about anything.

Had the squirrel avoided the nest the night before because of my presence, or because it was a male? As I said earlier, single members of either sex establish territories but only females occupy nests at breeding time. It was too early for young to have been born, since mating was still in full swing, but nests were being built all over the woods.

These small clues began to add up. If the resident was a male uttering territorial calls, this must have been his domain all the time. But this would not account for the nest, which would naturally be located in a female's territory, with the male visiting her at the appropriate moment to mate and depart. By a process of elimination I came to the conclusion that this squirrel was a male, that this was not his territory and that he was waiting for a female with whom he had formed a relationship before she was wounded or killed. The nest, therefore, would remain empty.

Satisfied I would learn nothing more for the time being, I left my treestump and wandered back, wondering about the identity of the other pair I had just seen.

As I neared the house I was recalled to the present by a violent trilling from the fir tree opposite the studio — Higi's tree. A squirrel was sitting on top of her box.

All squirrels within a species look alike unless one has been marked to set it apart. Even the darker male eye brackets are not an infallible sign and I wouldn't go to court on the evidence. With Higi, however, I had one sure method of identification. Only she would put her head in the bottle for nuts.

I rushed indoors to fill the bottle. Gingerly, half-fearing the outcome, I reached across to the tree, offering the tempting nuts to the squirrel still sitting there.

Higi, bless her, almost toppled off her box in her eagerness to get her head into the bottle.

My relief at finding her alive and well was so great that for a moment I forgot that a tragedy had been enacted and that some other female squirrel had fallen victim to a predator. I was tolerably certain it was not Higlet since it was too far from her territory. Her safety was apparent next day when she and her mother fought their usual battle for pride of place at the peanut tray. Her absence, like her mother's, was probably due to nest-building and I made a mental note to search for the site.

One question remained unanswered: the identity of the pair that had encroached briefly on the widower's territory. It did not take long to find out. Next evening they were dancing about in the trees inside Higi's domain. For a time they played on her tree-house and I was able to observe them closely. One was a strange male; the other was incontrovertibly Higi. They sat amicably side by side on a branch immediately over my head and Higi (quiet for once) clasped her little hands over her stomach in a gesture of such complacency I had to laugh. Then she turned her back on her companion, raised her tail to one side, skittishly, coquettishly, yet somehow still elegantly decorous, and moved her forepaws along the branch an inch or so, grasping it firmly. Her mate mounted her smoothly and after about five seconds the coupling was completed. They disengaged and ran to the ground, uttering delightfully soft little grunting noises, barely audible, and disappeared into the dim depths of the wood.

I found the experience enchanting and ambled back to the house in a state of gentle euphoria, to add a note at the end of my day's diary entry; and another note, forty days ahead, reminding me to watch for Higi's newest family. How lucky I was to have the date so precisely pinpointed for me.

*　　*　　*　　*　　*

Two months later one of the results of Higi's mating was literally round my neck, together with a close relative.

I opened my eyes after a short sleep in a comfortable chair. Two little hot spots against my skin came to life and uncurled themselves. Two pairs of bright inquisitive eyes peered out from the warmth of my sweater. A small contented grunting heralded a tentative sortie into a world bounded by the chair arms. Two baby squirrels, soft and supple, lithe, mischievous and hungry.

One — Douglas — was the son of Higi. The other — Sos (she was born on May Day) — was the daughter of Higlet and thus Higi's granddaughter. Their relationship to one another was complicated, since the father could have been the same for both.

Higi and Higlet had each chosen a bird box to nest in and I had kept close surveillance over them throughout their pregnancies. I found Douglas at the foot of his nest tree one morning when I made my rounds. He was very small and weak and his eyes were still sealed. The hair on half his tail was missing and the minute vertebrae were visible beneath the thin skin, which was beginning to look dry and brittle and would probably break off. This abnormality may have made Higi reject him and throw him out.

My familiarity with the mothers placed me in an unusually favorable position to observe everything that went on. It had been possible, without disturbing them, to look into their boxes through hinged doors, take nest temperatures and ascertain the number of offspring. The average litter is said to be four. Higi had seven babies and Higlet six.

I gathered little Douglas up and put him into the incubator, where he curled up and slept. He was so weak I feared he would die, even with constant care, since it was out of the question to replace him in his nest; he would only be rejected again. I felt that if he was to be hand-reared successfully he would need a companion not only to give him confidence when (and if) he opened his eyes, but to provide some stimulus of competition to provoke his appetite.

I decided to provide a companion from Higlet's litter. This meant breaking a self-imposed rule but the circumstances were unique. Higlet knew me so well she showed no concern when I visited her nest, nor did she worry when I touched her tiny offspring. Nothing would have induced me to interfere with the nest of an unknown wild squirrel.

Thus it was that Sos was picked out to be raised with Douglas. She was the smallest in the litter, the least likely to survive. That she was female was a lucky coincidence. Higlet, on whom I kept a sharp vigil, carried on as if nothing had happened, successfully rearing her remaining five babies. Higi also raised hers and all were normal.

Sos' eyes were faintly fluttering beneath their still-sealed lids: she was twenty-three days old and they were due to open in three or four days' time. Douglas was only thirteen days old and his would not open for almost two weeks.

Pioneering in infant feeding is a nerve-wracking business when one is not experimenting with control animals and the paraphernalia of a laboratory. So I set about finding a way to feed two infant squirrels much younger than Higi had been when she arrived. I found that nothing had been written on the subject of squirrel's milk, at least in North America.

Later I was to come by chance upon some information emanating from Jerusalem University, buried in a book without benefit of index, so that I would defy anybody to find it deliberately. My first day's formula proved to be too high in milk protein (casein) and the babies' tummies grew alarmingly hard. Directly I reduced this addition to their milk they grew comfortably plump once more. Douglas usually took his bottle lying on his back, holding it with both hands, while he lay in one of mine. Sos preferred to be held almost upright. Even at that tender age they had different personalities.

After two weeks in the incubator, Sos and Douglas were transferred to Higi's old house where Sos soon began to create precedents. According to one observer, young squirrels of this species are not weaned until 62-72 days and do not venture outside the nest before they are 45 days old. But Sos explored her cage at 37 days and rejected all but an evening bottle on the 50th day. Both she and Douglas were weaned by the 60th day.

They were easier to handle than Higi, who was much older when she arrived in our house. Douglas, who would have died if I had left him under his tree, became the more aggressive of the two, and I have no doubt that his steady growth was helped by the presence of Sos. They slept cuddled together and played endless games when they were old enough to explore Higi's old tree in the cage; they teetered on top of it as they tried to sit up on their tiny haunches to investigate a strange, long object that crackled when they bit it — a peanut in its shell. They romped round the living room as Higi never had until, tired out, they crawled to the base of my neck beneath my sweater, to curl up and sleep.

It was exciting to meet them every morning to learn what changes were taking place in their development. Douglas' teeth pierced his gums at twenty days (Sos' were already through when she arrived). They were a dirty yellow and at first flexible in their jaws. Later they became rigidly fixed, capable of gnawing through almost anything.

At first their faces were uniformly brown. The eye brackets began to show when they were two-and-a-half months old and the little white patches on either side of their nostrils did not appear until they were fully three months old. The soft baby fuzz gradually gave place to a soft grey fur tipped with brown but lacking the gloss of adult coats. As those grew, so did the black line dividing the light underparts from the rest of the body. Long black guard hairs sprouted and their legs and paws turned an attractive red.

Douglas' half-tail became very bushy, tipped with a tuft of pure white surrounded by black. This unique bottle-brush would, I thought, make him easily recognizable when he was released. Sos' tail reached to the base of her skull.

Although Douglas was aggressive he was also the most affectionate with me, coming readily to my hand and settling down quietly in a pocket when he was tired. He was also extremely independent, like most small boys, and would have got himself into all kinds of trouble had he not been carefully supervised when he was out of his cage.

Sos was skittish, naughty and much greedier than Douglas. She was easily coaxed back into her cage after a romp up and down the curtains and over all the furniture. But Douglas remained obstinately in an inaccessible corner of the valance where he knew I could not catch him. His natural curiosity served my ends, however. I only had to leave the room for him to come down to explore and I was able to foil his attempts to stay out of the cage. Once in it he found new occupations for his small mind; he began, for instance, to indulge in sex-play with Sos before he was off the bottle!

I discovered to my delight that these hand-reared baby squirrels tolerated being stroked. But Sos and Douglas, like Higi before them, detested being held, once they ceased to be held in my hand for bottle feeding. I feel sure there can never be any real rapport between them and me. They are always on the move, or eating, or grooming — or asleep. There is no leisure for making friends.

*   *   *   *   *

On a lovely August day precisely two years after Higi's return to the wild, Sos and Douglas were released. I took their large new cage to the balcony outside my studio and tied its doors open.

They ventured out slowly — unlike Higi who had shot out, never to return. They climbed the outside of the cage which was as familiar to them as its interior, and played around the tower before returning inside. Later they ventured out again and explored the balcony inch by exciting inch, until suddenly they saw the fir tree whose branches touched the railing. With prodigious leaps both babies reached the top rail, paused to regain balance on the slippery painted surface and then jumped easily into the tree. They were seen no more that day except as flying streaks of red-brown fur in the topmost branches.

For more than a month I left their open cage on the balcony and they returned to it at night to sleep and during the day to play and feed. For a time they continued to treat me as just another tree, tearing up and down me and holding onto my hair with their sharp little claws. Gradually this

93

ceased and by mid-September they were gone. Since Higi and Higlet still have their old territories adjacent to one another I assume that Sos and Douglas staked their claims elsewhere in the woods. On my walks I occasionally saw Douglas with his flamboyant half-tail and I think I heard Sos barking at the farthest end of the lake, a long way from the house.

And so, true to my unspoken wish, there are now three generations of Higis at Ravenshill.

With a little bit of luck Higi and her children and grandchildren will live to enliven our days for several years to come. When her time comes I, alas, will probably never know. The little tragedies in nature take place in stealth and secrecy. We cannot prevent them in the long run, however much we would like to. Even as I write, she has a wound healing on her back — a long, bloody gash, inflicted, perhaps, by a frantic bird whose nest she was trying to rob. This time she was lucky. She may not always be so.

Her small saga has been a success story and most of the credit must go to her ancestors. Of myself I can only say that I do not believe she suffered during her stay in captivity. She has survived, healthy, primitive and productive. To her forbears she owes instinctive, inherited behavior, as opposed to environmental, learned behavior.

Unlike Vixen who would have remained with her mother for ten months and therefore needed to be looked after much longer by me, Higi shot into instant independence on her release and knew what to do, what and who to fear, and was able to plunge straight into a full life in her natural habitat.

Of man she shows, I think, a kind of contemptuous tolerance, knowing she can safely risk putting her head into a bottle of nuts because she moves so fast nobody could catch her. Higlet, wholly wild, shows no awareness of humans except as useful sources of peanuts; in time she, too, learned to take nuts from the bottle. She frequently sits on the windowsill, eating or grooming for long enough to enable me to draw her. I find it gratifying, amusing and endlessly fascinating to live in unconcerned intimacy with such charming little wild animals.

Long may their generations flourish!

Chapter Ten

In goodly colours
gloriously array'd.

Spenser, SONNET IXX.

The hummingbirds are back!

News to be shouted through the house, to bring us running to the windows. These tiniest of all birds, these living jewels, have returned to Ravenshill and spring is here at last.

We talk about them through the winter, when all is drab and dark; in February we begin to count the weeks, to buy supplies of honey, to decide whether we should re-site the feeders or return them to their usual places. By the first week in March we are counting the days and in the last two weeks they usually begin to arrive. First a single male; the next day another; then two or three and finally any number up to about thirty, followed shortly by their mates-to-be.

Twenty-five seasons have come and gone since I saw my first hummingbirds, but the thrill is there every time — not just for the first arrivals, but every time I look out and see them dancing in the air — ten, twenty, a hundred times a day. I can never quite believe the evidence of my eyes when I see these minute miracles of bird-engineering hovering over flowers or at the feeders. Not only hovering but flying backwards. No other bird can perform this incredible feat.

And they have flown more than two thousand miles from their winter home in northern Mexico, along the whole coast of North America, over open sea, through mountain passes 8,000 feet high, in all temperatures.

Hundreds must perish on that perilous journey. Hundreds more are blown off-course by gale-force winds that buffet and bully these tiny morsels of flesh, feather and fragile bone. The survivors struggle on, dauntless in the face of unbelievable odds, driven by their internal timing instinct to their breeding grounds on Vancouver Island and along the coast of British Columbia to Alaska.

My first experience of these lovely birds, which are native only to the New World (Canada, the United States, Central America and the Caribbean Islands), was in eastern Canada in the sprawling city of Toronto where, smack in the middle of town, a group of Ruby-throated hummingbirds (*Archilocus colubris*) flitted amongst the white blossoms of a cherry tree. The ruby-red throats and green backs of the smallest birds I had ever seen scintillated as though dipped in molten metal.

I know of only one other creature that can fly backwards: the hummingbird hawkmoth, which I watched on summer evenings in England, hovering over flowers, darting its long tongue deep into the corollas of nicotina and other nectar-laden blooms, moving backwards and forwards with ease. Its brown and pink wings seem drab in comparison with its feathered North American counterpart.

The ruby-throat spends the summers east of the Rocky Mountains. The birds considered to be native to the west coast — because they breed there — are known officially as *Selasphorous rufus,* meaning rufous flame or, colloquially, the rufous hummingbird. Three and a half inches long from head to tail-tip, a single adult weighs three grams or about 150 birds to the pound! And there are still smaller species. Anyone interested in arithmetic might try calculating the number of movements involved in flying two thousand miles at speeds of up to thirty miles an hour at a rate of about fifty wingbeats per second for the female and seventy for the male. In courtship flight up to 200 wingbeats per second!

The hummingbird takes its name from the sound of its wings in flight. We regularly feed seventy or more birds and the sound of their massed wings adds up to a loud hum like a model airplane. Throughout the summer friends come to watch and even those who are not normally particularly interested in nature and are certainly not birdwatchers, sit on the balcony or at the windows, spellbound by what they see and hear. Birdwatchers and ornithologists come to Ravenshill by invitation with recording gear and cameras and even these case-hardened people cannot hide their sense of wonder at the annual display.

As for me, I am as one bewitched. I seem to spend more time preparing food for hummingbirds than for us and as my studio windows overlook their main feeding stations I am constantly but willingly seduced from my painting.

Can a mere human describe one of these birds? No classic poet ever saw one, so they have not been immortalized in verse like the nightingale. In all humility I shall try to picture a pair.

The cock is different from all other North American hummingbirds because he has a warm, cinnamon-colored (rufous) back and these feathers are not iridescent. His jewel lies on his throat — the gorget (from the French *gorge* — throat). He can flare it from either side of his head and it extends below his cheeks and under his chin to his throat and chest, like a baby's bib. The effect of the flared gorget is breathtaking — the bird looks twice its usual size and seems literally on fire.

Imagine a scarlet sequin, new and glittering in the sun. As you watch, blinded by brilliance, the tiny bird twists and turns his head and his throat feathers subtly change from flaming scarlet through crimson to an orange-scarlet that glows like a blast-furnace.

Suddenly the molten gleam disappears and behold! the color is all eclipsed, giving place to deepest black. The bird has turned his head from the source of light, which is no longer reflected in the sheen of the special feathers.

The reason for these dramatic color changes is that the feathers reflect light from layers of air-filled elliptical cells. Like millions of soap bubbles, these break up light and reflect it in rays which cover the full color spectrum — if you are lucky enough to see it. Individual gorget feathers look black but if you hold one and twist it to the light you can see the colors of the living bird. Vivid red and orange are most generally seen. For years, neither I nor anyone I talked to, had observed the full rainbow spectrum in the rufous hummingbird. Yet I felt sure it must be possible. The secret is to be in the right position vis-à-vis the bird whose gorget is made of feathers arranged like little shingles on a roof and which, under a powerful glass, seem to be covered with wafer thin metallic chips that glow from within.

I spent countless hours studying different males drinking within a few inches of the window, having placed feeders so that the birds at one were bound to face me, while those at others presented profiles from two directions. There at last I saw the whole rainbow in all its glory. The light caught the gorgets and turned them from jet-black through the rich reds and orange usually noticed, to yellow, bright green and finally the cool end of the spectrum — blue and purple, then back to black.

I suppose that given time and patience and eyes to see, all nature could be observed as closely.

But to return to the picture I was drawing. Below the scarlet gorget a white patch separates two scallop-shaped paler patches of the same cinnamon color as the back. And so to a tail of the same, which can be fanned out in anger or used as a stabilizer in flight, or when displaying. Metallic bronze-green spots adorn the tips of the adult male's tail feathers, while young birds have white spots on the tips of their three outer tail feathers, like the females. There is a tiny white spot beside the outer corner of the eye which seems to enhance its black brilliance.

The tiny body is completed by a long, slender bill, slightly curved, inside which is a most unusual tongue. I had read descriptions of this organ being tubular. As hummingbirds sip nectar this sounds apt. Yet I had observed rapid vibrations in the birds' heads as they drank at my feeders and I began to question whether the tongue was, in fact, acting as a pump. I enlisted the help of a young veterinarian interested in wildlife who sent a window-killed hummingbird to the University of Saskatchewan with a request for an exact description.

Shorn of technicalities, a hummingbird's tongue is long, narrow, forked and slightly hairy at the tip; two curled furrows divide it, creating tiny troughs along which nectar is carried by capilliary action until it is swallowed. So it is not tubular and I was right! It is suggested that the hairy tip helps to catch insects in nectar. However, my own observations tend to deny this and a very scientific observer of captive hummingbirds in Germany, Walter Scheithauer, agrees. Hummingbirds catch flying insects in wide open bills on the wing, like swallows. Far from drinking them in nectar, they are at pains to avoid doing so, as I proved when I tried to get a hummingbird to take squashed fruit flies in syrup during a period of temporary captivity following an injury.

Now I must turn to the little hen, who has an iridescent green back and head. Her throat is off-white with a peppering of cinnamon and a tiny patch of three or four feathers which glow like the cock's. Her flanks are pale cinnamon shading to a brown green-dusted tail with a white spot on each of its three outer feathers.

Nearly all our hummingbird visitors are of this species. One rare exception was identified by an ornithologist friend. He nearly fell through the window in his enthusiasm at the sight of an Allen's hummingbird (*Selasphorus sasin*).

The bird was feeding a few inches from the window while we sketched it and wrote notes. But we did not 'collect' it. Nobody may kill at Ravenshill. Our findings would go to experts for confirmation (nothing is left to one person's judgment) and would end as a small statistic in a minor report.

The Allen's is closely related to and difficult to distinguish from the rufous. The male has a solid iridescent green back and head and the female is distinguishable from her rufous counterpart only by her narrow outer tail feathers. You have to have a bird in the hand to see this feature.

Rare or common, our hummingbirds come in dozens to bathe and play during the summer when I turn the sprinkler to a fine spray. They fly straight up the jet, standing on their tails in the air, twisting and diving. If they ever reached the nozzle the force would be enough to blow them right out of the air. When they are wet enough they fly to a perch to preen with their long beaks and then return — for as long as I am willing to hold the hose.

Yet in spite of all their marvellous aerobatics and phenomenal speed, hummingbirds are subject to the oddest dangers. In fact, just being seems to be a hazardous business.

An unusual tapping came from the garage one day. A female rufous, caught in a mass of old spiders' webs at the window, was beating herself against the sun-heated glass. She was probably looking for cobwebs to secure her nest and the more she struggled the tighter the webs bound her body until she would have died of thirst and starvation.

I freed her and she lay still in my hand, eyes closed. Fearing it might be too late, I cast around for some means of reviving her. Since there is a danger of drowning so small a bird if one tries to give liquid from a dropper, I held her beak to the mouth of a feeder. Instantly her tongue shot out and she drank avidly. She began to recover as she drank, opened her eyes and looked at me. She was so tiny and fragile I was terrified of crushing her.

Her feet had been curled beneath her as she lay but she sidled up my finger when I opened my hand, her minute toes tickling my skin. She sat on my finger-tip beating her wings at full speed. A second later she was perched on a twig, preening her disarranged feathers.

Another time two babies, just half a day out of the nest, hit one of our windows, despite the paper cutouts I put on the glass to discourage them. Adults have done the same thing. Occasionally they break their delicate necks, but often are only stunned and I treat them for shock and release them, sometimes after half an hour cupped in my hand, sometimes after a few days' recuperation in a cage. Considering their size they are amazingly hardy birds who feed without protest in captivity. Other wild birds make much more difficult patients.

*　*　*　*　*

One hot day I lay sunbathing in a red-white-and-blue sunsuit, drowsily listening to a group of hummingbirds feeding overhead. One detached herself from the rest and flew to investigate me.

She hovered over my feet, examining them carefully. I could feel her beak on my skin. Finding nothing to eat she flew the length of my legs, fanning me coolly, and arrived at my shorts. There she darted at the red bits but, again finding nothing to eat, flew on to my face where she hovered, gently brushing my lipstick with bill and tongue. Her tail feathers almost touched my chin and her bright black eyes looked directly into mine. Frustrated, she backed away and streaked off to a bush, where she perched for a moment before taking off in search of more rewarding adventures.

How does a bird achieve this 'impossible' feat of flying backwards? I have often been asked about this and as I am neither a flight engineer nor a photographer with special equipment, I have done my best to digest what has been observed by others. It appears that the difference between the flight of an 'ordinary' bird and a hummingbird is that the former's wings beat up and down and the latter's backwards, forwards or sideways, describing a figure of eight. The power of the ordinary bird's wings is in the down-beat (on the lower face of the wing), the up-beat is just a return to position for the next down-beat. The hummingbird, on the other hand, has as much power in the up- as in the down-beat which enables it to hold a smooth, hovering position at any angle and in any direction, from a dead stop in mid-air to soaring, diving, rolling, moving forwards, backwards, upside down or right way up!

A hummingbird's wing is, as you might expect, also unique in that it is straight from shoulder to tip, rigid as a ship's rudder, although the tips can be manipulated into a braking curl. The feather structure is so strong and the shoulder joint has such powerful articulation that it doesn't matter which way the upper side of the wing faces: the bird still flies in any position it wishes. It is not surprising that this incredible flight requires equally incredible muscle power, and these muscles weigh one-third of the total body weight of the little bird.

So much for the technicalities. What I do know is that when I watch hummingbirds in flight I see them surrounded as by a little mist from the speed-blurred feathers. Small wonder they are so difficult to photograph. Add to this the sound which resembles a distant drumroll and the bickering of their peevish little voices which rise as the birds fly faster, and you have an experience worth the telling. I must say I find hummingbird voices far from musical and not at all in keeping with the beauty of the birds. A far cry from Keats' nightingale which sang of summer in full-throated ease. Our gawdy little bird has a voice like a bad-tempered hornet!

Flying at such speed requires an enormous amount of energy and therefore a vast number of calories to sustain it. In human equivalents — for those people who are condemned to the dreariness of reducing diets and the misery of push-ups and jogging — each bird would need 140 lbs of bread or 400 lbs of potatoes per day. There's a moral here somewhere, but I'm afraid it escapes me!

Hummingbirds feed on the wing because their legs and feet are so small they cannot function well on the ground. Occasionally a female lands if she needs grains of sand for roughage or specks of broken shell or soil. This happens at nest-building time and no other that I have been able to witness; and I have never seen a male on the ground.

These birds are enchantingly romantic, obtaining as they do a large part of their food from flowers. In fact each eats half its own weight daily in carbohydrate-rich nectar, while protein comes from hundreds of small insects, especially fruit flies, caught in a wide open beak which acts as a net (swallows feed the same way). As hummingbirds are able to manoeuvre in any position or direction it is also possible for them to take aphids, small spiders and so on from leaf surfaces, still on the wing. When I have to feed a hummingbird patient I have to collect tiny spiders and feed them by hand dangling from their threads so that the little bird can take them easily in a cage. No easy task. First find your spider. . . .

At the height of their season the hummingbirds at Ravenshill consume about fifty ounces of syrup a day in addition to natural food. Some observers say that refined sugar is better than honey, which is said to cause 'canker' (ulceration) of the tongue. There seems to be no scientific basis for this statement, however. The 'canker' found in cage-bred canaries and some wild birds is usually caused by a parasite. Honey does ferment more rapidly than sugar and for this reason I either boil it for a minute or two or renew the feed several times a day in hot weather, making sure the feeders are very clean. Honey contains vitamins and minerals and I prefer it to the over-refined product of the sugar factories.

But hummingbirds could not survive on an exclusive diet of sugar or honey syrup.

A few years ago little or nothing was known about hummingbird diets. Suddenly there seem to be almost as many diets as there are species. Two things are important in making their syrup: properly balanced ingredients and a homogenised solution so that the birds are not deprived of any one because it either floats or sinks.

When our hummingbirds arrive in the chilly, relatively flowerless days of March, I make them a fortified syrup from ingredients I would use for a captive bird. Their only source of nectar on arrival is the small white flower of Indian Plum; the first red one is the wild currant which does not bloom until early April.

Once they have grown accustomed to coming to a garden where there is food available at all times, hummingbirds develop habits so automatic that if I move a feeder from one location to another, they go to the exact spot where it first hung.

Before leaving the topic of feeding I must stress that anyone who puts out even a single feeder to attract these lovely birds is in duty bound to continue the practice until the last bird leaves for its migratory flight south. Once attracted to a site, to the extent of nesting nearby, birds come to rely on human-supplied feeding stations to augment their natural diet. So, if you're unable or unwilling to continue feeding these particular birds — and it's a lot of work when done correctly — don't do anything at all. If you can't keep faith, keep out of it altogether; that's the only fair thing to do.

Bird books indulge in a lot of discussion on the hummingbird's alleged predilection for anything red. My own conclusion — amateur, but based on years of observation — is that it doesn't matter a damn what color anything is if it contains nectar, although they do tend to investigate red coloring first. I watch them touching the red tail-lights of our stationary car, but if a tube of differently colored or colorless syrup is placed nearby, they soon find it. Once they know, they don't give a hoot what color their syrup is, where it is hung, or in what sort of container. My birds feed from glass tubes, plastic bottles, elaborate commercial feeders, or rolled-rim can caps. But they are not the only creatures who like sweet things.

Vixen's sweet tooth drew her to the feeders suspended in trees, in bushes, on poles and wires. With her innate cunning she succeeded in emptying them every night, leaving nothing for the little birds at dawn.

I tried all sorts of things to dissuade her, from vaseline on the poles to pieces of cone-shaped metal wrapped around them to stop her climbing. All to no avail. Her feet and coat were smeared with grease but she negotiated the poles nevertheless. She climbed over the metal cones with ease. I was getting desperate and tired of getting up before dawn to replenish feeders.

The solution came to me as I was hanging out some laundry: each night move the feeders from the terrace to the laundry line, which stretches from the house high across the lawn to a tree in the woods. Nothing can reach it from below. Instead of laundry, then, imagine about a dozen glass feeders of all shapes and sizes, each clothes-pinned to keep it from sliding into its neighbor. One night I inadvertently left one feeder too near the back porch railing and Vixen succeeded in getting it, but was thwarted from getting the rest.

To discourage insects, I put fine-mesh guards on the ends of feeding

102

tubes and spread salad oil around them. Hummingbirds are mortally afraid of wasps and dart fearfully to and fro trying to drink between their visits. They also dislike the small ants that appear in columns along twigs and branches, attracted by the sweetness. Honey-bees arrive in season and help to consume some of the syrup but are not usually a menace to the birds. Once, however, we were inundated with wild bees. The mouth of each feeder turned into a golf-ball-sized mass of heaving brown bodies. This was more than the birds could cope with.

Nothing kept these bees away, neither strong-smelling aniseed nor turpentine. I eventually found the bees' nest in, of all places, one of our wood duck boxes.

The hummingbirds needed their food and I could not bear to see them perpetually frustrated. They were also nesting and could not go elsewhere. The bees could. Peace was restored after an eager bee-keeper removed them in the box one night.

My hummingbirds also face competition from purple finches and orange-crowned warblers who have learned to perch on a twig below the tubes or even to alight on them. Since they cannot hover for more than a second, or fly backwards, they skid on the smooth glass and lose their balance but with wildly fluttering wings manage to steal a drop before falling off and starting all over again. One finch even succeeded in teaching herself to feed clumsily on the wing. Others caught on until eventually I gave them a special dish of their own to reward them for their efforts — and protect the hummingbirds.

The reputation of pugnaciousness and bravery attributed to hummingbirds is certainly borne out as they zoom in on one another at feeding stations, spitting vituperations, jerking face to face in the air, or attacking a marauder invading their territory. Yet their displays may only seem to be outbursts of anger and aggression.

Like many other animals, they are inclined to defend territory more than food. I watched a cock dart viciously at a warbler many times his size. The hummingbird was resting on a perch roughly at the centre of his domain, bounded by a thicket on one side and a feeder on the other. When the warbler flew to his shrub, the indignant hummingbird roared up from his perch and made a beeline for the intruder, spluttering with rage, zooming straight up on what appeared to be a collision course.

Hummingbird flew past warbler at perhaps forty miles an hour, then back again, right under the other bird's nose. What with the angry little voice, the ominous drumming from his wings and the surprise of sheer audacity, the warbler took fright and flight.

*   *   *   *   *

When the male hummingbirds arrive I am reminded that most descriptions of them include references to ''green on the head'' and ''varying amounts of green flecked on the back''.

Yet I have seen males that have bodies colored in solid cinnamon-brown without a speck of green anywhere. What is more, they seem to be dominant over other males who show green on head or body or both. At least the latter defer to what I believe are their elders, and have reached the tentative conclusion that each year we have birds of different ages. Those with green feathers are probably second-year birds (juveniles look like females for weeks before they turn brown). I believe that these young birds have experienced their first migration, led by the birds whose third or fourth year would entitle them to establish territories first. I also believe that some, at least, of the same birds return annually from the way they fly to a place that contained a feeder the previous year. Many of these are solidly brown-feathered and could well be from broods hatched two years previously. Their life-span in the wild does not seem to be known, although nine years has been reported for a bird in captivity.

On arrival all males feed amicably, there being no female competition. When the hens arrive each mature male guards his particular feeder. Any remaining feeders are free to all comers and up to twenty males and fifteen females may congregate in the vicinity of an unguarded feeder or feeders. Before sun-up and for about two hours before dark all feeders are free to all comers. An excellent arrangement since this allows all birds, whatever their rank or sex, to have a fair share at the two most critical times of day. It is then that my dwarf maple is adorned with specks of iridescent life, like a living Christmas tree.

At unguarded feeders the birds line up politely, with little of the petulant squabbling usually associated with them. But if one bird tries to approach a guarded feeder, the reaction is violent. The guardian, in a blaze of glorious fury, zooms up or down from his vantage point, straight for the interloper, who takes off in a hurry.

In cold weather the birds feed until after dark, in silence. In places where no food is available, hummingbirds have the ability to adjust to cold and starvation by lowering their metabolism almost to vanishing point. Heads shrugged deep into shoulders — but beaks pointed skywards — they perch with their feathers fluffed out for maximum warmth. They become rigid, as if in a coma, and can be picked up. They do this also when danger threatens, 'dying' until the coast is clear. But one year I witnessed the sad, strange death of two little hens in the middle of the nesting season.

The first was perched on the maple, waving her head about and holding her beak vertically, gasping — or choking, I did not know which. She fluttered weakly to a feeder, sipped a drop and staggered back to her perch. She was so obviously ill I fetched a small fish net and went out to see if I could catch her. But she had enough strength to elude me and rather than exhaust her further I abandoned the attempt for that day.

The next day she was still gasping and weaker. Again I tried to catch her and again missed her by inches. On the third day I was able to pick her up in my hand. She died an hour later, yet there was nothing visibly wrong.

I froze the tiny body and sent it at once to a university laboratory in the hope that some light could be shed on the cause of her untimely death. I was sickened by the thought that she might already have hatched her young, who would starve to death.

This at least was not so. I was informed that she had two eggs in her body and that there was evidence of some kind of infection in her throat, but not what had caused it.

Meanwhile another hen was showing the same symptoms and I was able to catch her on the second day. I put her in a cage with a feeder she could reach without effort, adding a drop of antibiotic to the syrup.

But again, whatever was in her throat prevented her from taking enough nourishment and she, too, died two days later.

I sent the small corpse to the lab. and with it, for comparison, the body of a normal hummingbird who had broken his neck against a window. The report came back as before. Nobody knew anything about hummingbirds and there were no known authorities in the country.

Mercifully there were no more deaths at Ravenshill.

Although these little hens both had eggs in their oviducts the mating season was still going on and we watched the males performing their amazing and spectacular courting display.

It begins a hundred feet above earth.

A tiny ball of fire pauses, stationary for a few seconds. Then he hurls himself downwards like a fighter plane at 100 miles an hour, gorget flared wide on each side of his head and flashing like a heliograph. Rushing air plays a high, whining tune on the reeds of his flight feathers.

At the very instant you feel he must commit suicide against a window, he swoops up, avoiding death by inches. He does not return to the starting point but stops short, having described a capital "J", and to this shallow curve — the tail of the capital — he returns several times before either zooming back to his starting-point, or down to his intended mate.

Whilst this display is going on the female sits still, beak pointed upwards. Usually she is on a low twig, occasionally on the ground, but nearly always protected by overhanging greenery.

Suddenly the cock arrests his flight a few inches from her, his tail down-flared. He begins a very curious ritual mid-air dance. Poised horizontally above and in front of his lady, he keeps his head parallel with the ground while the rest of him, from neck to tail-tip, curves in a sharp upward arc. In this astounding position he swings his body from side to side like a pendulum, while his head remains steadfastly towards the female as though tethered by an invisible string. He weaves his body with an intensity of passion that is matched by the vibrant, low-pitched thrumming of his wings — vroom-vroom — a deeper, more thrilling sound than that of his normal flight. As a violin string makes a deeper sound when played without finger-stopping — there being fewer, slower vibrations — so, presumably, the hummingbird's wing-beats, being slower, produce a deeper note.

The tiny green hen sits quietly, almost invisible against the leafy background. She moves her head from side to side to watch her mate's hypnotic gestures. Her body is rigid.

Abruptly he ceases his sensual, horizontal waving and shoots back into the sky. Again his flight differs from normal. His body shudders violently as he disappears aloft, so that he seems to stagger. At the same time he produces a sound like a stuttering outboard motor running out of gas. I hazard a guess that this is not so much a part of display as a matter of regaining balance after such an energy-consuming activity as his horizontal aerial dance-on-a-dime. The stutter on the upward flight is, I think, made by his voice, not his wings, but it is difficult to be certain. As the female has departed by this time, it cannot be intended to beguile her further.

So far he is still paying court, there has been no consummation. He may make many passes at one hen, or tire after a single dive and dance. The actual mating is quite protracted for a bird and plainly — though rarely — visible to a human observer.

After his dance and upward, waggling departure, the cock flies swiftly down to his mate. She turns her back to him. He mounts her deliberately and with several thrusting movements lasting less than five seconds, completes the act. She preens briefly before taking to the air while he departs like a fired bullet for pastures new.

Part of the fascination of observing nature is making one's own notes, then turning to various authorities to see if they confirm them.

Knowledgeable readers may comment that the "J" display flight belongs to Allen's hummingbird; that the rufous describes an ellipse, as shown in *Birds of North America* (C.S. Robbins et al), with a diagram to 'prove' it. Roger T. Peterson, in *A Field Guide to Western Birds,* says the display flight of a rufous is ". . . a closed ellipse . . .". The "J" is reserved for Allen's hummingbird.

This poses a question: are the textbooks in error? It sometimes happens that one authority takes the word of another authority without benefit of original observation. Or have we more 'rare' Allen's hummingbirds at Ravenshill than we ever imagined possible? I have observed hundreds of "J" flights at close quarters (by which I mean that I have been, as it were, on the receiving end of the dive). I have also seen the elliptical manoeuvre. Only one Allen's hummingbird has been identified at Ravenshill, yet the "J" displays are performed again and again by dozens of males during the mating season. The dive is accompanied by a strident sound, roughly tut-tut-tut-turre. The return wavering climb has another sound. This wavering climb is attributed to Allen's hummingbird by both authorities, yet I have observed it in the rufous.

With regard to mating hummingbirds one authority quotes a correspondent as having watched two rufous hummingbirds in what he ". . . believed to be the actual mating", and describes the pair closed horizontally in the air, swinging backwards and forwards. I have never seen matings like this. I have seen pairs closing in the air, vertically, face to face in what seems to be a form of game, since as far as I know birds cannot mate in this position.

Perhaps one day an extraordinarily patient photographer will succeed in making a slow motion film of the act.

In all my observations of nature I am, of course, aware of my amateur status. The word comes from the Latin *amare* — to love — so why should it now have a derisive connotation? Most of the great discoveries in this field have been made by amateurs — the Victorian era was particularly rich in the numbers of dedicated animal and plant watchers, not one of whom had a degree. I wish we could once more accept the validity of the amateur's statements. They have more time to watch and read, make notes and draw. Specialists are everywhere today and natural things are being observed in such inhuman ways that all beauty and wonderment is stripped from them. The language they use is mostly unintelligible to laymen, who consequently are denied a great deal of information and pleasure.

* * * * *

Each generation of nature-lovers accepts or rejects this theory or that but it makes no difference to the serene cycle of life that is enacted annually and at which we may marvel if we have the opportunity to observe.

The building of a hummingbird nest is a case in point.

Once the females have mated and are occupied with nesting, the males become less aggressive since they take no part in building the nest or rearing the young.

The nest is as lovely as its architect. Almost anywhere will do as a site, although none of the 319 species build on the ground. The rufous will nest up to fifty feet from the ground on the tip of a fir or cedar branch, sometimes in colonies, with as many as twenty nests in a small area. Another species may build on a knot in a rope hanging in a woodshed or some other similar place.

The nest dimensions seem more suited to a doll's house than to reality. The interior is a slightly ballooned cup averaging one inch in diameter; the depth is about seven-eighths of an inch inside and one-and-a-quarter inches outside. It is constructed of soft plant fibres woven together, anchored to the branch by cobwebs, which are elastic and slightly sticky. The outside is covered with lichens which render it almost invisible on a lichen-covered branch. Even when she is sitting on her eggs the little hen continues to decorate the outside of her nursery with bits of lichen bound by more cobwebs, using her beak as a darning needle and her tongue to smooth out protruding fibres. The inside is lined softly with small feathers, fibres and any suitable material she can find. To help her I hang out net bags filled with small pieces of soft string, cotton batting, lengths of fine wool and feathers leaked from pillows or moulted by ducks. One year I found a nest lined with strands of pure green silk, where it looked much more artistic than it had as part of one of my dresses.

One might expect the hummingbird to be a prolific breeder like the English 'jenny-wren' because of its small size; but although two broods in a season may occur, only two, occasionally three, pure white eggs are laid, like evenly matched pearls. The size of the eggs is misleading: hummingbirds lay the largest eggs in the bird world — in proportion to their body size. A beautiful iridescent blue tree swallow nested in a box I had placed on the balcony rail and when the two babies had flown I took the feathered nest; in it were two sterile eggs which measured nine-sixteenths of an inch by three-quarters: the bird measures five to six-and-a-quarter inches in length. Compare this with a hummingbird measuring approximately three-and-a-half inches who lays eggs averaging one-half by five-sixteenths of an inch. Incidentally the hen has another little trick in the repertoire of flight acrobatics: she is able to descend gently onto her eggs without using her feet to break her flight. Most if not all birds first have to land on some sort of platform.

The newly-hatched babies are no larger than bumble-bees who emerge after incubating for twelve to fourteen days. The tiny hen, with such a useless mate, is in the predicament of an abandoned mother of new-born twins — without the benefit of relatives and welfare service.

At the feeders, no quarter is given. Males feed both first and last. During the day hens with families must take nourishment whenever they have a chance and sometimes the pressure of birds is so great that four beaks may go simultaneously to the small hole in the bottle-top or glass tube and four tongues extend into the syrup together.

At least mother hummingbird is saved one chore: she doesn't have to clean the droppings from the nest as swallows do, picking them up and flying some distance before disposing of them, until the young are able to turn themselves round to eject straight out of the nest. The baby hummingbird ejects his droppings over the nest-edge from the start. But to do so he has to stand on his head. The sides of the nest are steep and he is very little, so he must climb up backwards to get his small behind over the rim.

As its occupants grow the tiny cup becomes too small. The sides are broken down until the nest is no more than a saucer. It also becomes a platform from which the babies hurl themselves into the air without benefit of lesson, as though they had been doing it all their lives. By this time they are replicas of their mothers. After a week or two it is possible to distinguish the males by their slightly darker throat feathers — a sprinkling of infinitesimal brown, vertical lines. The gorgeous metallic gorget requires weeks to develop and is not necessarily complete by the time of the southward migration.

When the young are fledged the adult males retire to the hills. Less, possibly, for their own comfort than to give the new generation, not to mention the exhausted mothers, a belated chance to feed without competition. They will have to increase their normal weight by fifty per cent in fat to sustain them over their incredible migrating flight. But nature, like art, has no hard-and-fast rules. Sometimes a few males are still with us days after the young start flying to the feeders and once a lone cock stayed for weeks.

Meanwhile the new generation whizzes round our garden, providing huge delight as we watch the shimmering bodies hurtle through the air, dart at feeders, indulge in mock battles and occasionally make a mistake — like the youngster who landed awkwardly on a twig, lost his footing and fell — bump — to the next twig a whole inch lower down. Tinier than tiny, they are the flower-children of summer. As mothers and babies probe the flowers for nectar they are sometimes unable to reach it even with their long beaks designed to explore deep corollas. Then the whole head almost to the shoulders disappears and one is treated to the delightful sight of a small tail-end supported by rapidly moving wings protruding from a flower that is moving gently in the feather-breeze.

By mid-August the last little birds have left on their maiden flight to New Mexico. Some stop off to winter in Montana, Colorado, Texas and the Gulf States. All are activated by the mechanism within them that triggers the decision to migrate — their biological clock, unalterably part of their makeup, that remains precisely timed, irrespective of weather conditions.

As I wash and store the feeders for another year I think back on the aerobatic displays of these darting balls of tropic fire; remember with wonderment the ineffable joy the first male hummingbird brought to a grey spring day. Above all give thanks to be alive and seeing and aware — and privileged to share a small corner of their fairy-like world.

Now we must wait through a whole fall and winter, looking forward to their return next spring and the next and the next, in all their glorious array of color, hoping their numbers will remain undiminished by pesticide, pollution or collectors. For a world without its hummingbirds would be without enchantment.

Chapter Eleven

*Accuse not Nature, she hath
done her part;
Do thou but thine . . .*
Milton, PARADISE LOST.

Ravenshill blends into hundreds of acres of wild country, its unfenced boundaries marked only by a few posts driven into the underbrush. Most of the original fir trees were logged fifty or more years ago, but the second growth is tall and thick. Here and there the forest thins to open scrub. Stunted Garry oaks find rootholds amongst the ancient moss-covered rocks. Yellow broom flourishes and open ground is carpeted with wildflowers.

Here herds of deer live and move and have their silent being. Several live within the sanctuary of Ravenshill. In spring pregnant does walk daintily across the lawn and skip down the rocks to drink from the lake. They bear their fawns in May and June. I know of few sights as enchanting as a sleek and shining doe with her tiny spotted baby trotting beside her, so appealing — and so vulnerable. . . .

One June day I answered a long-distance telephone call from a woman begging me to accept an "abandoned" fawn.

A few hours later a car drove up, containing the woman, her daughter with her baby, and a very small Columbian blacktail fawn. It lay curled in the daughter's lap, her own child temporarily relegated to the back seat.

The older woman got out of the car. There were no introductions, just: "He doesn't seem well and I don't know what to do. I know you look after wild animals. I picked him up by the roadside — he didn't even try to run away. . . ." Her voice trailed off unhappily. She turned back to the car and took the little creature from her daughter.

There were tears in her eyes as she explained how for two days she had tried to feed him before telephoning. She begged me not to put him in a zoo and I reassured her — vehemently — that I would give him sanctuary for the rest of his life. She thanked me profusely and drove away, leaving me with the fawn in my arms and a lump in my throat.

Alas, the story was all too familiar. A tiny fawn lies by the roadside, quietly watching an approaching human who cannot resist picking it up.

111

Unafraid, the baby deer allows itself to be carried to a car, innocent of any foreknowledge that in that moment its whole life has been changed. It will never see its mother again, nor suck her warm, rich milk, nor learn from her how to live wild and free like other deer.

I reflected on the fate of "abandoned" fawns. True abandonment by the mother occurs rarely and always for good reasons. Unlike humans animals have a positive, instinctive knowledge when one of their off-spring carries within it the seeds of death.

A bitch with a sickly puppy will unerringly single it out and nuzzle it away to perish of cold and hunger, or she will lie on it and suffocate it. To human eyes nothing seems wrong, although it is usually the runt. But if anyone interferes she will repeat her actions. The healthy puppies need her milk; the sickly must die and the sooner the better. It is the same with wild animals. Rejection and death of the unfit are their means for preserving the fitness of the species.

This fawn, however, had probably not been abandoned. A wild doe leaves her baby, usually though by no means always well hidden, while she browses nearby. I have been lucky enough occasionally to find one and it has always been lying alone. The dam leaves her baby alone for long periods and finds a new bedding place for it after each feed. Si-blings lie separately, minimizing the chance that both will be found by predators. Such behavior also reduces to a minimum the amount of scent left by the doe when she tends them.

During their first days fawns have no body odor; even a hunting dog could pass within a few yards and fail to pick up their trail. The mother's frequent grooming with her tongue eliminates any tell-tale scent her baby might leave when it is more than a few days old.

If the woman who found this lonely fawn had moved away to watch she would have seen the dam return to him or she might, if her hearing and awareness were sufficiently acute, have heard the doe call him. She would not fight for him, though, even in the face of a human about to steal him. Being newly born the fawn had no fear and could easily be picked up. Who can measure the mother's distress, or that of her infant if it should fall into the wrong hands?

I thought of the enormous responsibility this kind, misguided woman had placed on my shoulders. The fawn was not quite three days old when he arrived at Ravenshill. The woman's well-intended interference meant that this little deer would remain unafraid of people for the rest of his life — and man is a deer's worst enemy.

As I held the little buck his insides let go and I was glad I was wear-

112

ing old clothes. He was suffering from the scours just as Vixen had been when she arrived.

He stood shakily when I put him down to finish relieving himself, then he squatted like a bitch — a characteristic of deer of both sexes and all ages.

A newborn animal identifies with the first object it sees — its mother if it is left alone. But if it is removed from her at a very early age it can identify with anything — a log, a rock, even another species of animal or a human. There was therefore no danger that this fawn would run away since I was now his mother-substitute.

He was thin and wobbly, ill from diarrhoea and desperately in need of proper feeding, having spent two days on a human baby's formula which was totally inadequate.

I left him in a big cage on a bed of deep, warm hay, whilst I went indoors to fetch medication and the formula I had already prepared for him. My preparations included picking wild strawberry and stonecrop leaves for the scours. From these I made a strong 'tea' which I mixed with slippery elm to make a runny jelly. I put the mixture in a sterilized Coke bottle and snapped on a long black nipple intended for lambs, having first enlarged the hole.

He lay as I had left him, tired and weak. But when I offered the bottle he took it eagerly and drank the strange contents. Vixen had found the slippery elm unpleasant but the little deer was a herbivore. He probably found it unsatisfying after his mother's milk but for the moment it was the safest thing to give him.

After relieving himself again outside I put him back to bed and he rearranged his hay with a dainty, pointed-hoof forefoot, then folded his forelegs under his body, tucked his hind legs down and sank into it, as neat a package as you could wish for. He was very tired and fell asleep before I had finished dropping sacks across his cage to help him retain his body heat and give him some sense of security. Animals under the shock and stress of illness feel safer when housed in a warm, dim place large enough to move in but with boundaries that can be touched.

In planning his diet I had to take several things into account. Milk is differently constituted for different species. Human babies double their birth weight by six months and take years to mature, whereas rabbits double theirs in six days, puppies in seven to nine, and a fawn in ten to fourteen. The principle to follow is therefore that the more rapid the animal's growth, the richer its milk needs to be.

Countless fawns, puppies, kittens and other animals have been raised on cow's milk, diluted and sweetened. They have survived despite it, not because of it. In fact, *the milk is altered in precisely the opposite direction to what is required.* It is one of the chief reasons why so many young animals, especially wild ones, die 'inexplicably'.

Doe's milk, for instance, contains more than twice the solids of Jersey milk — which is the richest cow's milk; more than twice as much fat, three times as much protein, and twice as much ash (minerals), but — and this is very important — less sugar. *Added sugar in any form is the principal cause of scouring.*

Another potentially fatal danger for a mammal that has been removed from its mother at birth is that it is deprived of colostrum, the first milk after birth, which only the mother can produce, containing irreplaceable antibodies against disease. In bitches' milk the antibodies are active for nine weeks (when puppies should be given their first distemper shot). In deer the immunizing period is a mere twelve hours. In addition, during the first three days doe's milk is very rich in vitamin A, which must also be taken into consideration when preparing a formula for a fawn.

And so, armed with a formula based on evaporated unsweetened cow's milk fortified with fat, protein, calcium, slippery elm and herbs and vitamins — but no sugar — I went to see how my fawn was feeling.

I found him soiled, wet and miserable, the beautiful white hair on his rump green with scouring — yet even the single dose of slippery elm had produced some improvement.

Like all fawns he had a beautiful soft red-bay coat with lines of white spots — over two hundred of them — running from the base of his skull, down his spine and along his flanks to his hindquarters. These spots are composed of hairs different from the rest of the coat, coarser and longer, each hair brown with a white tip. In time the tip wears down, exposing the brown below it, which is why the spots gradually fade in summer as the baby grows into a gangling teenager.

I sat down beside my new patient and washed him with a soft sponge dipped in weak disinfectant, then dried him with paper towels. Suddenly he smelt milk. He uttered a short, weak, heart-rending bleat, a cross between a kitten's mew and a lamb's baa, without the tremolo effect — more like a short wha-a. As I picked up the bottle he struggled to get at it and when I gave it to him took the nipple between his lips and over his tongue and sucked to the last drop, hardly breathing in his eagerness.

I stroked him and talked to him quietly and after relieving himself once more he went back to bed. I left him in the dim light behind the sacking, hoping his eagerness to feed meant he would survive. Hoping, too, that by mixing formula and herbal medication I could short-circuit the semi-fast I imposed on Vixen.

Meanwhile he needed a name.

Edward murmured that every fawn seemed to be a Bambi, so that wouldn't do. Maybe he could make something out of his Latin name, if I happened to know it?

"*Odocoileus hemionus columbianus*", I said with glee.

He looked faintly shocked.

We eventually settled on *Cervus,* Latin for deer in general.

This, then, is the story of Cervus.

*   *   *   *   *

A newly-born fawn lives in a confusedly nebulous world, knowing only how to nurse from its dam while she lies down. In a day or two it stands on its feet for meals and can trot short distances beside the mother.

During the first hours after birth, which usually takes place in the early morning, the fawn is licked clean by the dam. The warm air dries it while it lies with its feet tucked under its body in some open glade where the sunlight is dappled with shade. Here the spots, so visible in the open, form a perfect camouflage.

Had Cervus remained wild, his mother would have groomed him for several weeks with her tongue. Her danger signal — a stamped foot and a coughing sound — would make him crouch low to the ground, head flattened, absolutely still. He would utter no sound while waiting to hear her call — a tiny reed-like sound, almost inaudible to humans.

True wildness develops when the fawn is between ten days and three weeks old. If it is caught at that time it will struggle desperately in its efforts to escape. After its spots have faded at about four months it will always remember its wild origins and remain shy and frightened in human company. Wild fawns at Ravenshill approach within six feet of me, but no further.

Scientific observations of wild fawns have produced various theories as to how often they suckle. Some say that because the doe's milk is highly concentrated fawns must feed 'relatively frequently' in the wild but only for short periods. Others are of the opinion that until they are ten days to two weeks old, fawns lie hidden by day and are only fed in the evening. After that they begin to follow their dam, sampling bits of green food as they trot beside her. Other sources state they suckle about two minutes at a time, over periods varying from two to ten hours, according to the observers.

My own experience, though limited to a small area, has been unusual in that the does at Ravenshill are used to seeing me around and bring their fawns out at an early age — probably about four days. I have watched them suckle at all sorts of odd hours during the day, for a minute or two at a time, with increased activity during early morning and late afternoon.

Lacking more precise information I decided to feed Cervus every four hours, on the theory that the relatively high fat content of the doe's milk would sustain her fawn for several hours, thus accounting for the long periods she leaves it alone. I further reasoned that should my formula need adjustment, it would be better for him to go slightly hungry between feeds than to have his stomach overloaded with too-frequent offerings.

Happily my calculated risk proved justified. Forty-eight hours after his arrival he began to pass almost normal stools.

His trust was infinitely touching. Although I knew, of course, that he was simply imprinted on me, I confess to feeling flattered when he showed no fear and he was so soft and warm to touch, and so eager to cuddle close to me. But no wild animal who has felt a human hand during infancy can ever be quite the same again. Something in its nature will have been dimmed, however slightly, a part of its instinct destroyed.

Thus bottle-raised captive fawns cannot be released safely because the only social relationships they have known are with people and because they are attached to the locality in which they have been raised. They grow into forlorn, unhappy deer, following humans endlessly for hand-outs, butting them with their antlers, pawing with front hooves at anyone who tries to drive them off. When the humans involved become tired of this and move the deer away to a new area, it succumbs quickly to dangers of which it has never been made aware. The only alternatives are a zoo — or death.

Yet if one has time and patience and guards vigilantly against one's selfish tendency to want to have and to hold, it is possible to rear wild creatures so that they become independent of their handlers, as I will prove.

I determined to raise Cervus as nearly as possible in his natural surroundings. I felt that, unlike Vixen who was not imprinted on me and therefore could revert to wildness on release, he needed to be free all day and as soon as possible at night, too, if he was to learn to look after himself.

In the morning I found him once more soiled and his bedding sopping wet. (Cervus is an ungulate who does not go somewhere special for his natural functions). After washing and drying him I set him down on the lawn and walked away from him, calling. He followed me into the woods, making little skipping trots in his effort to keep up with me. Still weak, he stumbled and almost fell. When he caught up with me he nuzzled my leg, so I bent down and stroked him on his back and under his chin. He stood still, raising his beautiful head to my hand in the gesture of a much-loved dog who wants attention.

I took two paces away from him and stamped my foot, at the same time giving an imitation of his mother's warning cough. Cervus looked at me inquiringly but made no move. I repeated the signals. He went down on his knees, tucked his hind legs under him, folded himself down into the ferns and mosses — and disappeared!

His camouflage was so perfect that even though I had watched the action I now had difficulty seeing him. Spotted coat blended into spotted shade; soft red fur absorbed light and blended into patches of bare soil and the cones and bits of bark scattered over the forest floor; his big ears lay flat as he crouched, neck extended, chin flat on the ground, not a muscle moving.

I walked quickly away.

From a distance I turned and looked back. There was no movement, no sound, to indicate there was a tiny fawn hidden somewhere in the undergrowth.

I had things to do, including a painting to finish, but I checked frequently from my studio window to see if Cervus had emerged from his hiding place. He did not reappear until I called him for his next feed. The problem of how to confine him was beaten almost before it had arisen. If he was free to move about all day I felt he would probably not fret if I penned him at night for a few days as a precaution against predators.

The next step was to introduce him to Mr. Bentley.

I fetched the old gentleman from the house and put him down a few feet from the new baby, who gazed at him steadfastly out of his huge, limpid brown eyes, twitching his sensitive ears and nostrils. He took a tentative step towards Mr. B., who had been cautioned to sit and stay. He remained obediently on the spot, blinking slowly into the sun, a benign expression on his snow-white face.

By the following day the elfin fawn and the veteran dachshund were friends. They were to remain so for years to come. Cervus thought Mr. B. was some kind of deer and did his best to play with him, while Mr. B. stood or sat, a little bewildered but prepared to accept him on trust, even when butted in the ribs by Cervus' small bony head.

The little fawn began to grow and put on weight. Soon after dawn I let him out and he roamed the woods, never far from the house, learning to feed himself with a little help from me. I only had to touch a leaftip here and there and he immediately investigated and nibbled. Fawns learn by example as well as by trial-and-error.

When they are about ten days old, deer begin to leave some scent in their tracks. For this purpose Cervus urinated onto his hind legs, squatting and at the same time drawing them inwards at an awkward angle, which caused him to wobble precariously as he sprayed himself. The object is to leave a scent that other deer may follow. Adults have three sets of scent glands, two in the leg area and one between the hooves. A fawn's urine is directed onto the inside of its hind legs, so that the fluid saturates the hair surrounding the outlet of the undeveloped tarsal gland.

Cervus' dam would have encouraged him in this performance by licking his hind legs just as she frequently grooms him all over. To imitate her I stroked his hind legs with a moist sponge, from time to time including his head, muzzle and most of his body. Like all baby mammals, he obliged with a bowel movement as soon as I stroked the area round the anus.

Days passed, sunny and warm, summer scents everywhere. The cascara tree on the lawn gave off a pungent perfume from its insignificant greenish flowers, resounding to the throbbing hum of bees. Cervus learned to browse some of the juicy herbs beneath it, then little by little extended his activities to include larger areas in the garden and woods, nibbling a leaf here, a flower there, always on the move and browsing at all levels. Deer don't graze, like sheep who crop the herbage close to the soil.

The bottle was his mainstay, so nutritionally his browsing meant little. It would be weeks before his stomach was conditioned to accept nothing but green food. Meantime nibbling could be regarded as a sort of practice run. His long, thin legs had grown straight and true, finished off with a set of tiny polished hooves. His body was well rounded but fine-boned, topped by an exquisite head and a pair of wide-set eyes with the softest of expressions. He was an enchanting sight as he wandered about nipping at plants — a charming prelude to more serious depredations when he grew older.

In two weeks he was transformed from a pathetic, helpless, wobbly baby to a lithe, supple, delicately-moving animal built of high-tension muscles perfectly coordinated for running and springing. He became very playful, in short bursts, putting his head down almost to the ground, then prancing sideways and back in a beautiful movement I never tired of watching. No matter where I was he always found me. When I was out with him he never strayed far from my side and if I bent or sat down he tried to suckle my ear-lobe. Thinking he might be in need of minerals or salt, I gave him a salt-lick containing cobalt and for a time he used it hungrily. I have never found wild deer to be interested in artificial salt-licks.

The weather changed to soft but persistent rain, the first that Cervus had ever seen. Here was a dilemma. Adult deer can stand no end of soaking. A fawn has softer hair and I did not think Cervus should get really wet. What would his dam do? Since I have watched does with tiny fawns wandering unconcernedly down our driveway in all weathers, I assume the baby is eventually led into the forest where summer rain would barely penetrate and there be licked dry. Certainly does groom their older fawns and are groomed by them in turn — a delightful sight — each licks a part of the other that is easily accessible as they stand together. I have watched times without number and observed the chewing motions of their mouths when they have finished the 'service' of de-lousing each other and eating the pests.

But my motherless baby tended to lie as near the house as possible whenever I went inside. He was then exposed to the full force of the rain and was likely to get soaked to the skin. So I put him in his pen whenever it rained heavily, then let him out after his meals and towelled him dry again: quite a chore.

As he grew older he would lose forever the dramatically handsome white spots; later still he would shed his coat to acquire his first winter coloring of brownish-grey. An adult deer's coat is made up of several different types of hair. Some soft and silky, wherever there is friction — under the legs and down them and on parts of the flanks and belly. The hair elsewhere is coarse, hollow and jointed, its texture feels like dry steel wool. It throws off water — a fact that can be demonstrated if one immerses one of these brittle hairs in water: it pops to the surface like a cork. A single fine red hair, however, rises to the surface slowly and the whiskers sink to the bottom.

Cervus' new coat would be water-repellant and by the time he acquired it he would be strong enough to withstand an occasional rainstorm before winter set in — I hoped.

When the rain finally stopped he had outgrown his pen and it was time he learned to stay outside all night.

With some misgivings I took him into the woods after his late feed and left him in the pale summer night, alone. I hated to go indoors, sensing his great eyes as he watched me leave. But for his sake I had to harden my heart.

I lay awake a long time trying to imagine his state of mind. About three o'clock I gave up trying to sleep and lay until daybreak, willing the night to pass. As light stole across the sky and the first rays of sun penetrated the trees, I sat up, and found myself looking directly into Cervus' eyes! He had made his way from the woods to lie beneath a weeping birch tree outside my floor-to-ceiling window. Wise infant, he must have sensed where I was and moved as close as he could.

He lay on the forest duff that matched his coat, protected by the green curtain of the deeply weeping branches. He looked very beautiful, like some elf of the forest. I stayed in bed for a few minutes simply watching, knowing he would rise when he saw me move. When I got up he cried out pitifully and I think his cry was of more than bodily hunger.

I dressed quickly then snatched his bottle from the refrigerator and warmed it in a jug of hot water as I went to meet him. He pranced eagerly towards me and soon reaped a just reward for his ordeal.

Chapter Twelve

Blessed is he who has found his work; let him ask no other blessedness.

Thomas Carlyle.

Cervus was still only three and a half weeks old, graceful, lithe, full of fun and infinitely appealing, with a bodily symmetry fit to inspire an artist. His white spots were sharply outlined, some spaced down his spine like dominoes, others spread at random over his body. His tail had not yet turned black on top, identifying him as a blacktailed deer but the inside of his legs were (and still are) pure white. He carried a white bib, and a narrow blurred black line ran under his chin from one side of his lower lip to the other. His ears were very large and still rounded, with soft curly hair inside. Later they became pointed and almost hairless within.

The eyes of deer, whether baby or relaxed adult, have an expression of such gentleness one wonders how anybody has the heart to shoot them. Dark brown, limpid, almond-shaped and corner-tilted like those of a beautiful woman in an old Persian painting, they are fringed by three-inch black lashes. Sparse black hairs sprout from the eyebrows and beneath each eye is a pear-shaped gland running obliquely downwards from the inner corner. It is lined with fine white skin and opens and closes whenever the deer experiences strong emotions, such as alarm or friendly excitement. This gland has no odor, at least to a human nose, whereas the scent glands on feet and legs give off a strong but pleasant smell like half-cooked biscuits.

I am always amazed at the silence of a deer's movement, even on hard surfaces. Cervus' hooves are soft and warm to the touch underneath, hard and polished above as I discovered when I held one of his dainty forefeet in my hand. He emerges from the woods with a curiously rolling gait, tail erect and waving. Behind each hoof is a pair of miniature hooves or 'dew-claws', similar to those worn by St. Bernard and Great Pyrenees* dogs and perhaps serve the same purpose — preventing the foot from sinking too deeply into snow.

Little by little my 'orphan' fawn learned the ways of his ancestors and in the process of eating green growing things gradually altered the arrangement of his digestive system, something only ruminants do. It is a most interesting phenomenon and I will return to it later.

---

* Known outside of Canada as Pyrenean Mountain dogs.

He had learned to accept my absences indoors, but kept me more or less in sight by making beds under all the windows in the flower borders. And then he discovered the front door. The first time he walked in I was so entranced I just stood looking at him. Disenchantment soon followed when he innocently soiled the carpet. He wasn't to know it was not meant for this purpose; after all, he was used to a toilet as big as all outdoors. On the whole, therefore, we discouraged him from coming into the house. Apart from the disastrous effect on my carpets, it was not good for him to grow accustomed to an artificial atmosphere.

The time would come when he would be large, strong and difficult to handle; deer are extremely stubborn and woe betide you if you try to make them go one way when they want to go another. And I had visions of disaster in the form of a panicky attempt to make an exit through the eight-foot double-glazed windows, which don't open.

Long-established deer trails criss-cross Ravenshill and I was interested to observe that Cervus followed them. If, as has somewhere been suggested, they follow underground watercourses, his instinct was running true to form, since many of these trails run in line with our well.

My herbal additions to his formula had long since been dropped as his intestines settled down to normal functioning. At this time his stool resembled that of a dog, but when he became a true ruminant he would pass dark pellets not unlike a rabbit's. It is important to notice such things when one is raising young creatures. You know how extraordinarily interested hospital nurses are in obtaining samples from their human patients! Disaster can often be averted merely by knowing what a normal bowel movement looks like; while great distress and illness can ensue if nature's signs are ignored, as happens all too often in the world of humans.

Cervus was looking thrifty, which is to say that his appearance was that of a fawn doing well on all fronts.

He had put on weight and height until at two months old he tipped the scales at twenty-eight pounds (two pounds heavier than Mr. Bentley) and stood twenty-one inches at his shoulder.

He stayed contentedly outside for hours at a time and one day met a wild doe with a fawn about his own size. He trotted eagerly towards them in obvious recognition of his own kind, with whom I am sure he merely wanted to play. But the doe gave him a light kick, then turned and led her baby deeper into the woods. Poor lonely Cervus, bewildered, returned to the lawn. It was his first lesson in the hard school of life. Henceforward he would be a loner. Our coast deer are not especially gregarious but even so form small groups. But Cervus, if the literature was correct, would never be permitted to join one.

Another lesson was due as summer was well advanced and he would have to be weaned.

Experimental experts believe in quick, early weaning at about two months. I don't! The initial shock of losing the mother, followed by an unnatural diet indicate to me that weaning should come slowly.

Experimental animals are captured at birth, taken from their mothers and raised in pens on artificial feed. From talking to scientists and reading learned papers I have gained the impression that early weaning is largely a matter of convenience and economics, rather than being geared to the well-being of the fawns. "They get along very well if you take them off the bottle quickly." Which means a crash program of just seven days.

In the wild state a fawn remains part of a matriarchal family for almost a year. The generally accepted time for its weaning is three and a half to four months but if the mother doesn't object it may nurse right up to the next mating season when it is five months old, and continue running with its dam until she is well into her pregnancy. As I write there is a lovely doe named Sarah feeding on grain beneath my window and with her is her seven-month fawn who even now occasionally tries to nip under mother's belly in hopes of a quick drink — but she takes the doe's rejection philosophically and returns to the grain, rubbing noses with her mother.

Cervus was weaned slowly. At four months he had finished with his bottle and had learned to browse for himself.

As I said earlier, a fawn's rather desultry nibbling of green foods has no digestive significance. He is learning by copying his mother — a leaf here, a blade there. An unweaned fawn has only one stomach (technically it is monogastric, like ours), which is not organized to cope with cellulose.

Adult deer, on the other hand, are ruminants and have two stomachs. In babyhood the upper of the two, the rumen, is cut off by special muscles. When the fawn begins to browse on leaves these gradually relax, opening a passage from his gullet to his rumen. As he grows, the rumen develops into a large chamber which takes up a sizeable part of the animal's interior. When he begins to chew the cud his rumen has begun to function and he leaves babyhood behind.

The expression 'chewing the cud' means that partly digested food in the rumen is converted into small lumps or curds. (*Cud,* or *cudde,* is a Middle English word deriving from a still older word *cwudu*). This cud rises into the mouth, where it is chewed and swallowed again, whereupon the whole process is repeated: up and down — down and up — endlessly. When Cervus reached this stage the process was easily visible as he lay quietly ruminating, converting into nourishment the tough, fibrous greens, which as a baby he could not have utilized.

The juices in our stomachs are acid and kill most bacteria. Those in Cervus' rumen are bland and encourage the growth of many kinds of micro-organisms. It is these — not the food in its raw state — which supply him with the energy he needs: they feed on the greenstuff he eats and what he uses for energy and life are the by-products of their action which pass through the wall of his rumen into his bloodstream.

I realize that this technical explanation is holding up the story but I think its interest warrants the digression. I should make it clear that I am not parading my knowledge; what follows is a 'translation' into layman's language of what I learned by reading stodgy textbooks and listening to complex and interminable explanations delivered by learned — and patient — scientist friends.

In the rumen different categories of microbes constitute a general mass of microflora, which is in a constant state of flux. Part of it is perpetually being washed down the alimentary tract into the true stomach which is known as the abomasum. There it is digested. The 'space' it has left in the abomasum is filled by new microbes which arrive with each new mouthful eaten. The result is a sort of free-for-all competition between new and old microbes and those which are best suited to the environment of the rumen thrive and become dominant. As long as the type of food eaten remains constant — in other words as long as the deer sticks to his natural greenstuffs or other food to which he has been slowly introduced — the microbes which are already dominant remain the best suited and those which occupy the 'space' will almost certainly be of the same kind.

I never offer Cervus candy or other tid-bits and I want to explain why.

A great deal of well-intentioned harm is done to tame deer in parks and zoos. They are often fed tid-bits by adoring children and adults and it is safe to say that none of the food they are offered is suitable.

When you change a deer's diet or feed him on tid-bits that you think are tasty, he may eat what you give him (and being bored in captivity he undoubtedly will), but the microbes in his rumen are not the right ones to deal with this new type of food. The dominant microbes which were accustomed to natural foods die off and other strains will have to develop and become dominant before the new food can be utilized.

124

Mr. Archimedes Dooley — saw-whet owl-in-residence.

Female rufous hummingbirds feeding.
The grills are bee guards. photo: Enid K. Lemon

Hummingbird ready for release.
photo: Enid K. Lemon

Cervus loved to visit but this had to be discouraged.

Youth and age: Cervus and Mr. Bentley, showing fawn's spots sharply outlined, spaced down his spine like dominoes.

Cervus, aged two years, with single spikes, becomes a little too friendly for comfort.

Cervus, lost and returned, mating with Tristesse.

Scarper (left) and Flo wait politely for the Admiral to take his bath, after hole had been pick-axed the thick ice—a daily chore.

After witnessing this scene, the boy vowed never to hunt.

While this is going on the deer is without nourishment.

What he has eaten cannot be digested for him by the microbes in his rumen; and so, deprived of their by-products, which are literally his life-blood, he starves to death.

Thus, to feed any new food suddenly in large quantities can be fatal.

This often occurs when bales of hay are thrown out in the snow to feed starving deer. They eat it and die of starvation — with full stomachs. If they had been left to forage they might have found enough to survive. Failing this, assistance can be given in severe weather and deep snow in the form of trees cut down so they can browse their natural diet. They may be thin, but they will live.

This is the basic reason why you should not feed goodies to deer.

In the wild, deer vary considerably in size, depending on the quality of the available food. In our locality they are fairly small. The heavy shade from the high conifers that cover a large part of their range minimizes sunlight and as a consequence the herbage is low in protein.

In view of his early deprivation Cervus needed all the help he could get to reach healthy adulthood so I kept a stock of rabbit pellets for him. These supplied him with additional protein in a form well balanced for his digestion. Unfortunately no deer ration as such is sold commercially. He quickly learned to find his feeding station — a tray under the balcony safely out of Mr. Bentley's reach. At first he merely blew on the new food. Some pellets stuck to his damp muzzle and in time he discovered they weren't so bad after all.

By this time storage of animal feed was becoming a problem. We possessed a battered old garbage can and nothing else that was rat-proof. One day Edward arrived with a shiny new one. When he took the car out the following day he glanced over at it, and looked again. The new can was not there but the old one was back. Rather sheepishly I explained that I had taken it to store Cervus' pellets. Edward shrugged and we continued to use the ancient relic we had inherited with the house. We still have it — and I have six new ones for animal feed!

*   *   *   *   *

Of all the wild creatures I have raised, none surpassed Cervus for sheer joy. Notwithstanding the fact that I was training him to be as wild as imprinting on me would permit, I took daily pleasure in his company out of doors. When I was gardening he sometimes lay curled up like a dog beside me, or skipped and pranced about, often round and over Mr. Bentley.

At ten weeks the pedicel or base for his future antlers began to grow in the form of two little bumps under his skin, half an inch high and hot to touch: they must have been tender as a teething child's gums, for he shied away if I touched them. In time they would erupt as his first rudimentary antlers — mere spikes which would fall off the following spring.

Contemplating my leggy buck I felt as so many parents do who would like to regard their large offspring as eternal infants. A very young fawn inveigles itself into the very fabric of your being, just by looking beautiful and helpless.

His winter pelage appeared gradually, starting at his shoulders. The new hair was grey-brown and very dense, coarser than his baby fur. The upper surface of his tail turned black from about half-way down to the tip, and wherever the hair remained white it had a startling brilliance. No matter what the weather or where he lay, Cervus' fine white hair was always pure as the driven snow. But each year, like all his kind, he would go through two moults, from the grey-brown of winter to the beautiful, shiny, cinnamon of summer and then back again.

In the meantime the season changed to a warm, brilliantly colored autumn. Cervus continued to follow me about like a faithful dog and to play skittishly, wanting everybody around to be fawns with him. When I went indoors he wandered about or lay ruminating under a window or in a warm hollow in the rocks from which he could survey his domain.

One evening, Edward and I and another couple were enjoying drinks on the balcony overlooking the lake. Cervus lay in the rocky hollow below us. Hummingbirds surrounded us. Conversation was desultory as we absorbed the blissful quiet.

Suddenly the silence was rent by the hair-raising screech of tires skidding to a halt on the road below.

Ever conscious of the peril to animals on this dangerous stretch of twisting road, I begged the men to go to see what had happened.

Presently they came straggling back, their earlier ebullience evaporated.

A doe, on her way to the wild land across from the entrance to our driveway, had been killed outright by a speeding youth in his new sports car who, too late, had seen her at the bend in the road. The boy was shaken and sorry; he offered to take the broken body to the proper authority. Our menfolk helped put the still-warm doe into his car and he drove off.

We went indoors sadly, each desolated at this useless loss of life.

126

I was particularly shattered for I knew that this doe had twin fawns still dependent on their mother for company, guidance and milk.

For days we searched the bush in the faint hope that we might come across the babies so that we could supplement their food. But we never found them. At any time they might have been only a few feet away from us.

We listened for faint bleats of hunger but there was nothing; nothing but the hot silence. Eventually, forlorn and frustrated, we gave up.

I prayed the twins had been healthy enough to survive and courageous enough to go to the lake for the water they would need to slake their thirst during the long dry summer. The alternative was too horrible to contemplate.

*　　*　　*　　*　　*

Deer-louse flies are picked up in the woods and have nothing to do with hygiene and they plague Cervus and all his kin. Nasty little six-legged creatures, flat and brown and sprouting wings in the fall infest the deer's body, running about on the skin of throat, neck, legs and anywhere else their tormented host cannot get at them. I kept Cervus reasonably free of these pests by dusting him with pyrethrum powder.

Wood ticks also plagued him. In spring and fall they climb aboard passing animals (including humans) and bury their heads under the skin. Being not much bigger than a pin-head, they are very hard to find until they bloat on the victim's blood into half-inch, shiny grey balloons. Then they fall off. Pyrethrum helps discourage ticks, but once they have started blood-sucking the only way to remove them is by hand — twisting them out anticlockwise. They won't come out cleanly any other way! A lighted cigarette applied to the tick's bottom is said to make it let go but I have yet to see this work. If you pull, the body comes away, leaving the head to fester.

Wild animals are also subject to various internal parasites whose invasions *appear* not to disrupt a healthy beast's existence. But very recent studies show that an animal can die from injuries which would normally respond to treatment unless it is heavily parasitized. Then, what are known as "shock bodies" appear in the blood vessels, causing coagulation and slow death. The injuries are not necessarily wounds, as I was to discover.

A three-and-a-half-month-old doe visited Ravenshill daily with her dam and enchanted us with her endearing ways and gentle beauty. But her mother must have been killed silently by a bow-and-arrow hunter because the little one appeared alone one day — and the next. On the third day I found her standing with head down, soaked to the skin and covered in mud. Normally she would not allow me near her but now she stood apathetically whilst I towelled her dry. Then I made her a bed in the garage and hung a heat lamp over her. Although I applied mouth-to-mouth resuscitation she gradually lost consciousness. There was mud in her mouth, so she must have fallen into the lake, struggled in the oozy mud and just made it to the familiar lawn where I found her at her last gasp.

No less than three young veterinary surgeons interested in wildlife generously came to help her but she died the following morning despite all our efforts.

I asked that an autopsy be performed so that we might learn something from this pathetic little fawn whose death seemed so useless and wasteful. Something that might help future cases.

The pathologist's report disclosed a horrid state of affairs. Her liver, lungs, bronchial tubes, intestines and muscles were infested by a fantastic number and variety of parasites and their eggs and larvae. Yet they had not killed her. Nor did she die of pneumonia from inhaling mud, as I had imagined. She died of "disseminated intravascular coagulation" — in other words shock. Had she not undergone the twin shocks of losing her dam and struggling to extricate herself from the cloying mud, she might have lived her normal life-span, her parasites notwithstanding.

When attempting to rid Cervus of external parasites which would be a natural part of his life in the wild state, I reasoned that he should be given every aid to achieve optimum growth and health. Skin parasites keep an animal in a constant state of irritation and nervous twitching. Wild deer, and dogs too, sometimes have raw patches on their faces and behind their ears where they have scratched to dislodge ticks or louseflies. Cervus undoubtedly had some internal parasites which it would be foolish to try to remove with drugs which would do him even greater damage. But I could at least do everything in my power to maintain the outside of him free of perpetual itching.

During the autumn I taught him to find mushrooms which he nibbled without much enthusiasm. But hanging from Douglas firs and from branches of oceanspray spiraea was a grey-green 'beard' lichen, a staple diet for deer at the end of the year.* Cervus ate it with relish. Yet even

---

* Two 'beard' lichens (*Alectoria sarmentosa* and *Usnea barbata*) are common but difficult to tell apart without professional help. Both are palatable to deer.

128

with his instinct for the right plants, he passed over many that were good for him. I had to touch with my finger to show him how to extend his menu.

I thought him the most adorable of creatures but there were times when I could have wrung his dear little neck, if you will pardon the pun. Such as when I found him calmly eating my dwarf cyclamen. To add insult to injury, when he had devoured all the blooms he sat on what remained of the plant. So comforting to an artist who paints flowers!

The next to attract his insatiable appetite were the runner beans. Master Cervus ate the lot in one early morning splurge. Then came my autumn-flowering crocuses and after that he turned his attention to various rare shrubs. Finally he waded into my raised herb bed, standing on his hind legs, front feet firmly in the soil. All disappeared down the gullet of my darling fawn.

It simply isn't possible to keep herbivorous animals who are not under any kind of restraint and hope at the same time to have a garden. If you want a garden or even a small vegetable patch you have to enclose it with chicken wire, including the top.

Very few items are permanently excluded from a deer's diet and when autumn days grow cool and they eat hungrily to put on fat for the winter, garden plants that once seemed immune from their depredations suddenly become desirable. There appears to be no rule of thumb to make life easier for gardeners.

Broadly speaking I find that strongly aromatic plants are the least attractive to deer. But even these must be protected as seedlings.

Watching wild animals come and go takes priority over gardening and I was almost resigned to the loss of most of my shrubs and bulbs. But not quite. During the months which followed I talked to many people, read books on the habits of browsing animals and here and there found a ray of hope, to which I will return later.

Chapter Thirteen

The heavens are draining,
it's raining and raining,
 and everything couldn't be wetter,
and things are so bad
that we ought to be glad:
 because now they can only get better.

Piet Hein, GROOKS 5.

Sunny autumn days turned to rain. Cervus' need to be near his humans was so great that day after day he lay ruminating in the open near the house. When he shook himself he produced a halo of fine spray that enveloped him in a little private cloud. As long as I stayed with him he would stand under cover but as soon as I left he traipsed forlornly to a place from which he could keep an eye on my comings and goings. I tried drying him with towels but gave up the futile exercise, he was wet again within minutes.

The temperature was falling as steadily as the rain and a cold wind blowing on his wet body could have dire consequences. It was a temptation to bring him indoors or at least under cover but an animal subjected to sudden changes in temperature is more likely to become ill than one living naturally.

Cervus came eagerly to his tray under the balcony for his daily ration which consisted at this time of a bowl of undiluted, unsweetened canned milk, a piece of home-made whole-wheat bread, a carrot or an apple, and his pellets.

He had gained so much weight I could no longer pick him up to stand with him on the bathroom scales. (One does not, as some have discovered to their cost and amusement, try to put a struggling animal on the scales). He was in fine fettle but his resistance to the hazards of winter was about to be severely tested.

Day succeeded soaking day and night followed night of cold, pelting rain and howling wind.

One morning, after a week of this, I found Cervus standing with his head hanging, his coat dull and wet, muzzle dripping and eyes inflamed and discharging pus. He was hot to touch and probably had a temperature far exceeding his normal 102.1°F. Artificial rearing had doubtless predisposed him to sickness and if I was not quick and careful he would go the way of so many hand-reared fawns.

Now I had to get him under cover.

Deciding on the indoor garage, unheated but dry and easy to keep clean, I evicted the cars, including Edward's pride and joy. We then dragged in some heavy planks and placed them across bricks to create an airspace between them and the cold concrete. On top of them I put piles of hay, first tossing it to free it from irritating dust.

This done, I called Cervus.

He came, a sad, bedraggled little deer. Gone his joyous skipping gait, flag-tail erect; gone the eager search for the morsel in my hand. There remained a lonely, suffering waif.

I had no problem getting him inside since he was always trying to enter the house. He sniffed his new bed and then, aided by a gentle shove from behind, mounted the low platform and sank into the sweet-smelling hay, looking utterly woebegone.

I towelled him dry and left him with a bucket of rainwater and an armful of his favorite greenstuffs. Drastic treatment was needed if he was to live.

With human children one expects the 'usual' illnesses and generally they recover quickly. But with wild animals there are no 'usual illnesses', apart from parasites — which are not diseases, though they may bring one on.

Here was, for me, a classic instance of when not to be adamant on the subject of herbal-versus-orthodox treatment. Herbal medicines work slowly and without drama. Cervus would die if a dramatically speedy remedy was not found. One of the antibiotics was his only hope.

To give him a large dose by mouth would not only be difficult (a deer's mouth is tight-lipped, making force-feeding almost impossible) but would probably play havoc with the microflora in his rumen. This left the hypodermic needle which could be tricky if he started to buck and kick. But I had no intention of tying my fawn up or restraining him in any way which might cause him added stress.

I calculated his weight, then telephoned Peter Davies, a young and brilliant bio-chemist who, fortuitously, was doing post-graduate work at the University of Victoria. (Now Dr. Davies, he is at present engaged in valuable research at Harvard University.) I hurriedly explained my problem and Peter readily agreed to produce the appropriate dose of penicillin-streptomycin, a combination which would act directly against the main infection if it was bacterial and prevent secondary infection.

Being an animal lover, Peter drove over immediately. I distracted Cervus' attention while Peter swiftly injected his thigh muscle. He barely twitched when the needle went in. He even let me take his rectal temperature, which was very high.

131

Since humans often get splitting headaches when they have high fevers, I think animals may also suffer from them. Closed eyes usually indicate pain in animals and Cervus' were shut most of the time. I made up a solution of dried rosemary leaves and lavender flowers, chilling it to bathe his face and head. I douched his eyes with a strained solution of clear, weak tea, followed later by eyebright-saline. Eyebright is a herb for eyes, as its name indicates and the solution is prepared by pouring one cup of boiling water over one-half teaspoon each of the herb and rock salt, then cooling. To relieve the pain of his sore and running eyes I squeezed in a cream anaesthetic after bathing them. The 200,000-unit dose of antibiotic was designed to 'hold' for four days, during which there was nothing for me to do but wait and keep my patient as comfortable as possible. Every day I rubbed his body with a rough towel to promote circulation and smoothed oil of wintergreen or eucalpytus on his chest so that he could breathe the vapor. A mild nose ointment went into each nostril morning and evening.

Fever made Cervus shiver violently; there was a dreadful rasping rattle in his chest and his eyelids flickered with pain. It was vital that he keep warm, yet it was useless to try to blanket him: he would have thrown it off as soon as my back was turned, so I had to rely on the heat-generating hay and a heat lamp hung high overhead.

Sick animals are so long-suffering and silent. I feel guilty for not having more understanding of what they need. Humans ask; their babies yell; but animals just lie looking at you as they wait to die and you never know whether they are thinking anything at all. Dogs are trusting and show their love, which if anything makes it worse. At that time there were no local vets interested in wild animals. The three who came to the dying fawn were later arrivals. All were women and it is comforting today to know that there is someone to call on in an emergency.

Cervus had to be nursed without further help, and I was determined he was not going to die.

The once-proud head drooped as he coughed and panted, flanks heaving. He sucked up water and the herbal infusions I prepared from garlic, slippery elm and honey to quench his burning thirst. Garlic contains an essential oil (crotonaldehyde) which passes through the wall of the stomach into the bloodstream and is a natural antibiotic.

Bravely he nibbled the fresh greens I picked and held for him as he lay. I took heart from his appetite, poor though it was.

Keeping him dry presented a problem. Since deer roam by day and night, sleeping in different places without benefit of bedding, they need not worry about soiling their quarters as might a badger, for instance, who takes elaborate sanitary precautions in his permanent home or set. Cervus' bedding was soaked with urine and had to be changed daily and the platform scrubbed with disinfectant. The weather was mild so I let him out for a time to breathe fresh air and gently exercise his limbs. He even had appetite enough to browse on a few plants but he was pathetically weak and very willing to return to his bed and a towelling.

On the third day he was worse. His breathing had become even more labored, mucous bubbling audibly, and he coughed quietly, closing his eyes against the pain that must have seared his lungs. His muzzle was hot and tender, the black skin peeling where it had cracked. With difficulty I tried bathing his inflamed lips and gums, using a weak solution of fresh lemon juice.

And then his coat began to 'stare'. His hair, though not shedding, stood away from his body in a lumpy sort of way, quite different from its appearance when he was healthy. Beware a staring coat in any sick animal, it means real illness. Once seen it is never forgotten. In Cervus' case it undoubtedly signified that his infection had reached its peak. During the next twenty-four hours he would either succumb or turn the corner.

The waiting was awful. My once-lovely fawn looked deathly. His legs were weak and his face had grown puffy, which gave it a curiously square look. His great sensitive ears were crimson-veined, hot to touch; from his limpid eyes ran a thick discharge and when he blinked it was slowly, painfully; they must have felt like hot grit.

Ill though he was he seemed to be putting up a fight to live by dint of the sheer effort of chewing his cud. I scoured the woods for things to tempt him but there wasn't much at that time of year. A few arbutus shoots, medicinally valuable for sore throat; some yellowing branches of thimbleberry; a little lichen, a handful of chickweed and a late mushroom here and there. It wasn't much but it was eaten willingly, which was half the battle.

I also spent time each day just sitting with him, his head in my lap. I stroked him and talked to him and did my best to convey to him that his substitute mother had not abandoned him.

In the middle of the third night I went down to see if he needed anything. He looked the same, bedraggled, ill, drooping. Fingers of fear tightened in my stomach.

The fourth morning dawned cold and fine. I woke with the same sick fear and went breathlessly downstairs, dreading what I might find on the other side of the door into the garage.

As I reached for the handle there was a tapping on the door. I opened it to find Cervus standing there, hoofing at its fire-proof metal surface. My relief at finding him alive was so great I put my arms round his neck and hugged him. He responded feebly with a hot wet lick to my face.

I examined him as he drank from the bowl I held.

Lungs: his breathing seemed a little easier; his flanks still heaved but not so hectically. Eyes: a little less discharge. Coat: a little less staring but still dull and lifeless. Mouth and muzzle: no better but at least no worse.

He wasn't going to die. Something more than wishful thinking told me so. I let him out for a few minutes and watched as he squatted shakily, noticing how thin he had grown in so short a time — his ribs were starkly visible.

The next day cold rain greeted us once more. Cervus had to stay indoors, restive at his confinement like any sick child. He spent another wretched week in the garage, while outside it rained and the wind blew the last leaves from the bushes. I had to bring him bucketfuls of bright yellow fallen poplar leaves, which he ate for their sugar and cellulose since they lacked green chlorophyll.

In two weeks he had recovered enough to return outdoors, though he would need careful watching.

Death had nearly claimed my fawn. For a few days I found myself strangely drained of resources. Serious illness is a testing time for nurse as well as patient.

Hoping to persuade Cervus to sleep under cover while the cold weather lasted, I transferred his bedding to his feeding station under the balcony. It was a bright idea but it didn't work. In the garage, ill, he had nowhere else to lie but free once more he spurned man-made shelter. He had almost a dual personality; he wanted to come indoors as my pet but would not accept artificial comfort from me outside. In time the hay became a home for rats, which Mr. Bentley was cajoled into dispatching. Cervus' sick-bed ended up on the compost heat.

*　　*　　*　　*　　*

In November the rain turned to sleet and finally to heavy snow. Our lake froze and the woods became silent and white. The outstretched limbs of cedar and fir, dogwood and pine received their shining mantles. Traffic noises blurred and were finally silent as the road became impassable. Under the moon the land was an enchanted place, ethereal and beautiful. Dozens of birds came to our feeding tables and some of the smaller ones roosted in Cervus' food tray or flew into our tool room to avoid the bitter cold.

Snow was a new experience for Cervus. Each morning his delicate tracks showed clearly where he had been during the night. But when I felt his feet his hooves were always warm, and soft underneath.

His tracks were so neat one could be excused for thinking they had been made by a two-footed animal. His hoof marks lay exactly in two-paired lines, since he set his hind feet precisely into the imprints made by his corresponding front hooves. Up to the age of about two years a buck's tracks are indistinguishable from those made by a doe. After that his hoof marks are larger than a doe's, his stride longer and he no longer places his hind feet exactly in the imprints made by his front ones. The scent glands in the legs and feet of adults of both sexes enable them to track one another easily. Cervus always shook the snow from his body but one morning he appeared for breakfast wearing jewels in his hair! The night temperature had dropped to 14°F (−10°C) and as he moved through the bush snow must have melted on his head, where it froze into a diadem of small icicles which tinkled faintly as he walked.

Three fawns from the current year's crop appeared on our lawn. A buck with little spikes about three inches long, another with only the bumps visible, the third a strange-looking doe. She was not only much smaller but stunted and malproportioned, with short legs, too-short neck and a general appearance of unthriftiness. She followed behind the others as they took the familiar route across our driveway.

Had she been born deformed, she would have been abandoned by her dam. Therefore something must have happened to her later.

I thought of the tragedy of the previous summer, when a nursing doe was killed by a car; of how we searched in vain for the twins I was sure she had hidden. Was this stunted doe one of them and the smaller buck her brother? If so — and it seemed possible — it was a miracle they had survived the hot, dry summer without parental guidance. It was curious, too, that only the buck had grown to a reasonable size — though he was considerably smaller than Cervus. What had dwarfed the little doe? Another of nature's mysteries I would never unravel.

As the snow deepened food grew scarce. Deer do not dig for edibles; at most they paw ineffectually at the snow. So I began a weekly program of supplementary green feed. Grocery storekeepers are glad to dispose of their vegetable trimmings and they often gave me a bonus in the form of a bunch of carrots. I emptied a huge box of these greens onto our snow-covered lawn and not only the deer but our geese and ducks made merry. And I was happy to see the orphan twins occasionally eating when there was nobody about.

Cervus usually finished his breakfast before strolling over to the pile on the lawn, where he competed with the ducks for choice pieces. Mr. Bentley also waded in on his short legs because he loved the sweetness of carrots or cabbages. I worried that Cervus might kick him or the birds when they were all wandering under his feet. Occasionally he bunted the old gentleman and frequently stooped to lick his head and ears or butt him playfully. Dear old Mr. B. He was thirteen but still a going concern.

The weather grew steadily colder. Wild mallards flew in and joined our residents for grain. Cervus, too, decided he would like some. I found him at the feed trough, happily munching a mixture of whole corn, wheat, barley and oats. In small quantities these natural foods did him no harm. But for the rather timid geese, his thieving was serious. The poor birds already had to compete with the mallards, who could fly into the trough and sit on the grain, shovelling their bills along like little vacuum cleaners, and with our large domestic ducks who were tall enough to stand on tip-toe to reach in, since they couldn't fly. Even Mr. Bentley joined in. Dachshunds are notorious scavengers and anything remotely edible is grist to their mill, but the raw grain, which Mr. B. ate simply because it was there, passed through him unaltered and sprouted in the spring.

Here was a problem.

I solved it by scattering the grain over a wide area so that the small birds had to take their time searching for it. This meant clearing a lot of snow but it prevented the greedy few from hogging all the grain.

Poor Edward, unable to negotiate the icy, twisting road leading to Ravenshill, perforce spent many nights in city motels or with friends. Meanwhile I revelled in the beauty and silence.

I am always excited when snow blankets everything and can hardly wait to go out to wash my face in its chilling freshness and to explore the ground for animal signs and the trees for birds and dangerous broken branches. These 'widow-makers' can live up to their name when high winds blow, although by tearing down branches and uprooting trees the wind is doing nature's job of pruning. But to a human caught outside in it, a gale can and often does spell death.

Death for a man, life for a deer. I have mentioned the life-giving lichens. These, growing on branches torn from their trunks during gales, supply feed for deer at a time when there is little else to sustain them.

Whenever I picked up a fallen branch when Cervus and I were in the woods together, I offered it to him before piling it away and he nibbled his way daintily along it, taking not only the 'beard' but other lichens as well as fir needles. These tough, spiky leaves form a significant part of the deer's winter diet and in the spring they relish the young shoots. They will also eat small quantities of cedar, although it is well known to be poisonous to humans.

Wind, flood and bitter cold ushered in the new year. Our lake overflowed its dam, flooding the road. Winter miseries, including some bone-chilling power cuts, assailed us. We had to cook in the living room fireplace, which was fun, though it didn't do the saucepans much good. And without electricity the well pump ceased to function and, of course, since such disasters always arrive unannounced, we had no reserves of water in bathtub or buckets. Edward, who spent years in the desert of North Africa managing on half a gallon of water a day for everything, including sock-washing, found no difficulty accommodating to the shortage. But I, accustomed to lashings of hot water, was thankful I had to melt snow for only a couple of days.

Birds flocked to icicled feeders, including a strange Oregon junco with white circles round its eyes and a white necklace where only black should have been. Downy woodpeckers competed with nuthatches and chickadees for the suet.

One bitter February morning Cervus, now eight months old, shed neatly into my hands the four-inch baby spikes he had grown the previous summer.

By the middle of May he was growing a lop-sided new pair and moulting his winter hair; so what with odd antlers and a motheaten coat he looked a sorry sight. He also had a small V-shaped nick out of one ear which was to prove very significant indeed.

But soon he was once more sleek and shining of coat. He had survived a particularly wretched winter and was gradually managing to become a wild deer. My natural desire to pet and make a fuss of him had to be rigidly curbed. I held back when he appeared from the bush, contenting myself with spying on him from indoors. I hated to disappoint him when he came to the house for food or company, yet he had to learn complete independence. Far from feeling rejected when he trotted back into the woods, I was delighted to see him behaving more and more naturally. The deer who grows too tame, too reliant upon human handouts, almost always comes to grief.

This was my fawn's first spring and he was healthy, despite his near-fatal bout of the previous fall with what was probably pneumonia. He browsed far and wide as a wild deer should, no longer needing me to point out what to eat. He began to disappear for days and I worried about him crossing the road. But he always returned for his pellets and grain, which by now were the only food supplements he received. The charming days of babyhood were left behind forever.

I began to anticipate his second summer, during which he would grow his first pair of adult antlers and, completely outfitted, become a credit to his proud and unashamedly anthropomorphic 'mother'.

Chapter Fourteen

A deer wears antlers. Not horns.

Horns are permanent, unbranched structures that project from the heads of male and female cattle, sheep, goats, antelope and others. They consist of a bone core covered by a layer of tough, fibrous protein, called keratin.

Antlers are much the same, but they are shed annually. With two exceptions they are worn only by the male of the species. The exceptions are caribou and reindeer, in which both sexes carry them.

They are at first covered with thick black skin and short, soft red hair, which looks and feels like felt and is known as the velvet. Late in the summer, when the antlers have attained their maximum growth for the year, blood ceases circulating to the covering velvet and the buck rubs it against trees and bushes to loosen and shed it. After it has been rubbed off he polishes his antlers against the bark of trees and shrubs until they acquire a fine patina. By October he is ready for the mating season.

The doe's readiness to mate is not nearly so obvious. She gives no outward indication until about two days beforehand, and even this is dependent upon the presence of a buck. Once she has come positively into heat she starts running at a fast trot until she is panting, her tongue lolling. She has an extremely short receptive period, lasting less than a day, and running increases her chance of locating a buck if one is not present when she is ready. She can cover a wide territory, marking her trail by the heightened activity of her leg and foot glands as well as by urinating at frequent intervals.

Does of Cervus' species reach breeding age in their second or third autumn. After the first heat, they come in again every twenty-four to twenty-eight days, beginning in October or November and lasting until early March. The end of their season more or less coincides with the dropping of the bucks' antlers. Their gestation period is roughly seven months. The majority of fawns are born in late May or early June, but climatic differences influence both breeding and fawning dates. It is also believed that the number of fawns born to each doe is affected by the food supply.

During the mating season the buck defends his territory by fighting other bucks, using his antlers simply to push with rather than as active weapons. His most potent weapons are his front hooves which can tear a man from neck to navel in short order.

An angry antlered buck is a formidable sight. The hair along his back and neck stands up like the hackles on a dog; likewise the hairs on his tail, which he carries high. With hunched back and lowered head he presents his antlers to his opponent, coughing and stamping or pawing at the ground with his front hooves before charging. Then there is always the danger that the antlers may become locked and, unable to disengage, both bucks die a lingering death from starvation or predation.

During the rutting season bucks can become extremely dangerous. Even tame ones change their docile, trusting natures, becoming fierce, suspicious and prone to attack.

Directly the antlers fall off in the spring, a tame buck reverts to his docile, trusting self. When I say 'directly' I mean it literally: one moment you have a dangerous animal with pounding hooves anxious to pin you to a wall by the sheer weight of his three hundred pounds; the next instant the antlers have fallen off, their own weight pulling them from the rotted stumps and behold! you have the charming creature you knew before the mating instinct took over. All that remains is a little bright blood in the sockets to show where the proud antlers once grew. Usually, of course, they fall off in the bush, where mice feed on the outer covering and in time only the hard core remains to bleach with exposure.

Cervus' antlers gradually evened out until they matched as a lyre-shaped pair of single spikes, still covered in velvet, which he shed in the manner described above — having taken fourteen days to rub the velvet off (some bucks do it in a matter of hours). In late October he was ready to mate.

Mindful of warnings about a rutting buck's ferocity, I watched him closely, careful to keep facing him, remembering never to bend too close to his sharp points. Common sense bade me heed these warnings — it would be stupid not to — yet I felt instinctively that Cervus would be docile with me during the rut. Famous last words? Perhaps. Time alone would tell.

His second summer passed without incident and I felt as proud as he looked. But he was still a loner and his one attempt to team up with some visiting wild does met with rejection.

In late October his visits to his feed tray became erratic. Needless to

140

say I worried. I have already mentioned the ever-present danger of the road and in addition it was still the hunting season which for some reason overlaps the mating season and in this area the open season allows the killing of blacktailed deer of *any age or sex* with bow-and-arrow — a diabolical weapon if ever I saw one, and generally in totally unskilled hands, whatever the regulations may say to the contrary.

On Armistice Day Cervus reappeared, after an absence of ten days, walking on three legs. When I ran out, he limped painfully towards me, then stood, head down, thin and exhausted by the agony of walking. Heaven knows how far he had trekked to reach home.

My mind flew back a year almost to the day when he had nearly died of pneumonia. Here he was again, victim of a different kind of disaster. He could have fought with another buck and, being inexperienced, been badly beaten; perhaps with a kick, perhaps with a sharp butt from antlers longer than his, backed by the impetus of greater weight. There seemed to be no other explanation. There was no arrow or bullet wound to tell of a hunter's near-miss. No torn flesh to conjure up a vision of his being hit by a car. Just a grossly swollen knee joint and a tiny flesh-wound, hardly deep enough to bleed, on the inside of his leg. Even a dog's teeth would have made two marks.

Patiently he allowed me to feel him all over, never once lowering his head and its dangerous spikes. He could no longer fend for himself and once more I made his bed in the garage.

He settled gratefully onto the hay and drank thirstily. As I held the bucket so that he could drink lying down, I could not help wondering whether he remembered his earlier illness.

Unlike a dog, which can be taken to the vet., X-rayed, bandaged, splinted and nursed, a wild deer cannot be put in a car and driven to hospital, nor even X-rayed with a portable machine on the spot, since he cannot be restrained by any means except a tranquillizer gun. This is a ticklish business, not to be undertaken by amateurs. Cervus, therefore, had to be nursed at home as before.

I obtained and administered a massive injection of the same antibiotics as before, only this time I was alone and not without trepidation. But Cervus hardly flinched when the needle pierced his thigh.

I sat for hours holding ice-packs to his leg. The rest was simply a matter of waiting for the drugs to do their work. Much of nursing a wild animal — or indeed any animal — entails waiting to see what nature will do. An injured wild creature of any size is the more difficult to tend properly without specialized equipment. It would have been pointless to try to splint Cervus' leg: he would have struggled violently and done

141

himself even greater injury. I hoped he would recover with complete rest and regular feeding, even if, as I suspected, there might be a hairline crack in the bone.

Wild plants are nutritionally poor at that time of year, so Cervus had to go back on his pellets to help him rebuild his tissues. Not having had any for a while, he did not take to them very kindly at first.

The swelling slowly subsided, without complications. I decided to pen him under the balcony where he normally fed, to free him from the dead, cold air of the garage. But I had left the urgent call of the rut out of account. When I opened the door he took to the woods on his three good legs as though he had never had need of the fourth. For hours I called him in vain. Eventually I had to give up and go to bed, in a state of frantic anxiety. He returned, however, the following morning and, limping painfully, followed me to his newly-constructed pen.

He remained there, docile enough, for ten days. Presumably there were no does running to tempt him. He ate well, the swelling was almost gone and I grew more optimistic about his future. Each time I entered his pen to clean and feed him I remembered the warnings and shut the gate with my foot in order to remain facing this antlered buck who might attack me.

Each day I relaxed a little more until one morning while I was inside the pen he suddenly lowered his head menacingly. I wondered if my last moment had come. But he merely gave me a playful butt on the hip, producing an enormous bruise, which fooled me into thinking he only wanted his breakfast. He did. But as soon as I opened the gate a few inches to let myself out, he slipped past me. The gap was not more than a foot wide. Looking at Cervus no-one would dream he could squeeze himself through it.

There was nothing to do but resign myself to doctoring him as best I could whenever he decided to reappear. When he did, no amount of persuasion would make him go into his pen again.

For two days he remained in the wild; then home for a day; then missing for a week. Hearing shots in the vicinity (strictly illegal) I dreaded he might not return, but he always did. He fed himself on lichens, trailing blackberry, stonecrop and Douglas fir tips. At home he ate pellets, whole grain and carefully rationed home-made mash which he loved as it contained molasses. But he still limped painfully, unable to do more than barely touch the tip of his forefoot to the ground. He spent much of his time resting on the rocks.

He limped all winter, never able to put any weight on his injured leg. By spring I feared he would be crippled for life. Otherwise he was

142

healthy. He ate well and appeared and reappeared at will, always friendly and gentle. At no time during the rut did he try to attack me.

On March 1 he shed his ten-inch spikes, a week later than the previous year. Unfortunately they dropped in the woods and I never found them. Twelve months later I had the good luck to be on hand when he shed his two-point antlers right into my hands when I touched them, not realizing they were on the point of dropping. I have them still.

During the spring following Cervus' injury a pregnant doe roamed through the Ravenshill woods, still accompanied by her last-year's fawn. Was the new life within her part of Cervus? Had he found time to mate before being injured?

Once more spring crocuses adorned the lawn and in the nick of time I discovered the antidotes to Cervus' depredations.

There were three: dried blood sold as fertilizer, hung in old nylon stockings on shrubs prevented Cervus and the wild deer from eating the leaves for a time. When it rained the blood dripped and was absorbed into the soil and had to be renewed constantly.

Next I tried mothballs in little net bags and these, too, kept him away until, all too soon, they disintegrated.

Finally the longest-lasting deterrent of all — human or dog hair clippings in nylons. These cost nothing and lasted many months. I think the unpleasant spikiness of hair-ends sticking through the nylon deterred Cervus more than any possible odor.

*   *   *   *   *

In May the fawn left her pregnant mother and wandered alone. In June the dam appeared on our lawn accompanied by twins. Two exquisite little spotted sprites trotting beside their mother, agog at their week-old world; stopping when she stopped, nursing briefly within sight and sound of me. The lovely doe stood quietly until they had finished, aware of my presence.

A few weeks later Cervus lay beside the lake. His new, still velveted antlers tall and forked, his light summer coat sleek and shining, glancing frequently at the doe who lay beside him while her twin fawns — their twins — lay tucked down a few yards apart in the long grass nearby, asleep. Presently he rose, stretched, and walked off a few paces, magnificently proud — and no longer limping.

I crept silently away, afraid to disturb the idyllic scene. My questions were answered. He was accepted by his own at last.

Chapter Fifteen

Everything that lives,
Lives not alone, nor for itself.

Blake, *BOOK OF THEL.*

When you involve yourself intimately with nature you must accept her laws and take the rough with the smooth; the many dramas and tragedies which go hand in hand with the bounties and delights. Ravenshill, being a microcosm of all outdoors, produced its share of the dark side of nature and this I learned to accept as the price exacted for the privilege of enjoying all that was wonderful. I also learned the hard way that to attempt to interfere with nature's balance is to invite inevitable disaster.

Some ot the harshest lessons concerned a fatal meeting of hawk and duck and a man-made tragic drama with unique elements concerning Canada geese. But all this was in the future. At the moment it was summer, dry and hot.

The forest was no longer a place of cool, dripping trees and damp, lichen-covered rocks bedecked with flowers; now the trees were potential torches, the mosses crackly dry and slippery. The ancient rocks radiated warmth late into the night, making it pleasant to lie on them listening to the midnight owls and on moonless nights to breathe the magic perfumes rising from the ground. Our woods have a scent, resinous, tangy, yet sweet and langorous. It is not the same as the sharp sweet breath of Mediterranean pines. It is different again from the leafmold odor of England's beechwoods. The smell of a larch copse is different yet again. Our heady distillation is made up of mosses, lichens and flowers, resins, pungent aromatic leaves and honeyed nectars. It has an exciting, memory-provoking quality so strong I have but to shut my eyes to recall it, even in the dead of winter.

Over all hangs a great calm. Lying in the sun in a moss-cushioned rock pocket, drowsily watching a swallowtail butterfly or a sleeping garter snake, coiled and striped, one's mind turns from city noise and everlasting worry to thoughts of a vast, almost untouched land, still rich in forests where cougar, moose, deer and little squirrels roam, as they have done for countless centuries.

Ravenshill is privileged to play host to many creatures including a great variety of birds. Raven and eagle, hummingbird and chickadee come and go according to their various habits and seasons. Evening grosbeaks thump down at feeders to devour hundreds of sunflower

144

seeds, chomping the husks off with their huge yellow or white beaks. Raucous-voiced, cheeky, thieving Steller's jays dressed in royal blue and black hop about jerkily, moving earth and debris with strong beaks, looking for grubs.

On a smaller scale the green or yellow or blue-grey warblers flit among the shrubs looking for insects. Purple finches and white-crowned sparrows feed on land while song sparrows run and flit over broad-leaved water weeds as well as taking seed from our bird-tables — as does the occasional Fox sparrow.

A scarlet-crested pileated woodpecker, largest of his kind and jet black of body, swoops heavily to the trunk of a dying cedar, left standing for such as he. So intent upon his carpentry is he that he pays no attention as Edward stands below taking photographs. The loud hammering continues for half an hour and we wonder why the bird doesn't suffer from headaches, although we know he has a special cushioning device in his head to absorb the shock to his bill as he chisels great rectangular holes in his search for ants, grubs, or to make a nesting site.

In charming contrast to this big bird a cloud of little whispering ghosts descends on a cherry tree, hanging upside down and softly twittering; bushtits dressed in Quaker grey are surely the most soft-sung of all birds.

A handsome red-eyed rufous-sided towhee scratches the ground with a sharp backward hop; a young one surprisingly devours a bumble-bee. Shy, exotically marked wood duck walk timidly about the lawn with mincing steps, looking for grain. They were joined once by a fabulous Mandarin duck, astray from some private collection. Pooh-Bah, as we named this Asian bird, tried to steal their females who were stoutly defended by their drakes.

From the terrace a few rustic steps lead to the rocks which fall steeply to the lake. There is a little beach, verdant with western buttercup and yellow flags stand stiffly at the edge while in the water pale waterlilies offer their geometric chalices to the sun.

Here in the evening Cervus drinks. With supreme grace of down-curved wings, great blue herons glide to the lake and stand looking in silhouette like bronze Japanese statues of themselves. The liquid laugh of a woodpecker carries clearly over the water and is echoed by the gargling rattle of a belted kingfisher who flies to a dead branch and waits, motionless, for unwary movement of frog or snake or leech in the water below him. The only other sound is the sudden whistling dive of a nighthawk.

Solomon, a turtle who has been sorely mistreated, is learning that he need not be afraid any more. Until he was rescued and brought to Ravenshill, he was deprived of the water in which he must swim to stay healthy. Tied to a stake by a wire threaded through a hole drilled in his shell, this shade-loving reptile was forced to exist on a patch of bare lawn, foraging for what food he could find within the radius of his tether. His owners were convinced he needed neither food nor water. As a result of this treatment the markings which should have identified him were absent from his shell.

The speed with which this sorry creature made his way into our lake was astonishing and pathetic. He swam and swam. Hours after his release he was still soaking water into his parched body. Strangely I never had to feed him. He ignored the tempting things I set out for him and lived exclusively on whatever he found in the water or on land and in time doubled his weight and grew healthy. We see him occasionally as he ambles slowly about near the lake or pond but most of the time he is invisible, hidden in the bush.

Heralded by Higi's scoldings, Vixen trundles into the quiet scene, and the ducks scatter in alarm until she has moved on. A bald eagle sails lazily overhead.

I whistle softly and a half-grown crow — Poe II — flaps across the lake to perch on my wrist. Once fed, she selects a branch and preens her feathers. Higi arrives, collects nuts from the bottle and rushes to a branch to eat them. Looking down I see a little brown mallard softly quacking to draw my attention. She was found as a day-old duckling, separated from her mother and siblings when they crossed a busy road. I raised her and she lives at Ravenshill where she found a mate — another of my orphans. She is fed with six others who have flown up at the sound of my voice. They are permanent residents — 'The Group of Seven'.

It is an enchanted place. The woods draw about it a curtain of secrecy and wild creatures come and go in their sunlit depths, unafraid — at least of we who dwell here. We have given what we can to Canada and our gifts have been returned a thousandfold in kind. Life is good here.

*   *   *   *   *

As summer gives way to another fall the animals feed heavily to put on fat to keep warm through winter's cold and none more so than birds with their high metabolic rate. Autumn yields them a rich harvest of bugs and seeds and inevitably the predators are busy.

146

Late in the afternoon of a November day a pool of weak sunlight filtered through bare branches of red alders beside the pond. Leaves scattered on the coarse grass were brown and frost-crisp. Apart from the usual bickering, life on the pond was 'business-as-usual'. Young mallards in bright new plumage ate the grain I scattered or swam about the pool and in general played ducks and drakes.

Dusk was relinquishing to night — that period of half-light when it is difficult to distinguish one thing from another.

Suddenly there was a commotion near the pool, a sound of metal violently banged, a rush of wings. Then silence.

By the time I reached the window the pool was empty of birds. Only the swirling water told of the sudden thrust of bodies into the air; and the swaying laundry line bore mute testimony to the body which must have hit it; another body had hit the metal garage door.

I made out a mess of pale feathers near the edge of the pool — too many to have been shed casually. A little farther inland another cluster of feathers, and the dread cause of my ducks' panic.

On the ground not twenty feet from our front door was a goshawk — the biggest hawk I had ever seen. In flight he would have a wingspread of three-and-a-half to four feet.

Brown body against brown leaves; only a slight movement enabled me to discern him with one of my mallards clutched in his talons.

The light faded and I turned away.

Early next morning I looked out expecting to see merely traces of the previous evening's havoc — feathers, a little blood perhaps, but nothing more.

Instead I saw the big hawk still crouched in the same position, clutching the partly eaten body of a mallard. His heavy shoulders hunched over the prey as the scimitar curve of his beak dug into its flesh. I could easily see how he wrenched each mouthful free, aided by the muscled column of his neck. His wings were folded and his long tail stretched behind, its tip resting on the ground. I could imagine his black, sickle-shaped claws, razor sharp, needle pointed, flexible and immensely strong, pinioning his prey invisibly beneath its feathers.

I could imagine, too, the scene of the night before. Mallards feeding on the grass or swimming peacefully. Then that split-second of rigid terror when they became aware of the deadly bird high above. The instinct, individual and collective, to seek safety on the wing. Bodies exploding from land and water, upthrust by panic-driven leg muscles into an almost vertical ascent.

One duck was too slow.

Out of the dusky sky the hawk would have hurtled with the velocity of a bullet, head down, legs down, feet and claws braced for the anticipated impact, evolved and conditioned over hundreds — thousands — of years to reach the pinnacle of adaptation in the performance of its function. Supreme co-ordination of eye and mind, directing the tautly muscled body in a perfect dive upon the hapless, terror-stricken duck. A hunter so perfectly evolved that it is a model of lethal efficiency, its proud mastery of the air a source of such deep wonderment that there is no room to regret the ruthlessness of its descent upon its prey.

To our eyes a hawk kills ferociously. Actually it deals death with lightning speed, aiming talon and beak at the spine at the base of the skull. It is doubtful if the victim is aware of anything after the first terrific blow and even that is probably cushioned by the hypnotic force of terror. Is this not preferable to a slow, painful death from hunger or disease?

Much of our thinking about animals and their appearance is based on imagination rather than fact. The impression of implacable ferocity we attribute to a hawk standing over its prey is produced by its round, staring red or yellow eyes, cold and expressionless. Birds have no expression in the human sense. They neither frown nor smile; nor can they move their eyes in their sockets — they depend on turning their heads to see. Which is why birds that have eyes at the sides of their heads (unlike owls who have them in front) cock their heads in what seems to us an appealing gesture, quizzical and charming. In fact they are merely trying to see!

For two days the hawk stayed a mere twenty feet from the house devouring his prey until he had reduced it sufficiently to be able to lift it and fly to safety among the trees.

The wild raptorial bird kills only to assuage its hunger. Whether any animal ever kills for sport is pure conjecture. That some kill without visible necessity is bloodily illustrated by that symbol of peace, the ring-dove, who mercilessly attacks her mate. Sentimental stories abound about delightful little squirrels; beautiful, stately deer and other animals. It is seldom mentioned that these, too, have their tough side. Squirrels are nest-robbers. Zooed roe-buck have been known to disembowel their own kind, females and young alike, if penned too closely with them, which would not happen in the wild.

It does not help wild animals to attribute 'darling' sentiments to them. Yet I find one of the most tiresome aspects of scientific observation is that, in falling over backwards to be purely objective, something is overlooked: anthropomorphism per se is both natural and acceptable if it is kept within bounds. That is, if it does not affect the animal or the study being made of it.

There is surely no harm, scientifically, in indulging one's imagination occasionally by seeing Higi anthropomorphically as a little pot-bellied old lady holding her too-tight coat together, scolding the observer? You are aware that in the "objective" reality of scientific parlance you are looking at a squirrel sitting on its haunches, its fore-paws across its abdomen, indulging in territorial calls. The squirrel is unaffected by the comparison. But the observer shows he is first of all a human being, not a data processing machine. It seems to me that a love for animals must go hand in hand with a sympathetic understanding of their natural habits. I love the swallows whose nest-boxes Higi raids. I also love Higi. Both are doing what comes naturally and both feelings are compatible. I love Vixen, despite her depredations. I love the screech owl who nests in my wood duck box. Yet I had one of her victims in the house for days before he was well enough to release. I had found the baby deer-mouse with one eye sealed shut, a bloody gash on his tiny head, trying to eat a corn kernel he had bravely fetched from Cervus' tray. I do not hate the owl for pursuing her prey but I love the mouse too, although he steals my grain and will gnaw through anything that gets in his way.

Today wildlife 'management' is a term much in use. 'Experts' proclaim the necessity of culling herds to prevent overpopulation and resulting degradation of their food range. Yet even with developments encroaching on their natural habitats, herds of game animals would be kept in check if only we would leave their predators alone.

Wolves, cougar, coyotes and others prey on the weak, the sick and the old and so ensure the maintenance of high standards of physical and mental health within the herds. But Man relentlessly kills these predators to the point of near extinction, so that he may select — not the weak the sick or the old to fall before his rifle — but the best, the tallest and most magnificently antlered (or horned, as the case may be). He takes no pride in shooting a doe, legally or otherwise. And so the very animals whose virility and stamina would be most likely to improve the herd are killed for 'sport'.

To his everlasting shame, Man the hunter can be seen every year in season outside local newspaper offices, standing by his car. Lashed ignominiously to roof or trunk dangles an animal whose once beautiful eyes are glazed in death. Full of pride, man and gun await the flash of the newsman's camera. But he only poses for pictures with the antlered stags he has shot, never with the does.

Wanton killing for sport, or euphemistically, for 'management' seems to me a poor way of demonstrating our higher intelligence. Predators hunt to live. Only man hunts for the sheer triumph of killing. It is a fact that only man is uplifted by the spectacle of an animal's death. I know a man who was once attached to a government conservation department who stated publicly that to kill was for him a "religious experience".

In this context I felt my efforts on behalf of our wildlife were worthwhile when Timothy, a twelve-year-old, said to me after meeting Cervus and Vixen: "I know how to hunt deer and raccoon and when I'm old enough my father is going to give me a gun. But now I've seen what they're like *close up and free* I'm going to ask for a camera instead. I've decided I don't want to kill any more".

*   *   *   *   *

Winter brings birds flocking to feeders and I never know when some rare species may appear, driven off-course by high winds. Such rare birds are exciting and impart an idiotic sense of achievement, as though I somehow had something to do with their being there.

We once sighted an eastern blue jay which was hundreds of miles off-course, far from its normal habitat in central and eastern Canada and the United States.

We telephoned the local natural history society purely to inform them for the record but within the hour several strangers began tramping, uninvited, about our property.

Upset as we were by this invasion of privacy, it was nothing compared to my fury when a man telephoned to ask if the jay was still here as he wanted to come and collect it. He was not far away, he informed me, and he and his gun could be with us almost immediately.

I gave him a blast I hope will stay with him for the rest of his life and perhaps make him think again before needlessly killing a wild creature — for which 'collecting' is a favorite euphemism. Since then I have never revealed the presence of any rare creature at Ravenshill to anyone but friends who think as I do. A pity, because I like to share such experiences.

I keep my feeders filled with many kinds of food: suet, cracked grains, sunflower seeds, dried or frozen berries, chopped eggs, whole wheat breadcrumbs, nuts and any useful table scraps. To prevent them from freezing to the trays I construct special ones out of seed flats covered with thin plywood. Underneath I put a light bulb which gives off enough warmth to keep the food on the lid loose. When the weather is

150

freezing day and night I add a little coarse sand to the feed, since birds need grit to digest their food.

The fat-eaters take their meals from net bags hung out of reach of predators like Vixen. I do not use wire mesh as it can damage the birds' feet and eyes if they touch it in sub-zero weather. Incidentally, birds refuse fat which has been too long in cold storage, even though to my nose it seems in good condition.

To keep their drinking water free of ice I add a little glycerine. Even so, it freezes during the night. When there is snow, drinking is no problem because the birds eat it. But even in cold weather they love a bath and it is worth taking the trouble to fill the bird bath daily. If this is done at the same time every day they learn to take advantage of it before it freezes over.

I buy the grain and special seeds for our creatures from my good friends Doug and Art at Clark & Cordick. They are knowledgeable about all types of livestock and never seem to mind spending time helping me.

I have always loved feed stores. There is a friendliness about their dusty, sweet-smelling bales of hay and straw, piled to the roof. Interesting little banks of odd-sized wooden drawers with round, worn handles, open to reveal golden pools of millet seed, so tiny, round and satin-smooth to touch; black-and-tan striped sunflower seeds which make satisfying little noises as you run your hands through them, like the clicking of small finger-nails; all kinds of grass seeds, some so minute and light that a handful feels like thistledown; others so polished they run through your fingers like silk. Then the giant bins that let down from the counter, rich stores of golden corn in their depths; or hard wheat which somehow looks efficient even before it has had a chance to nourish livestock. Barley, long and slender, an elegant grain, and oats, divided down the middle by a furrow — beloved of horses which grow stout on them, while men (and women, too, these days) prefer to sow them wild. It is sad that bulk-buying has put an end to many of the old-fashioned bins, supplanting their friendly wooden depths with fifty-pound or twenty-kilo, double-thickness paper bags. More efficient but less romantic.

Even such reminders of our polluted age as bottles of pesticides in serried ranks behind locked glass doors cannot destroy the general air of personal friendliness that is the hallmark of this store. If you take the trouble to ask, its owners actually say they enjoy being there all day even though it is cold and drafty in winter. They love the hustle and bustle of traffic flowing endlessly through their vast barn of a depository.

Doug and Art, both middle-aged, never feel tired and the days are all too short for them.

They even shut their store for a day when an old and valued employee died. Think of it — a whole day without earning precious dollars! Nice people, part of a dying race, more's the pity, who manage to imbue their place of business with an atmosphere that makes you want to browse around, looking for surprises.

Such as the day years ago when I discovered an odd-looking metal feeder for fifty cents; something Doug had no idea he had in stock and which I adapted for some creature's needs. And the time I asked for chicken leg-bands to try out on a young gosling. Art brought out about a thousand on a piece of string and when I laughingly told him I only wanted one little ring, he ceremoniously removed a plastic circle and put it on my finger as a keepsake, saying he couldn't be bothered to work out the number of decimal points to find the price of only one.

As a small child I used to enjoy going to the feed store with my father to buy grain for our chickens. We went to the local miller, who usually appeared covered in flour; the air in his store was misty-white with suspended particles which settled on everything and everybody. I used to wonder what would happen if it rained on the miller. Would he end up covered in mucilage? He always let me roam around while he completed his business with my father and I have loved such stores ever since.

There were always cats wandering about to control rats and mice. They were shy, almost wild; most of them were born on top of bales of hay. I tried to make friends with them, but they were too wary, exposed to too many strangers, to be anything but distant. It is the same today.

And of course there are the seeds. Seeds in pots, in bins, in buckets. Seeds in painted packages adorned with impossibly green leaves and improbable flowers which rarely come up to expectation. Each spring I am drawn to the revolving stands with their racks of enticing packets, buying far more than I need because the urge of spring is too strong to be denied. I am not really a seedling gardener. I haven't the patience, for one thing, to prick the hair-like plants into flats and later into pots or beds. I like trees and shrubs which, if they do take a long time to mature, at least stay where I first planted them.

The trouble with feed stores is that my eyes are always bigger than my purse and since one can't have everything I gaze at the things I can't afford. But still I come home feeling rich as I pour golden grain into my bins (all six of them!) knowing it will feed my creature dependents who in turn will make life richer for me by just existing.

152

This digression on the subject of feed stores for which I have a soft spot brings me back to food generally and the fact that fresh, unadulterated food is as vital to animal and human well-being as maternal affection and body warmth are to an infant's mental and physical welfare. Both are far-ranging in their effects and we pay a life-long price in illness if we are deprived of either.

Today, so much reliance is placed on scientific nutrition for animals that people have come to believe the only safe, balanced ration is a commercially produced pellet. These are convenient, admittedly, but how much of the vital quality of fresh foodstuff must be missing from these dehydrated, compressed, sterilized, vitaminized, homogenized, 'enriched' products — not to mention the dangerous chemical preservatives added to them? I would never condemn a creature to the sheer boredom of such a diet!

Animals so fed are supposedly healthy. But what is health? Is it merely the absence of disease? Or is it an optimum state of vibrant joy and brilliant eye and alert, questing mind? Sometimes it seems that health, like beauty, is in the eye of the beholder. All too frequently animals which are alleged to be 'perfectly healthy' appear to my eye to be lackluster and in poor shape. So long as I have strength to boil a pan of water I shall feed us and the animals in my care with foods whose ingredients I can see, touch and taste, and as far as possible know where they were grown.

If you care for animals you have to be interested in their food. You can hardly expect to arrive at a proper diet unless you have some understanding of what the animal eats and why. It is unfair to feed it what comes first to hand. Occasionally, for the animal's own sake, one has to resort to force-feeding but it will be much happier if it is provided with its natural food. A wild creature stands a far better chance of recovery if it will eat voluntarily.

It helps to comprehend why one should feed one thing to one animal and something else to the next if you understand something of the process of digestion. I have described Cervus' rumen and how it functions but here I would like to begin where all eating must begin — with the mouth: what kind of mouth, for instance; whether the teeth are flat for chewing as in sheep; or sharp for tearing as in dogs and other canines. Some jaws can be moved laterally as well as vertically: canines move their jaws up and down; cows and sheep sideways as well; while birds swallow without chewing at all. Nor do all mouths contain saliva. Dogs salivate and so do swallows; but grain-eating birds appear not to.

Chewing plays a major role in the feeding habits of, say, flat-toothed plant-eaters (herbivores), but practically none in the sharp-toothed dog, which bolts its food. If it doesn't there's something wrong. Chickens and other birds take rapid pecks at small grains, which they neither smell nor taste much; they are attracted mainly by color and lustre. Fruit-eating birds seem to have a sense of taste; they and the insect-eaters are much harder to please when one is hand-feeding.

As a child, I used to wonder how cows, rabbits and horses managed to thrive on nothing but greenstuffs and grain. It seemed to me impossible that gigantic carthorses, so tall and thick, could pull their enormous loads on such a meagre diet when I, who did far less work, was fed on a much richer diet containing meat. Now I know that these animals have digestive systems different from ours.

You and I, like Cervus when he was very small, are monogastric — we have only a single stomach, which cannot digest the tough plant substance cellulose. The raw foods we eat consisting of cellulose, minerals and water, act as bulk rather than food. (I am not referring to peas, soy beans and so on which are loaded with starch and protein and are real food).

Horses and rabbits are non-ruminant herbivores. They don't chew the cud but can utilize cellulose after it has passed out of their stomachs and intestines into a special organ known as the *caecum*. True ruminants such as cows and deer, chew the cud — a process I have already explained.

By paying attention to the plants wild animals choose, one can learn what is most palatable to them at each season of a normal year. Times of famine produce abnormal eating behavior. The plants of winter and spring are low in protein and high in water content; animals must eat almost continuously to keep alive at these seasons. Summer plants are the most nourishing for leaf-eating herbivores. Root-feeding animals like muskrat fare best in the fall when nutrients are stored in roots and tubers. All this is just as true of vegetables for human consumption.

I love to cook and often my best meals are produced when I have to improvise, using bits and pieces from all over the place, including wild plants in season, and I love the time when my herbs are nearing maturity and my hands are perfumed from handling them.

A scented garden is a lovesome thing, bringing quiet joy as one brushes against some aromatic herb. Brought indoors and air-dried, one can have an endless variety of teas, butters, sandwich spreads, and to open a sealed jar of pot-pourri on a dull cold day is to awaken the scent of summer, a momentary preview of things to come.

How I wish I could have had, not a preview but a presentiment of the incredible drama that was about to take place — so that it could have been avoided. What I am now going to describe is a classic example of tragedy that usually occurs when humans meddle with nature.

Chapter Sixteen

When sorrows come, they
come not single spies,
But in battalions.

Shakespeare, HAMLET.

There are few creatures as supremely wild as Canada geese, their chevron flight etched in witches' black beneath the moonglow. The soul-compelling cry issuing from the throats of twenty or thirty birds exerts a pull that reaches down to very earth, and dull of soul is he who in his heart does not respond.

The big grey or brown 'honker' has enormous dignity; his sagacity, courage and fidelity are legendary. I love these magnificent birds over all other native waterfowl and I longed to see some of them at Ravenshill.

My dream was realized when a friend who raised geese offered me a gosling from a clutch of incubator eggs.

He was ten hours old when he arrived at Ravenshill, a ball of golden down with soft black eyes and enormous black feet. Being an incubator baby, he was already firmly imprinted on humans. "Dooleykind" immediately took over our hearts and a heated pen in the utility room.

This entrancing baby liked to sit on my shoulder and groom my hair with his tiny, serrated bill: he even nibbled at my eyelashes. When he settled to sleep in some warm spot he turned his little head onto his back, having no wings to tuck it under. His silky down, which he groomed assiduously, would not be waterproof for many weeks since he lacked the oil which his mother would have supplied, had he known her. She would have groomed him from her own preen gland until his developed.

I had to teach him how to eat, as I have taught many an orphan duckling. It is an arduous business. Dooleykind had to be taken outside where I 'pecked' with my finger at grasses and herbs until he followed suit with his bill. From the outset he followed my feet wherever I went and if I was walking too fast he uttered a small, shrill, peep-peep. Opening his inch-long wings, he tried desperately and ludicrously to use them to propel him as he ran. Frequently he tripped over his feet, which were plate-sized in comparison with the rest of him. A bird's feet extend up what look like its legs, as high as the first feathers. The legs proper begin only above that point.

Dooleykind soon graduated to a larger pen outside. There he spent the nights and those times during the day when I could not be with him. When he grew big enough he was allowed total freedom. Canada geese, even incubated ones, do not like to be penned; they lean their breasts against the wire, to the detriment of their feathers.

Donning hip waders, I taught Dooleykind to swim in the lake. To stimulate his preening instinct, I found it necessary to duck him several times until he was wet all over, then fetch him ashore and into the sun where he could preen his down dry. If he did not do this properly I had to bring him indoors to dry as otherwise he would have become dangerously chilled.

He lost the exquisite yellow and olive-grey down bit by bit until, in the final stage of feathering he appeared to be wearing an unravelled knitted sweater. All the while he remained gentle and friendly, following me around, in or out of the water, and coming when I called him for his food. He learned to graze on the lawn and to roost beside the pond or lake at night.

When Dooleykind had grown to the point where he was softly and smoothly feathered in delicate shades of grey, his primary feathers almost long enough for him to begin to practice flying, some old friends arrived from the interior of British Columbia, bringing with them their ten-year-old son Graham. He was a quiet boy who liked reading and wandering about outside, alone. He spent hours watching Dooleykind and was thrilled to feel his gentle beak taking grain from his hand.

But the little gosling was missing on the third day.

Graham and I called and called. No small voice responded with its musical whistle; no satin-textured gosling came running eagerly to us. We searched everywhere, combing the edges of pond and lake, fighting our way through dense wet underbrush. Finally, in pouring rain, we returned to the house, tired and dispirited.

Two days later there was still no sign of Dooleykind. I explained that he must have fallen victim to a predator.

The rain continued to keep us confined. Graham, who was becoming restive as a captive animal, disappeared into his bedroom. When he emerged again he came shyly to me and handed me a folded paper. When I opened it and read what he had written I was deeply touched.

Here, precisely as he wrote it, spelling mistakes and all, is Graham's epitaph in memory of little Dooleykind, the Canada gosling who had no chance to grow up:

In Memory
of
Our
Dear
Friend
DULINGCON WARD-HARRIS
From egg to gooseling, is thought to be in mouth of
Preditor. R.I.P. Amen.
Passed way at the age of only 9 or 10 wks. old. Amen.
And know we will remember Dulingcon with <u>love</u> forever!

Amen.

*　　*　　*　　*　　*

Dooleykind's death made me pause to wonder whether such was to be the fate of all tame waterfowl at Ravenshill? Vixen might have taken him. Or there were mink and other predators who could equally well have been responsible. Much as I longed to see Canada geese on the lake I decided it would not be fair to try again until I could provide them with protection until they were fully grown, when they would be able to take care of themselves.

By now Ravenshill's reputation as a wildlife sanctuary was becoming increasingly widespread. My painting was often neglected (to say nothing of Edward) and I began to find myself very overworked and short of vital equipment for nursing sick creatures. A great deal of ingenuity, improvisation and time were called for simply to keep going. I desperately needed a breathing spell.

But one day I was asked to give sanctuary to a pair of domestic ducks who would otherwise have to be killed because the family of the little girl who owned them was moving to a place where pet ducks were not allowed. Had her parents asked me over the telephone I would probably have refused. Instead, they turned up on my doorstep, complete with a large carton containing the two ducks. Behind them slumped their young daughter, who was crying bitterly. Moved by her distress I capitulated.

And so Scarper and Flo, as Edward renamed them, were introduced to the freedom of Ravenshill's waters.

I am unwilling to admit domestic ducks to a wildlife sanctuary because they tend to cross-breed with the wild ones, which is bad for the latter. But Scarper and Flo were at least a pair and they provided us with welcome comic relief and I decided not to worry about breeding since they would mate together.

They waddled about, preened themselves, cavorted ponderously and raucously quacked their way through life, unhampered by cage or care. Scarper was purebred but Flo's parentage was highly suspect. They were mallards but Flo was black and white in all the wrong places. Mallard feet are orange; Flo's were orange blotched with black. Purebred Scarper had a white neck band; Flo's neck was black — like her beak, which should have been yellow. Both had the heavy bodies and short, flightless wings of birds bred for the table rather than for life, which rendered them doubly vulnerable to predation.

Mallards are dabbling ducks but Flo thought she was a diver and swam yards underwater, almost leaping out with abandoned joy when she surfaced, gloriously untrammelled by any self-consciousness as to what she ought to be doing. On land she propelled herself with a marvellously nautical roll which was extremely funny. She looked like one of those toy wooden ducks on wheels.

Scarper and Flo were an affront to the dignity of Ravenshill. But I had accepted them and that was an end to it.

Shortly after their arrival I was asked if I could provide a permanent home for a pair of Canada geese whose owner had fallen ill. I agreed — gladly — to take these pet birds because, being adults, they would be strong enough to look after themselves. They were used to living free on their owner's large pond but their wings had been severely clipped to prevent them from flying away.

Delighted at the thought of having wild geese and thrilled at the prospect of someday watching them rear their goslings, I drove over to fetch them. They were superb birds, strong, healthy, darkly brown of feather.

We named them Lester and Judy.

They spent their first three weeks at Ravenshill confined behind a fence enclosing an area half in and half out of our pool to permit them to swim and graze at will. Once they had grown accustomed to their new surroundings and, I hoped, to me, I let them out onto the pond.

Ignoring Scarper and Flo they settled down once they had thoroughly explored their new territory — as later they were to explore the larger lake. They were of breeding age but as yet had produced nothing more than a few sterile eggs, forlornly deposited on an old raft at their former home. Their owner had neglected to provide a nesting site so they had not been very happy. Canada geese like to nest where they can see their surroundings, preferably high up. Their natural nesting grounds are on flat prairie, where all they require is a small hillock to enable them to see for miles. Coastal British Columbia is too densely treed and the only safe places for geese to nest are on small islands in the middle of large lakes. So I built them a raft which I anchored in the centre of the pond. A large wooden box filled with hay, nailed to the raft, made a reasonable nest-site.

Cervus appeared on the scene and at once expected Lester and Judy to play fawns for his benefit. But the first and only time he tried to play with them, they simply marched into the water and swam away. His expression was a study in innocent frustration, as if to say "Fawns don't do that sort of thing!"

Throughout the rest of the summer they swam happily and preened in the sun, eating copiously and sleeping with their heads tucked snugly under their wings. After their annual moult — when both were naturally deprived of flight — their primary feathers began to grow back and I had to make up my mind whether or not to clip their wings again.

All their lives they had depended on rations from humans in addition to the food they had found for themselves. They had never flown and I had doubts about their chances of survival if ever they left Ravenshill. On the other hand, the thought of mutilating their wings filled me with horror.

I wanted very much to keep my new geese. I had the necessary government permit to own game birds and I knew that breeders of geese always clip their wings because they cannot afford to lose valuable stock. Once the birds have flown they revert to the Crown and cannot legally be caught again. I assured myself that the operation was not painful — the flight feathers are cut in such a way as to render flight impossible but without injuring the bird; the feathers grow back each year when the old ones fall out and so must be clipped annually. There is another method employed by breeders, known as pinioning, whereby a bird's wing is partially amputated when it is very young, making flight permanently impossible. I longed to build a flock of my favorite waterfowl — not for any commercial purpose but simply to see and hear them from day to day.

Yet still I was not sure. Rather desperately I sought advice from Art and Doug at Clark & Cordick. They did not help much. Doug said "Clip" — for my sake. Art said "Don't" — for theirs. My dilemma was unresolved.

Back at home Lester and Judy, still flightless, took to following the ducklings as they trailed behind their mothers. At dusk several separate processions wended their way through the woods to roost on the lake. Lester and Judy usually brought up the rear, flirting their long black necks this way and that, rolling their large bodies slightly, looking self-important and rather incongruous as they paraded under the tall trees. Neither goose had ever flown, but would they not feel frustrated when the male mallards emerged newly feathered from their moult? Or when, even in their period of eclipse, they flew up for grain? (Unlike geese, mallards can still fly during the eclipse or moult). The ducklings would soon learn to fly and my geese would surely grow agitated with an urgent desire to follow them into the sky.

Moreover, if their wings were clipped, would they not be in danger from predators? On the other hand I had observed them repulse Vixen easily, many times. They were powerful birds, well able to take care of themselves against anything small, even a dog, and there are no large predators near Ravenshill.

To clip or not to clip. The battle raged in my mind.

In the end I reached a compromise. I would clip their wings just enough to prevent distance flying but not enough to keep them from flying altogether.

And so Lester and Judy were soon sailing majestically from the pond to the lake below as though they had been flying all their lives. They had the width of the lake for take-off for the return trip to the lawn for food. The distance is only about fifty feet but if Lester flew up alone, Judy set up a honking from the lake as if to say "Hey, wait for me!" My compromise seemed a good one — at the time.

Canada geese are essentially grazing birds and require a large area of varied greenstuff to nibble at. They take a blade of grass near the ground and tweak it off neatly with a sharp backward motion of the head. A flock will keep a lawn trimmed and I hoped I might one day have acquired enough of these voluntary lawn-mowers to save us having to cut it ourselves.

Meanwhile Lester and Judy spent most of the day on the lawn, grazing and eating grain. They were rarely out of one another's sight. During the day they held long conversations in attractively husky voices; the wildly beautiful honking is reserved for flight or, on the ground, when the geese are anxious, or to greet one another after an absence. There is a different tone for each occasion.

At dusk they walked across the lawn to the rocks above the lake, stood on the brink conversing as if undecided which way to go, then lifted to sweep over the branches to the water below.

They grew fat and feathered and were content to be together. As winter drew near they acquired a layer of goose grease to keep them warm.

Life at Ravenshill gradually slowed down with the year's approaching end. Then one day, not long after the dramatic episode of the goshawk's descent upon the mallard, I was awakened at dawn by goose honking.

On and on went the haunting sound until I could bear it no longer. I dressed, shivering. Half awake, I slithered down slippery rocks to the lake in an eerie half-light, surrounded by a thin, penetratingly damp mist.

Judy stood on the roosting island, a tiny patch of mud surrounding an old tree stump. She was still honking, her head raised high. She seemed to be pleading because she was quite alone. Lester was nowhere in sight and the intensity in her voice made it plain that this was no ordinary absence of a minute or two. Canada geese mate for life and their faithfulness is legendary.

I searched the lake shores for Lester, clawing through dense underbrush and shoulder-high salal. Panting with exertion, I returned to the house and put on chest-high waders to go into the icy water. Perchance he had become imprisoned in swampy growth, like the trapped mallard I had once rescued.

An hour later, dirty, dishevelled and despairing, I clambered back to the pond to search the surrounding bush. But Lester had vanished, yet there was no sign of violence, no tell-tale drop of blood, no scattered feathers to indicate that he had been attacked, no footprints in the mud — nothing. Only a single set of fresh tire-tracks near the lake. It had to have been made that morning, before dawn, since by the time I was up no vehicle was visible. And the previous night's heavy rain would have obliterated any earlier tracks.

A dreadful thought forced itself into my unwilling mind. Poaching. Would anyone dare to take a big goose off a private lake, risking being seen from the house? Was there anyone so callous as to shoot or lassoo a bird so obviously tame? Yet it was inconceivable that Lester would have taken off of his own accord. He was happily mated to Judy and would never have left voluntarily without her; and his wings were partially clipped.

Judy quietened down, perhaps exhausted by her long calling. But that evening, when dusk fell, she began honking again. It is a wild and lonely sound at the best of times; now it held a tragic undertone of calling-for-what-cannot be. I redoubled my efforts to find her missing mate, alerting the police, the local radio stations, humane societies, my neighbors — everybody I could think of who might remotely be expected to see or hear of a lost or stolen goose.

The following day there was still no sign of Lester and no report of his having been found. I decided I had to act quickly on Judy's behalf. She might go looking for him and come to grief.

I phoned a breeder who said he had a disconsolate male whose mate had been poached a year previously. I bought him immediately. Within an hour he was installed in a large pen on the lawn where Judy was bound to see him. His wings had been severely clipped. We called him The Admiral and I hoped that, recent though her loss had been, Judy might take an interest in this new companion.

Alas she did not meet her prospective groom. Some boys arrived at the lake to fish and their voices must have spelt danger to a goose who had so recently witnessed the abduction of her mate. Spreading her great wings, she rose almost straight from the water like a mallard, gaining enough height, despite partial clipping, to clear the brush at the end of the lake. Helpless, I watched her rise higher still, heading up the lake and out of sight.

Darkness frustrated any thought of searching for her. But over the next few days I scrutinized every open body of water in our neighborhood, without result. Judy, too, had vanished.

I had dreadful visions of Lester dead and roasted and anger raged within me as I thought of his faithful mate, alive but alone, searching and crying as only a goose can cry. When wild geese flew over Ravenshill I listened to their honking, wondering if Judy was among them.

But she did not return.

With my geese I realized I had adopted an attitude nearly as anthropomorphic as any pet-owner. They do seem to hold conversations amongst themselves and the idea takes hold all the more strongly when one imitates their voices and they respond. Then, too, their sagacity, their proud domesticity, the charming way in which they groom one another, and the infinite politeness with which they accept food, make these soft-eyed, elegant birds paragons of the feathered world. There is also an element in all of us which responds to the enchantment of the wildness implicit in their honking. A formation of Canada geese etched against the sky, necks stretched, legs tucked up, wide wings slowly beating in uniform rhythm, calls forth an atavistic urge to follow their haunting clarion-call, growing fainter as they pass, heralding a life of untrammelled primordial wildness.

The Admiral, too, showed this urge as he swam in lonely splendor or mounted the raft to stand as if on a ship's bridge—hence his name.

When wild geese flew over his pond he honked loudly and I felt for his wing-clipped loneliness. I hoped a wild one might come down in the spring. But the hope was faint; there are too many trees at Ravenshill to entice such big birds to make safe landings.

The Admiral was not like Lester. He was not tame, for he had lived without much contact with humans. There were no lone females of the right age available to purchase for him and he had to continue to live alone. But he struck up a strange friendship with Scarper and Flo.

Such is the sad state of affairs when humans interfere with the natural ways of wildlife. And the lesson was to be hammered home later on when The Admiral became a leading actor in a drama which was probably unique in wild goose lore. But before I tell that story let me dispatch the winter which, that year, was a severe one.

*   *   *   *   *

Snow descended on the land, blanketing everything with a white pall. Even rubber boots proved useless as the snow rose higher than the tops and the drifts were deep enough to hide a man. The cold was bone-chilling; our woodpile grew steadily smaller. We wondered whether winter would be endless, whether we were doomed, whether God had somehow forgotten to change the season. Mr. Bentley stayed firmly indoors. He loves heat and always lay close to the hot air register. He was growing old, so I carried his basket to whatever room I was going to be in and put it close to the warmth. His principal activities were eating and sleeping, dreaming of spring when he could once more scour the countryside. Perhaps he dreamed of last year's triumph over Fred.

The ice on the pond and lake thickened, making it more and more difficult to maintain a section of clear water for The Admiral, Scarper, Flo and the wild ducks. Fortunately for the surviving, dormant young goldfish, the pool was deep enough to leave them plenty of water at the bottom. Because of them we kept the ice open only in another pool beyond the dam. Had we axed through the ice on the big pond the shock of the blows, reverberating through the water beneath, could have killed the fish.

A flock of mallards landing on ice is a sight to see. They land at speed and it's a wonder they don't break their feet with the impact. Somehow they manage to touch down smoothly, skidding until they slow up sufficiently to dig in with the nails on the ends of their toes.

As fast as I scattered grain it froze to the ground and had to be pickaxed. The waterfowl also ate the fresh greens I imported for Cervus.

Each morning the white carpet of snow became as pages in a book, wherein we could read the nightly doings of our creatures. Higi's tiny footprints near her tree, evidence of her sometime wakefulness. The Admiral's large, three-toed signature, flat and impressive; repeated several sizes smaller by the wild ducks.

Cervus, fooled by snow lying on ice, walked across the pond. I

164

nearly had a fit the first time I saw him standing in the middle. There was ten feet of water beneath him and many a deer has drowned because it was unable to extricate itself from deep water onto ice. But he strolled across many times and the ice held his weight.

Vixen and Mo ceased coming into the house, for reasons best known to themselves. Their feet left tracks like a barefoot child's which made it easy to trace them to the bird feeders.

One morning the frozen lake displayed the curious, dragging track of muskrat; little five-toed footprints running parallel on each side of the broad tail track. I had to look closely to see the mark of the minute fifth front toe.

Early one morning I watched a sleek, slim marauder crossing and re-crossing the muskrat's trail. He was a beautiful black mink with a small white blaze on his chest. When I first caught sight of him he was sitting up on his haunches, muzzle held high to sniff the wind, looking like a little dark pillar driven into the ice. His dark color identified him as an escaped ranch animal; native wild mink have paler fur and light brown noses. I had caught sight of him in the summer so he must have been on the loose for some time. I thought of mink coats and was delighted at his freedom.

The muskrat's den was hidden beneath the bank at the lake's edge and had an underwater entrance. The owner was evidently safe inside, for although the mink circled the telltale tracks on the ice, stopping now and then to sit up and look about him, or read the scents in the air, he failed to locate his prey. At last he danced off in another direction, bounding along and arching his body caterpillar-wise in graceful curves. Next day the muskrat came out for provisions and the mink gave chase but was out-maneuvered and again went hungry. His daily peregrinations were easy to trace by the trail of his round paw marks. If the icy cold persisted, he would be a very slender mink indeed.

A few days later I saw him on our terrace, trying to fish the icy pool. Despite the cold I opened the door to the balcony and went to see if I could watch him more closely. To my astonishment he came straight towards me, mounted the steps to the living-room door and walked past me into the house. Dumbfounded, I followed. Edward was in the room watching, an expression of incredulity on his face.

The lithe cylinder of black fur walked across the room with unhurried, undulating movements. Down the long passage to the bedrooms, which he investigated; back to the kitchen and utility room; then once more into the living room. He went carefully round our bookshelves, where he presumably found nothing to suit his taste; then across to the large, low windows which he touched in turn with his forepaw. Finding no exit there he located the door, ambled outside, down the steps, down the rocks and so to the lake. There was no explanation and it never happened again!

More snow fell, drifting under the balcony, fine as icing sugar, soft as down. White-footed deer mice, tip-toeing in Cervus' wake for grains of corn from his tray, left infinitesimal footprints, the embodiment of invisibility, as it were.

Birds by the dozen left every kind of mark in the snow, from the slight traces of tiny red-breasted nuthatch looking for sunflower seeds and fat on top of the feeders, to the fan-shaped tail marks made by rufous-sided towhees. And always the ubiquitous mallards, who stamped about the snowy lawn until no single print of theirs was left visible.

Vixen and Mo ceased their activities and I had visions of them curled up somewhere, keeping each other warm. Raccoons are not very bright about denning and are quite likely to sleep in a roofless hole high in a tree, with snow falling in on them. That they don't appear to mind testifies to the density of their magnificent coats.

During a brief period of semi-thaw, a neighbor told me he had seen raccoon tracks near his house. Vixen — if it was she — was apparently feasting on a barrel of apples, throwing half-eaten fruit about with wild abandon. Thrift and economy were entirely foreign to this voracious prodigal.

Christmas came and went. The days were clear and very cold, the nights crackly and glistening, silent with that perfect silence only deep snow can bring. The mercury stayed obstinately down below freezing. Mercifully our deep well continued to function and life was joyously filled with the comfort of huge log fires, hot soups, and the blissful sense of isolation brought about by a total absence of road traffic.

The Admiral, Scarper and Flo tucked their heads under their wings and snoozed all day, waiting for spring. At night they slept on a pile of hay under a stump. With difficulty we managed to chop their swimming hole, which was only large enough to permit the big birds to wet their feathers, but not to swim. The natural gentleness of all the birds, allied to lack of space, made their bathing an orderly ritual: while The Admiral, who was the biggest, took his time maneuvreing his body in the constricted circle, Scarper and Flo waited patiently on the ice for their turn. When our birds had bathed the wild ones rushed in. flapping and floundering and shoving one another under water. None of the water birds minded the cold so long as they remained dry and protected from wind while they were on land.

Our daily hacking at four-inch ice had made that part of the pond look like a silver battlefield strewn with chunks which gradually piled up and froze into multifaceted turrets that shone in the moonlight.

Wild deer foraged. As their hooves are not adapted for digging, like those of caribou, they rely on growth visible above the snow. In bad winters trees are marked by browse lines as high as the deer can reach and the following spring someone may find dead animals, pathetic witnesses to winter's hunger.

It is never dull in the country. Even when conditions make it difficult to go out there are things to delight mind and eye. The beauty of blue shadows on snow; the tracery of naked branches; the precarious shapes of snow piled in every nook and cranny, on every branch and twig, softening all outlines. Indoors are books to read, sketches to sort, paintings to plan and dreams to dream, waiting for spring.

Meanwhile nothing stirred in the woods. No bulb pierced the frozen soil. Only the mink danced his graceful dance of death on the white surface of the frozen lake. The rest of our little world slept.

Almost imperceptibly the temperature at last began to rise. Winter gales which had driven great banks of snow against every exposed object, lessened and finally died away. Rain fell and the sun reappeared and suddenly, to borrow Oscar Hammerstein's joyous phrase, "spring was bustin' out all over" — begging to be painted.

Indian plum, the first wild shrub to respond, put on a veil of tender green leaves, followed quickly by clusters of tiny white, scented flowers hanging like waxen earrings from every twig. Snowdrops, green-tipped and fragile, drooped their virginal heads above the sodden soil. Aconite, rising from the earth with bent heads already in bloom, lifted cupped yellow faces, green-ruffed, to the sun. Crocuses pierced the grass with colored swords, embroidering the lawn in purple and yellow. The lake came alive again. Yellow skunk cabbages, furled handsomely in green, sprouted in swamps everywhere, dotting the watery ground with palely shining lamps. Winter-starved creatures crept forth upon the burgeoning earth.

Cervus had come through with flying colors. He tore about in youthful springtime exuberance, leaping over rocks, around trees, and effortlessly clearing tall plants without disturbing a leaf.

Soon all the Ravenshill residents were accounted for. Except for little Mo, and, of course, Lester and Judy.

Chapter Seventeen

He who has never hoped
can never despair.

Shaw, *CAESAR AND CLEOPATRA*.

With spring came once more the haunting cry of wild geese flying over Ravenshill. I listened to The Admiral trying to call them down. His honking became an almost hysterical screech of despair. But his wild relatives always flew on.

I became accustomed to his nightly plea for company, so one evening when a group flew over with more noise than usual, I neglected to go out to watch them. The voices of the flying geese were growing louder, not softer with distance. The crescendo of honking rose to such a pitch that I finally went outside to see what was going on.

Directly overhead were seven wild geese, flying in circles over the pond, while The Admiral stood on the grass stretching his neck to the sky. He was beside himself with trying to make them understand how badly he wanted company.

Once, twice, three times the little flock circled — and flew away. Once more The Admiral's hopes were dashed and he was condemned to another lonely night.

At dawn the following day the seven geese were again circling. Two detached themselves from the skein and flew low over the lake, their heads down-bent as they scanned the area. Geese have marvellous eyesight and can identify objects on the ground from enormous heights.

They watched The Admiral, honking his heart out, as he started his trek to the lake. Usually it took him ten minutes of careful progress but this time he broke all records, half running, half flying along the ground, using his mutilated wings to help propel his feet as he ran with outstretched neck, crying desperately.

Yet again, just as he reached the lake, the others flew off, leaving him in a paroxysm of frustration. But he calmed himself and swam round the lake a few times with quiet dignity before climbing onto the beach to roost awhile. Wearily resigned, he closed his eyes, laying his head backwards against his big brown body with a graceful, sinuous movement of his long neck.

That evening the seven geese returned, circled once, and again flew away.

Early next morning the performance was repeated — with a difference.

The flock's calling grew wilder and The Admiral, already on the lake, swam with rapid strokes of his powerful legs to keep them in sight. Suddenly they veered round and flew away — but one goose peeled off and began circling high up, craning its neck downwards as though looking for something. The Admiral's call grew more clamorous — a raucous, high-pitched scream.

The lone goose answered in a voice lower in pitch, softer, and, to my mind, feminine.

The stranger rose higher above the treetops and circled once more, calling without interruption in the strangely seductive voice. Then the beautiful wings curved down to brake flight as it dropped, feet down, neck stretched full length as the tail became rigid. The big goose made a perfect landing, barely rippling the water.

As fast as he could The Admiral swam towards this strange goose he had called out of the sky. With neck stretched parallel to the water he uttered his greeting — the greeting of all Canada geese — a harsh, high-pitched excited shriek. Floating close to him with wings folded, face to face, the stranger made gentler sounds. Their necks reached eagerly towards each other until their bills almost touched. The formalities completed, they swam side by side, exploring every bay, every tree-stump and plant around the edge of the lake. And so they continued the whole day long.

Little work was done that day. Every few minutes I found an excuse to stand at one window or another to watch the geese. They remained on the lake all day, from time to time emerging onto the beach to preen each other — a charmingly affectionate gesture.

Early next morning I ventured out, leaving Mr. Bentley shut in the house in case he upset the visitor. The birds were standing on the beach, each on one leg, relaxed.

There was something about the stranger that seemed familiar.

Long experience with animals has given me a sixth sense concerning them, anything from signs of ill-health not apparent to a casual observer, to recognition of one in a group of similar individuals.

Since all Canada geese are much alike in form, plumage and coloring and since there is only a very small difference in size to distinguish the sexes, this instinct was all I had to go on. There are other ways of determining sex, but all require close contact with the birds.

I told myself not to be a sentimental wishful thinker, yet I suppose I had always retained a faint hope that if she was still alive Judy might return.

Armed with a tin of grain I crept slowly to the rocks overlooking the lake. The new goose glanced up at me, curious but not alarmed. I called

169

softly: "Judy!" Again she looked up, with that flirting motion of the head which is typical of geese when they are interested, alarmed, or about to take flight. Which was it?

Slowly she turned to face me.

"Judy, come!"

The Admiral took a few steps in my direction, then stopped, as if wanting to know what his companion wished to do.

I retreated to the lawn, calling as I had always called them at feeding time. The trough was still where it had been when Judy had used it. I filled it and waited.

Both birds were silent. The early morning air was damp and cold. I shivered — as much from nervous tension as the chill.

After what seemed an interminable interval The Admiral appeared over the brow of the rocks, advancing with purposeful steps, slow and dignified.

The stranger followed. Slowly, cautiously, pausing at each step to look around, long neck upstretched, head cocked, eyes brilliantly alert.

"Judy!" I tapped the grain tin softly.

She came on. With agonizing slowness. Thirty feet away. Twenty. Fifteen.

She stopped, looked at The Admiral on the lawn and veered towards him, wagging her head, her wings lifting a fraction with each step as though to be sure they were in working order, her whole body braced for instant flight. All her feathers were held tightly against her body, denoting the tension in her. She was taut as a bowstring and I, as acutely aware as if I had become one with her, stood rigid with the same tension.

Suddenly she lowered her head in a gesture typical of an inquiring goose. She curved her neck into a shallow sideways 'S' and ran the last few yards to the grain trough.

Surely only Judy would have gone so eagerly to her old feeding place? Surely no wild stranger could be so brave? But I was still not quite sure. There were other tests I could make.

Our garage door is metal and swings up on a cantilever, making a terrific racket. Certainly enough to scare a strange bird; but it had never worried Judy.

Leaving the geese to feed, I opened the big door. It went up with a metallic roar.

At the trough the geese ate on, unconcerned.

Lester, Judy and The Admiral had always regarded Mr. Bentley as part of the scenery, and never minded when he moved near them. So I let him out and he ambled over to the pond. An extra goose made no difference to him and he ignored them both.

The Admiral and his companion looked up. They regarded Mr. B. with a long stare, then quietly resumed their feeding.

I surely needed no further proof. This must be my dear Judy who for five long months had been lost.

Later that day she was standing on the lawn after a good meal. She stretched first one wing and a leg, then the other in a slow, sensuously lazy movement, the kind we make when we wake in the morning. She was relaxed at last — nervous birds don't make such movements.

All her wing feathers were clearly revealed. Six of the ten flight feathers were shorter than they should have been—had they not been clipped six months ago.

This was incontrovertibly Judy.

Chapter Eighteen

*Absence from whom we love is
worse than death,
And frustrate hope severer
than despair.*

Cowper, HOPE, LIKE THE
SHORT LIV'D RAY.

Judy the beautiful, Judy the gentle, Judy the intelligent, Judy the half tame. In the near-past she had grazed at my back door; then had become part of a wild flock of her own kind, high in the empty sky, flying in formation as though she had done so all her life instead of spending it in dull security as a semi-domesticated bird. During the five months since she disappeared she must have flown many times over Ravenshill. Then the vibrant urge of springtime had awakened The Admiral to cry to the skein of wild geese above him. And she, the odd one, had responded.

What had she thought as she flew, strong and free, with her kindred? What passed through her mind when suddenly, from below, came the sound of a love-call? Did she recognize the place? Geese have long memories.

How greatly she must have been torn between her deepest instincts. A male voice called to her from a place where she had known the most terrible tragedy of losing her beloved mate. Should she break from the flock anyway, obeying the instinct to breed? Were her nerves taut with fear as she descended to greet The Admiral?

How long had it taken this goose of two worlds to reach her decision and at what cost to her integrity? How many reconnaissance flights over Ravenshill did it take her to reach it? To exchange her new-found freedom for a voluntary return to a life near humankind? A mind-searing experience. A widowed goose or gander only rarely chooses a new mate, usually spending the remainder of its life in sexual abstinence. The Admiral was a widower and Judy had lost her mate under mysterious circumstances. So their enthusiastic greetings and their immediate ac eptance of one another made this an extraordinary event.

At dusk there came a great honking. Judy was running across the lawn to lift away over the laundry line, which she tipped with her feet and nearly broke her flight. Why was she flying away from her new-found companion? The flightless Admiral screamed in distress as he watched her.

172

Judy landed gracefully on the lake and called a strident, imperious summons, to which The Admiral responded instantly, running ponderously overland to join her. They swam serenely for about half an hour. Then Judy began honking and shaking her head in the characteristic pre-flight gesture.

She rose in a run-and-lift movement over the tree-tops and out of sight.

The Admiral, in shocked disbelief, screamed and cried disconsolately for nearly an hour before dragging his weary way back through the woods to his customary roosting place beside the pond. I thought of lovers' trysts. The wild eagerness of anticipation that lends feet wings. The heavy, lifeless, meaningless hours after the beloved has gone.

It was all wrong. Judy should have stayed if she intended to take The Admiral for her mate. And he should have been able to follow her if she left. It is the female who chooses the breeding site, so this, too, was all wrong. Once more Man had interfered in the lives of two of nature's most imperial creatures and the results were instinct with distress. Judy's fear of the lake at night, from which her mate had disappeared, must have proved stronger after all than desire.

At dawn the following day Judy glided in tight circles to the lake, honking on a low, restrained note and landing with a splash which sent wide ripples chasing across the surface. The Admiral gave a joyous shriek and swam with all his might to greet her, his sturdy breast cleaving the water like a ship's prow, his raucous voice echoing across the lake. She, too, was greeting him with outstretched neck almost before she had finished folding her wings tidily.

Once again they spent the day swimming and preening themselves and each other. From time to time these otherwise dignified birds dived for food, their large black and white rear ends pointing comically skywards. In the afternoon they emerged to feed quietly from the trough. As evening approached they returned to the lake. Judy seemed to take her cue from The Admiral, and dutifully walked. Heads erect and eyes alert, they started the slow, cautious trek through the woods. It is an incongruous sight to see two huge geese wandering about under trees, but in spite of their webbed feet these big water birds are capable of walking for miles and rough surfaces do not seem to injure their tough black skin.

Arrived at the lake at last, they entered the water together and pushed off to the centre. But alas, Judy suddenly again took off for parts unknown, leaving her companion bewildered and disconsolately crying for her.

And that night, to make matters worse, Scarper disappeared without trace, not so much as a dropped feather.

His mate set up a harsh, deep-throated quacking that lasted well into the night. We never saw Scarper again and were forced to the conclusion that either Vixen or the mink had killed him. Since both these predators drag their kill to a safe hiding place if it is not too heavy, his body could have been concealed in a dozen places impossible to search. He had been ill-equipped to elude them.

From that time forward, Flo attached herself to The Admiral. Although she had mated with Scarper many times, she did her best to get her new friend to breed her. Sad though the circumstances were, we could not help smiling at the antics of this ill-assorted pair. Poor Flo would sit or swim beside The Admiral, making all the proper gestures of a duck willing to mate — the sideways dipping of her head towards the drake, the fluttery runs across the surface, the general air of coy expectancy. But The Admiral took little notice of the lonely mongrel mallard, his mind centred on his new-found goose.

The extraordinary goose routine continued on the same lines that Judy had already set. She flew in each day at dawn with noisy greetings and took off again every night, leaving The Admiral as bewildered and unhappy as ever. During the day they slept a great deal, folded down onto the grass, their heads laid to rest upon their backs. I was intrigued by the way their white-feathered eyelids closed upwards. Beneath them is a second, transparent lid, which protects the eye from wind and sun or when diving; it moves sideways from the inner corner, across the eye.

Gradually a change came over my geese. I observed them commencing their curious pre-mating ritual. It was plain that this unusual pair was about to consummate a marriage which, by all the laws of goosedom should never have taken place.

The Admiral approached Judy with his head held close to the ground, his neck extended and weaving like a snake. He opened his bill wide and hissed as he moved towards her, ruffling his feathers until they stood bristling all over his body. Had a rival appeared at this point, he would have attacked it. Then, the preliminaries over, the two birds entered the water. The Admiral dipped his head deeply, raised it with a quick backward jerk, tossing water over his back. Judy responded in the same way. It is a gesture that geese and ducks also make when they are bathing, except that in the mating ritual they hold their wings closed.

Judy, who had never been far from The Admiral's side, swam still closer until she came alongside him. She dipped her head beneath the surface quickly — down-up — down-up, in a sort of coy invitation, much as Flo had done. This lasted about two minutes. Then, while Judy

174

was still making her desires known, The Admiral swam to one side of her until his breast was mid-way to her back. Then he mounted her, pushing her down and grasping the nape of her neck in his bill until her head was submerged. The mating took three or four seconds. When it was finished Judy rose again, her neck still held securely in The Admiral's beak. At last, when all was completed, they swam about a little, dipping and bathing, then walked onto the lawn for a prolonged preening session, snaking their necks gracefully over their backs to their preen glands to collect oil to spread upon their feathers. And then they settled down side by side to a well-earned sleep. And very nice too!

Edward and I turned away from the window, happily confident that after so much heartache and frustration Judy was settling down with her new husband. In time, we hoped, they would raise a family of downy goslings. We were impatient to see a troupe of little Dooleykind replicas swimming behind their devoted parents.

But Judy again took off that night.

This was astonishing behavior. They had already broken the goose law enjoining widows and widowers to remain in their bereaved state, although that law is not entirely inviolable — widowed geese have occasionally been observed to take new mates. But for a newly mated female to leave her husband was extraordinary indeed.

Again Man's interference was to blame. Judy must have been split right down the middle, the desire to remain with her chosen mate pulling against her need to nest somewhere safely distant from this place of remembered terror.

Day after day her unnatural behavior continued. Happy days spent with The Admiral. Unhappy nights spent apart from him — each partner surely as lonely and disconsolate as the other. But the thrust of her fear was too much for Judy. Usually in Canada geese the strength of family attachments overcomes all outside fears; in fact the mating bond is so strong that a gander will guard a nest even after his goose has been lost to a hunter's gun. That a goose should choose to leave her gander after the consummation of their nuptials must mean that the loss of her first mate, Lester, had happened in circumstances of unbelievable terror.

An even stranger change began to manifest itself in Judy's behavior. Instead of staying with The Admiral all day, she took to flying in and out several times before finally leaving at dusk. Was she searching for a place to build a nest? It was the obvious conclusion. The gander will guard the nest faithfully but he has nothing to do with the choice of site or with building.

During one of Judy's nightly absences I added an old tire to the raft I had earlier made for Judy and Lester. It raised her nest-site even higher and I filled it with hay for comfort. When she returned next morning both geese swam interestedly round it. Eventually Judy mounted and sat down, while The Admiral carefully pulled out bits of hay and dropped them into the water. But I thought 'At least Judy is behaving properly now and will settle down here and lay her eggs and brood them'. Again I was wrong.

She left again that evening, to roost I knew not where. The Admiral cried in misery. Little Flo strove to comfort him and be comforted. The two spent their night as usual on the bank, each wrapped in bewildered, separate loneliness.

Yet Judy was back again next day and she and The Admiral mated several times, behaving like a devoted couple so long as they were together. I was becoming used to these unnatural events, yet I was not at all prepared for what came next.

One dawn I was awakened by the familiar honking of The Admiral crying greetings to his wife. Or so I thought. But then a third voice joined in. I looked out to see — not Judy — but two strange Canadas swimming belligerently round the lake, harassing The Admiral. By now my eyes had become acclimatized to slight differences in form and color and it was plain that these were a mated pair. The male was a strongly dominant bird; The Admiral, beleaguered on his own territory yet unable to use his powerful wings adequately, was compelled to dive deeply and swim several yards under water to escape. The new pair took over his lake and he was forced to submit to the indignity of having his territory disputed and won from him.

Just as I was beginning to wonder whether she would return at all, Judy flew in. The Admiral greeted her joyously — he was no longer odd man out. The wild strangers stayed at Ravenshill, greeting, honking, chasing one another and mating. They also walked up through the woods to graze and sleep. Harmony reigned.

It is not for nothing that hunters set out decoy geese. The presence of Judy and The Admiral must have been reported amongst the wild flocks and so this strange pair was attracted to a body of water they would not normally have visited.

Excitement and tension grew. It was no good taking anything for granted with these magnificent birds, who were always up to something new.

The early morning racket grew deafening as Judy, accompanied now by the two newcomers, came circling down to the confused Admiral; their loud voices and the great rushing splashes as they chased and played over the lake ensured that we would be up and taking notice.

And so we saw the fifth goose land.

We were treated to the unprecedented spectacle of five huge geese sailing majestically on our little lake, where no wild goose had ever alighted before. The brown-and-black plumage of Judy and The Admiral, the paler buffy-brown-and-black of the three newcomers, the long, slender black neck-stockings of all, their handsome flirting heads with white cheeks and chin straps made a breathtaking picture of wild beauty. We felt vastly privileged to be honored by the willing presence of these proud denisens of the north and hoped that all of them would stay.

But human hopes ran counter to nature's dictates. A day came when our lake was devoid of geese. Even The Admiral disappeared for two days and nights.

Had he gone looking for Judy at night, on foot, perhaps to be run over on the road?

A single wild goose returned. Was it one of the pair that had stayed with us a few days? If so, where was its mate? Or was it the odd man out? It was all very confusing.

The Admiral reappeared — alone.

The following morning Judy at last flew back to spend the rest of the day with her lawful husband.

The Admiral's behavior towards her was charming. Whenever she emerged from the water he greeted her with outstretched neck and high-pitched cry. When she settled on the grass to rest and preen, he stood guard over her on one leg, alert and wary. Only when she awoke did he risk tucking his head under a wing, or laying it along his back for a brief nap.

Sometimes she played around the raft nest but did not seem seriously interested in it. Then one morning I watched through binoculars as she fiddled with the hay around the edge of the tire, picking bits up in her bill, poking and rearranging. At last she's getting down to business! I thought. Even as I watched she turned away, stooping low so that her breast touched the hay, lifting her rear end high. She seemed to strain a little, then suddenly sat back. In that brief interval I distinctly saw an egg leave her body, its creamy whiteness glinting for an instant against her dark feathers.

Geese lay their eggs over a protracted period, at the rate of an egg every day or day-and-a-half. They start incubating them only after the last has been laid.

In the evening, as usual, Judy took off. Long after dark, when I was sure she had left for the night, I untied the raft and pulled it inshore, using a flashlight to examine it. To my astonishment the nest contained a single off-white egg, not much bigger than a mallard's! I couldn't believe the evidence of my eyes. A Canada goose egg is white and more than twice the size of a duck's.

I replaced the raft without touching the egg. The next day Judy returned to her nest. By the end of the week there were six eggs. Clutch sizes vary from two to nine, but the average is five, so she had already laid more than her quota.

The following day she did not appear at all, leaving the eggs to lie cold in the nest. This would do no harm, as she had not yet started to incubate them. But once she began to sit in earnest, her eggs could not be allowed to cool: to keep them warm waterfowl cover them with down plucked from their own bodies.

Her absence made me wonder if this unhappy goose was trying to run a separate menage elsewhere? Yet I had never heard of a polygamous female of this species and only rarely has a male been observed with two mates. Canada geese are the epitome of morality.

After two days passed and Judy had still not returned, I began to worry about her and her eggs. She was disturbed and divided in her loyalties, consequently there were no guidelines for predicting her behavior. Anything might happen. Including total desertion.

Birds' eggs can be hatched artificially, although in the case of waterfowl successful incubation requires knowledge and skill. They must be kept at a temperature between 100.4°F and 101.3°F (38.0°C and 38.5°C) and be moistened regularly to prevent the inner membrane from sticking to the shell. Even with all this taken care of, they will not always hatch.

Nevertheless, I decided to have Judy's eggs incubated professionally. So I rang up a friend who proved willing to take them to a hatchery in Vancouver. He came to the house and we pulled the raft in.

He took one look at the clutch of eggs in the nest and began to laugh.

"Why . . . they're DUCK eggs!"

This was too much. I recounted the whole story and he listened patiently. I was certain I had convinced him that the eggs were Judy's when he said: "You must admit you wanted them to be goose eggs, didn't you?"

"Of course. But I saw her lay one of them. At least, . . . I think I did."

"Well, if these are goose eggs I'll never disagree with anyone again as long as I live."

He took them to Vancouver anyway. Hatching would take twenty-five to twenty-eight days.

Eventually Judy returned but her behavior was growing more and more erratic and abnormal. Sometimes she stayed from dawn till dusk, sometimes for a few hours only, and occasionally she didn't come at all. She continued to mate frequently with The Admiral but no longer mounted the nest. Yet I kept finding eggs, a further twelve in all. This was far too many for a goose. I desperately wanted them to be Judy's, but. . . .

One morning The Admiral and his wife were sunning themselves on the bank as contentedly as if they had never been parted. Flo was sitting on the grass a few feet away. Beside her lay a solitary egg. Its color and size exactly matched the others. Had she — incredibly — mated with The Admiral? Goose and Mallard? Against all reason I still clung to my belief in Judy's eggs.

Then I saw a mink loping along the edge of the pond. These animals are fast and vicious, they swim well and are avid egg-eaters. Vixen also swam well and was a lover of fresh eggs. There would be no tell-tale scent from the raft; but how long would it be before one or both of these ever-curious predators swam out to investigate it?

The following day all the eggs were smashed. Fragments were scattered around the nest and in the water; the hay was a sticky mess of half-eaten yolks and slimy whites. And to this tragic scene of devastation came Judy.

She swam to the raft and climbed up. The Admiral remained in the water and together they spent the morning cleaning up, picking at the soiled hay and depositing bits in the pond, eating the broken shells until at last the nest was tidy again. Remembering my friend's caustic comments about the eggs, I felt smugly that here was further evidence they were Judy's — otherwise why would she take such pains to clean up the nest?

Silly goose — if only she had stayed to incubate the eggs all would have been well. No small predator can penetrate the defenses of a goose's powerful wings and bill. And an enraged gander guarding his mate is another formidable opponent.

But even as I put her down as silly I knew her absence bespoke a deep inner turmoil. All the instincts of a mother-to-be must tie her to home-site and mate. Against them pulled the fear that this was no safe place in which to raise babies. Judy was evidently caught helplessly between two sets of conflicting emotions, each as strong as the other.

After cleaning the nest she abandoned it, reverting to her early pattern of mating in domestic felicity by day and desertion at night.

But then one morning she flew in accompanied by another gander, who attacked the helpless Admiral. Again he was routed in his own territory. Judy led her new partner up to the pond, her old love following disconsolately at a distance, to look on without protest while they mated.

I had attempted to put myself in Judy's place when she first flew from the sky to join The Admiral. I tried now to penetrate his thoughts as he sat on the grassy bank, cuckolded under his very eyes. Words like 'faithless hussy' ran through my mind. Surely he must feel ashamed for his depreciated masculinity? Fearfully impotent in his proven incapacity to hold a mate? Surely he was wishing the earth would swallow him?

As to Judy — here was behavior unheard of amongst Canada geese (at least I have never heard nor read of a similar case). A faithful bird widowed; a lonely widower. Brought together through my intervention, they paired and should have lived for the rest of their lives in happy harmony. But because Man had interfered with their wings, they were unable to fulfill their natural destiny. Judy, the urge to produce a family strong upon her, had done the only thing possible under the circumstances — taking yet another mate, her third. The fact that she had two of them simultaneously was no fault of hers. I felt obscurely that it was somehow mine. Yet I had not clipped The Admiral's wings and the key to this situation was that he had been unable to follow his mate to some other nesting site. Judy's torn loyalties were tragic but The Admiral's tragedy was by far the most poignant.

The event was unique in its very unnaturalness. Regardless of the fact that wing-clipping is the general practice among owners of geese; regardless of the fact that the operation causes no pain; regardless of anything anybody could say to comfort me, I still felt guilty — on my own behalf for ever contemplating following such an example; and on behalf of all bird mutilators. I vowed that I would never again clip a wing as long as I lived.

Meanwhile the drama continued to unfold.

Chapter Nineteen

*I shall remember while the
light lives yet
And in the night time I
shall not forget.*

Swinburne, EROTION.

Had Judy been possessed of human expression, her face must have betrayed the ravages of split loyalties.

During her visits to Ravenshill, sometimes accompanied by her new mate, sometimes alone, she looked for new nesting sites.

One morning, for instance, she flew to the top of a wood duck box in which, as so often happened, a screech owl was rearing her three young. Judy stood on its roof, surveying the landscape, then bent to peer in through the small entrance hole — which must have caused the owlets no small alarm!

That afternoon I became aware of curious stamping sounds on the roof of our house. When I looked up I found Judy leaning over the edge of the gutter. Canadas certainly nest on rooftops, but ours was too steep, so she turned her attention to the far side of the lake. There, an overturned tree stump rose high out of the water and she seemed interested in it.

It was very late in the season for her to be looking for nesting places but there was just time before fall for her to raise a clutch of goslings, providing she was left undisturbed.

Judy was having difficulty manoeuvreing on top of the stump. Anxious to do all I could to help her, I rigged a nest from a large crate, lined it with hay and staked it into the upturned roots. She watched me as I worked and as soon as I was finished, climbed in to investigate my makeshift nest. She began rearranging the camouflage I had erected around it. Geese accept artificial nests readily, even in the wild, but they are scrupulously fussy and must arrange them exactly to their liking. Judy was spurred by the desperate urge to deposit her eggs and incubate them before summer was too far advanced. With a heart-felt prayer that she would at last be able to settle, I left her to her domestic duties.

On this occasion she was alone with The Admiral (goodness knows what her second mate did when she came here by herself). While she fussed and fiddled with the new nest, he swam in tight circles at the foot of the stump, from time to time climbing up to assist her. I watched from the opposite bank, wondering if my geese were at last to enjoy a state of married bliss. If any goslings were born of these strange unions, nobody would ever know their paternity; I doubt if even the experts know whether a goose can conceive from two males. But in view of the fact that many matings occur over a long period and egg-laying is staggered, why should not two males fertilize one female in the course of a week?

Although Judy left for the night as usual, she returned the next day, still alone, and continued her activities at the new nest. The Admiral took advantage of her solitary presence to pay assiduous court to her, showing his affection in many charming ways. Vibrant with eagerness, he swam back and forth at the foot of the stump, crying to her in a loving voice; then, when she joined him, groomed her gently with his bill, and generally behaved like a newly-wed. She seemed content, submitting gracefully to his ministrations. In the evening she walked with him to the lawn, instead of flying in to feed, as she had lately been doing. The Admiral must have been grateful for this small crumb of comfort, since he always became agitated whenever she took to her wings.

Our anxiety for a happy ending for these star-crossed lovers caused us to spend endless hours observing them. On the evening of Judy's second day of activity at the new nest we watched them fondly as they grazed. The declining sunlight glowed on their warm brown feathers. If only Judy would stay the night with her husband and discover that she need no longer be afraid!

Flirting her head slowly from side to side, she started to walk away from him across the lawn.

With baited breath we watched her walk slowly, sedately, to the top of the rocks. The Admiral followed, on foot, of course. Judy looked about. She turned to The Admiral and they conferred together in low, grunting voices. Suddenly she jumped into the air to glide — not away over the trees — but down to the lake and her new nest. The Admiral honked as he climbed carefully down the steep rocks.

Judy mounted her nest. The light of the setting sun turned the surface of the lake to fire. Through it The Admiral swam, silhouetted against the red-gold glow, to join his mate and perform at last the function for which he was born: to guard her against all dangers, and thereby to ensure the continuance of his kind.

Our beloved geese had literally swum into the sunset. The idyllic scene seemed to be the perfect ending to a near-tragic tale.

*   *   *   *   *

Suddenly branches snapped. Voices were raised in excitement. The sounds reached us all too clearly across the water late in the afternoon of the following day. Through the trees on the far side of our lake we saw a man, a woman with a baby and two walking children burst through the undergrowth.

"Look, it's a goose — a big goose — and it's on a nest!"

They were standing immediately behind Judy's stump, within a few feet of her.

I screamed at them to go away — please, PLEASE GO AWAY!

The woman shouted an obscenity. A child jumped up and down; dry brush crackled and snapped. The man asked loudly who I thought I was, to order them off? Desperately I told them that this was private property, that the goose must not be disturbed. For God's sake — GO.

Too late.

It was all over in a matter of seconds.

Judy rose on her nest and leapt straight into the air to crash down into the lake a few feet below. The Admiral screamed, cupping his great wings, half rising from the water as he rushed to her defense.

Judy did not pause to acknowledge his presence. Gathering momentum she took a few pattering steps over the surface, her great wings beating faster, faster — then rose, outraged, into the air. With loud, protesting honks she disappeared over the tree-tops. The Admiral set up an anguished cry as we watched in helpless rage.

The sun sank behind the trees. The intruders, muttering, crashed back to the road. Car doors slammed, the motor was gunned in anger, tires screeched, and the trespassers roared off, little realizing the damage their presence had caused.

With infinite slowness The Admiral walked back to the lawn.

Judy never returned.

*   *   *   *   *

Did Judy rejoin her second, wild mate? Did she succeed in finding another nesting place in time to raise a family? We could only conjecture. Her wild love would be better able to defend her than the partly crippled Admiral. With the full strength of his wings, he could have routed even human marauders, providing they came unarmed.

But one thing was devastatingly certain: Judy would never again venture near the lake where she had been subjected to so much terror.

She would have remained faithful to her first mate, Lester, had not

Man put an end to him. She would have stayed with the Admiral, had he been able to fly to her chosen nest site. His heavily clipped feathers had not had time to moult and grow again.

He spent days and nights by the pond, lonely and apathetic, 'widowed' for the second time. In due course the mating urge died down and he began to moult. Flo kept him company as best she could; the death of Scarper had brought her close to the big brown goose and perhaps the protection that he could offer. He turned at last to the little mongrel duck. The ill-assorted pair swam and fed and roosted together, bound by a common tie of loneliness.

A few days later the mystery of Judy's eggs was explained.

Flo disappeared.

Mr. Bentley and I were wandering near the pond when I noticed him intently eyeing something near the base of a big rock. Thinking it might be some small creature he wanted to hunt, I went to pick him up, hoping to give whatever it was a chance to escape. Too late. He lunged and began to drag something out.

It was Flo.

I yelled at Mr. B. to drop her, but his primordial instincts were stronger than his lifelong domesticity. He held on to the struggling duck.

I grabbed him by the scruff of his neck with one hand and tried to pry his jaws loose with the other, an act I have performed successfully with many dogs. This time I met a jaw too strong for me. In the following minutes I did things I have never done in my life. I grabbed his ears, I twisted his tail, I hammered his nose with my fist. All to no avail.

Flo was weakening. Her wing dripped blood. The ground was befeathered. And still Mr. B. hung on.

Desperate, I spotted a short length of wood nearby and reached for it. With this I managed to prize Mr. B's jaws open. Dripping blood from a wound in his lip inflicted by one of his own teeth, he finally let go. Flo flopped away to the water, one wing hanging limply to the ground, broken.

Exhausted and trembling, I took Mr. Bentley into the house and ordered him to his basket. Morally he was in disgrace.

Yet was he really to blame? Had Flo been in her customary place beside the pool, he would have treated her with his usual indifferent courtesy. But, as I immediately discovered when I returned to the scene of the crime, she had been sitting on her nest. I must have passed unsuspectingly within a foot of it a dozen times.

The spot she had chosen was a cunning one. An old, half-rotten ladder lay on its side, backed by six feet of solid rock. Between them, protected by the rungs, was a cavity in the ground; ferns and grasses grew closely about it, making it invisible. Only when I parted the greenery was Flo's large, round, feather-lined nest revealed. In it were fourteen eggs exquisitely arranged — and they precisely matched all the other eggs I had found scattered around Ravenshill that summer, including 'Judy's' on the raft. I estimated that she had laid a total of thirty-four eggs. Poor, dear old Flo!

She, too, had known frustration and despair. And just because she was 'dear old Flo', we had taken little notice of her quiet comings and goings, save to feel sorry for her loneliness after she lost her mate. Because, of course, the eggs were hers and Scarper's.

The mystery was solved. I had indeed seen Judy lay one solitary, creamy-white egg on the raft — but it must have been devoured by Vixen or the mink sometime in the early evening. The egg I found later the same night — the smaller egg with a deeper tinge — must have been laid by Flo in the interval between the predator's visit to the raft and mine.

Understandably she deserted her nest and the eggs in it grew cold and died. I brought them in to cook for other creatures in my care. It was just as well that mongrel Flo had never reared the brood fathered by the purebred Scarper. I cancelled the incubation of the first eight eggs.

Flo's wing dragged and she was clearly in pain. But she was so nervous that I could not catch her to bind her injuries and so the wing healed in its drooping position.

The friendship between her and The Admiral deepened and they became inseparable. He displayed a new protectiveness towards her, as if to compensate for the mate he could no longer guard. On land he stayed close enough to Flo to touch her and he never allowed her to enter the water alone. When she climbed awkwardly out of the water onto a log, The Admiral would climb up beside her if there was room; if not, he sat in the water near her. He even ceased to peck at her when she stood on tip-toe to feed from his trough.

In this manner these ill-matched birds spent the rest of the summer. When fall came The Admiral's new feathers grew long and beautiful and sleek. He needed no encouragement to practice and spent days flying back and forth between the pond and the lake.

One lovely evening, just as the light began to fade from the sunset, a formation of wild geese passed high overhead. Once more their haunting voices were heard by my lonely goose as he paced the ground near his pond.

With a great cry The Admiral ran for the last time across my lawn. He lifted on curved, sweeping pinions, his long neck outstretched as if in anticipation of the freedom he could at last enjoy. Freedom to fly, gloriously, for the rest of his life.

Tears ran down my face as I watched him go, wishing him godspeed.

Only Flo remained.

Three weeks later she was dead. A sorry trail of feathers led deep into the bush, where I found a little pile of them: all that remained of a valiant duck who, mentally and physically battered beyond repair, hadn't the agility (or maybe the heart) to elude an enemy.

I still have a few of her feathers and some goose quills, mute reminders that the line between good intentions and moral indefensibility is sometimes very thin indeed.

186

Chapter Twenty

The price of survival is education and vigilance.

J. W-H.

I pray that Judy and The Admiral have been reunited and that, being long-lived birds, they may dwell in conjugal happiness for the rest of their lives. Whenever I watch flights of Canada geese winging their way over Ravenshill towards some other lake, and hear their wild dark crying, a great longing surges in me to know. Judy had no special markings; The Admiral had a black plastic band on one foot; so I inquire hopefully of everybody who might have observed geese on land whether or not they have seen my vanished goose. I explain how special he is.

Alas, nobody has.

*　　*　　*　　*　　*

And now my story is almost done.

I set out to tell the tales of a few of the wild creatures who have come to my door, partly to share the pleasures and rewards they have brought me, but also in the hope that by using them as archetypes of all wildlings who come in contact with humans, I could show how our interference with nature must inevitably give rise to sadness and tragedy. Ravenshill has known both. Some of the original animals are still here. Some have passed on and left their progeny. Some have provided us with fascinating sequels to their stories.

The orphan mallard has a wife and is only distinguishable from the rest of the flock by the red band on his foot. He also has two more female companions, both of them raised from infancy at Ravenshill. They bring their wild mates and so we have a little home-bred flock.

The deer mice still feed on Cervus' grain and in turn are prey for the screech owl.

Two baby rabbits who came uninvited have multiplied greatly. But wise nature adjusted the balance and prevented a plague of rabbits by sending a number of great horned owls to prey upon them. Yet they manage to keep just ahead of their predators: there are always a few lolloping about at dusk, their little white scuts bobbing as they dash about the lawn, before settling to feed in earnest on whatever they can find, such as my crocuses in spring.

Two weeks before Christmas I was watching Cervus who was chewing his cud whilst lying on one of his favorite rocks opposite my window. Suddenly a white mongrel dog about the size of a Labrador retriever appeared on the lawn. I rushed outside to shout at the dog. If Cervus had only kept still, all might have been well. But he saw the dog and naturally took off into the woods. Simultaneously the dog gave chase. By the time I reached the scene both animals had disappeared.

Cervus' fear made his loose droppings easy enough to track but they ceased at a steep rock incline which forms one of Ravenshill's boundaries. From that point I could only guess the route he might have taken.

I climbed onto a plateau but there were no signs of tracks on the rock and no sounds of scuffling. I wandered about looking at the ground carefully, calling Cervus, until it was clear that I would achieve nothing. He had bolted deep into the bush and as there was no sign of the dog I could not tell whether Cervus had been attacked.

Restlessness drove me out of the house an hour later, but the woods were silent still. Pushing through tall salal was not only exhausting but futile: if Cervus was injured he could be a few feet from me and I would not see him. Instinctively I felt he was far beyond the sanctuary of home. However, he came home once before with an injury and I would have to wait to see if he did so again.

Meantime I alerted neighbors over a ten-mile radius and searched and called daily.

On December 23 the owner of a small golf course just down the road telephoned to say he had found a dead buck in the bushes behind one of the greens. Could it be Cervus?

I tore down in the car and he took me to the spot. It was not Cervus but a much younger buck. The little animal had been brutally shot through the stomach with an arrow. He was then left to crawl — how far? — to where he died — after how many hours of agony? He had not even been killed for food. His body was soaking wet and stiff. There was nothing to be done for him. Bitterly I railed against a new municipal law that permitted this dreadful 'sport'.

I drove home furiously angry and with no heart at all for Christmas.

Months rolled by. A year. Another year. Cervus did not return.

In December of the third year a young doe who had grown up with her dam at Ravenshill and was now of breeding age was eating grain alone on the lawn. Her name is Tristesse—we say "Bonjour" to her every day.

Behind her a fine buck strolled out of the woods, wearing four-pointed antlers. This was not unusual. We often see wild bucks passing through Ravenshill during the mating season.

What was amazing was that this one joined Tristesse at the grain. No wild buck had ever done that. This was exciting in itself but there was also a sudden hammering surge of hope that had to be satisfied.

I opened the door quietly to go onto the balcony above them. The buck stood his ground.

I crept down the steps. Still he did not move.

I stood openly within six feet of him and still he did not budge.

This buck was not young. The white hair of his muzzle had spread to just below his eyes but he was in superb condition and must have weighed over two hundred pounds. His antlers were polished to a fine lustre, his hair dark for the winter. There was nothing immediately recognizable to raise my hopes except his extraordinary tranquility.

And yet — was he favoring one leg, ever so slightly, taking his weight on the other three — or was it my heightened imagination at work? I looked at his ears for the tell-tale nick. There was one — but suddenly I realized that after three years I was not quite sure even which ear had been damaged.

"Cervus — Cervus, boy, is it you?"

He looked at me attentively, then turned and walked a few steps. Was there just the slightest limp? Three years ago Cervus' leg was healed but then he had not been chased.

Tristesse was not ready to mate that day and the two deer walked quietly into the woods and disappeared. The same thing happened during the next four days.

In the meantime I had looked at my photographs of Cervus and there was the little hole in his ear exactly matching the nick in this new buck's ear.

This was Cervus — of that there was no longer any doubt.

On the fifth day things happened.

Tristesse turned from the grain, put up her tail and began to run in circles.

Cervus' head went up and his nostrils flared, catching both her mood and scent. The hackles rose along the ridge of his long, exceedingly powerful neck as he stretched it parallel to the ground. His whole expression changed and he became a rather frightening, very strong male animal whose eyes were no longer gentle but staring wildly. He raised his upper lip, baring his teeth in an ugly snarling expression.

Tristesse continued running coquettishly with Cervus following closely with long easy strides.

She stopped to urinate; Cervus stooped to inhale the scent.

Suddenly Tristesse became still, her back to Cervus, tail raised, feet firmly planted and well apart on the grass.

Cervus approached her from the rear, breathing hard and fast. In one awkward yet majestic movement he mounted her, his big heavy body covering her small one. He gripped her haunches with his knees, allowing his relaxed forelegs to dangle on either side of her. She staggered a little under his weight, readjusted her feet and was still again.

The mating lasted perhaps thirty seconds: I was far too fascinated at being privileged to witness this incredible scene to bother looking at my watch.

The December light was poor but Edward nevertheless took photographs from the back porch. We knew the results could not be perfect but they could easily be a unique record.

When the mating was over both deer shook themselves and wandered calmly off. I brewed coffee and tried to sort out the jumble of my thoughts and emotions.

The first and most important thing was that Cervus had proved beyond all doubt that I was justified in my original thinking: a hand-raised fawn could, if correctly treated, be rehabilitated and become completely independent — even though originally imprinted on a human.

Cervus is now true to his own self with undivided loyalties.

How strong is a deer's territorial instinct? Had Cervus returned to his home ground during those three long years of waiting, I would have known it. It was a reasonable assumption that he had not done so. Was the push of fear greater than the pull of home—like Judy's? Or was he perhaps made to run so far beyond all his usual boundaries that he actually was lost and forgot his territory? Did he return merely because he had chosen a doe who just happened to be in his old domain? Having mated at Ravenshill would he remember and return in the spring when his antlers dropped?

They had mated on December 4. Tristesse fed regularly on the lawn during her seven-month pregnancy. On July 15 she brought her ten-day-old baby to feed on the lawn. How many ordinary people can be so fortunate as I was to have this precise information about a wild animal? First Vixen, then Higi and now Cervus.

I observed the fawn's progress through teaching and grooming and weaning. He is a little over four months old as I write and is sprouting two knobs under the skin of his bony little head. Cervus II.

He lies or eats some distance from his dam but watches with her in the mornings from the terrace. They can see me through the window as I dress. They turn their heads to listen for the grain-bin's rattle and arrive to feed—she with long strides, he at a charming, very young-looking prancing trot, tail high. They groom each other between mouthfuls. This is how it should have been for Cervus I.

This is the fourth year since Cervus disappeared and he has returned, but only for a day. It is December again and once more he follows Tristesse. His son ran away from his unknown sire and for a few days was a lonely fawn.

This time Cervus is in competition with a younger buck and as I have seen Tristesse running in season only once and alone, I cannot tell if she has mated, or with which buck.

Cervus is nine-and-a-half years old and his face is considerably whiter than last year. Strong and healthy as he seems to be, it is probably time for a younger male to supplant him.

Cervus lived with me for five years and I almost broke my heart when he disappeared. But he lived and returned for two brief visits a year apart, and he leaves another son to carry his bloodline.

The experience has left me with feelings compounded of pride, thankfulness, admiration and a great welling of gratitude that Cervus' tragic beginning as a needlessly sickly fawn has culminated in this supremely beautiful, princely buck.

The woods are by no means always sad. Higi and Higlet danced about, always at the double, always busy, for nearly six years. Both have borne litters each year in one or another of our nest boxes. Sos disappeared after she was released with Douglas and I never saw her again. But two years after they were given back to nature I noticed a squirrel busily eating from Higi's nut bowl, which was in its usual place at my feet. Since Higi and Higlet were regular visitors I took no particular notice.

The next day the same thing happened, except that I was more observant. The squirrel at the bowl was a full-grown male. This was extraordinary. No male squirrel had entered the house since Douglas left — with his half-tail distinctively white-tipped. This one had a full-length bushy brush of brown and black hairs.

He continued to eat, regarding me out of bead-bright eyes.

I ventured a hand towards him — slowly, slowly. He held his ground. I touched his head with my finger, fully expecting to be bitten. He went on eating calmly as though I was not there.

The following day he reappeared. I casually strolled over to him. (A casual-seeming approach to animals nearly always works best — especially when there is some question as to how they might respond). The squirrel looked up but went on eating. I sat down and held out a peanut at knee height. He hesitated, then leapt up my trouser leg onto my knee, gently taking the nut from between my fingers.

Who could he be? It was past the breeding season; Higi and Higlet were already nursing families nearby. So why should a male turn up, unless perhaps he had been dispossessed of his territory?

After a day or two I ventured to stroke him. Cupping my hand, I ran it down his head to the nape of his neck, then on along both flanks, even to his delicate paws.

By now I could stand the suspense no longer. Boldly I took his tail between thumb and forefinger and gently felt my way up it, feeling the flexible vertebrae like minute beads on a string. When my fingers reached the mid-point they encountered a lump — a most palpable lump.

Was I expecting it? It's hard to say. It was so improbable. Mammals don't (surely?) sprout new tails? Yet the evidence of my fingers — and later, when I could part the hair and look, of my eyes — told me that this must be Douglas with a new tail, complete and properly colored all the way to its tip. The fact that he had been imprinted on me in infancy would account for his remarkable tameness now.

Nature gives as well as she withholds. Once more I felt profoundly grateful for her sometimes inscrutable kindnesses.

*   *   *   *   *

There remains one more wildling whose tale is not yet all told. Vixen. Her depredations upon our population of wild birds were so great that for a long time I had worried what was best to do for all concerned.

The decision was more or less made for me abruptly one morning when I looked out to see that a family of wild mallards was short yet another member — from eleven to seven in two weeks. As if that was not enough, two of the survivors had badly mauled feet; the poor little things either hobbled along on one leg or dragged themselves on their bellies, the injured foot trailing painfully. Vixen again, I feared.

I remembered Dooleykind — the orphan mallard — and some baby pheasants. I had never dared to leave them in their pens unguarded lest Vixen arrive; she would have pulled their heads through the wire to certain death. I remembered, too, the little owl she had killed.

Now another screech owl was raising her brood. It would probably only be a matter of time before she got them. Meanwhile our swallows, not to mention a golden-crowned kinglet and various juncos, robins and doubtless other birds, had all had their nests robbed of eggs or young by this sly little marauder — so elegantly furred, so agile, charming and fascinating to watch.

Vixen, a minority of one, was taking appalling toll of a majority of peaceful creatures. She had to go. The sentence must be exile from Ravenshill.

Which meant that she had to be re-located. But where? And how? I thought of various places to take her, discarding them for equally various reasons: not enough food; too many people; too near home, and so on.

I would miss her, I knew, and was still half inclined to let her stay — until I recollected that by accepting her at Ravenshill I had introduced a predator into the sanctuary I was striving to create. Admittedly wild raccoons inhabit the surrounding woods and had always done so — I had released one there myself — but they ranged over their own territories. Vixen would stay close to hand, probably hunting a smaller range than theirs. Wild raccoons, in any event, were discouraged by Mr. Bentley's presence. But Vixen was used to him.

As if to help me make up my mind, she appeared at the door, churring softly and charmingly. Very disarming! I fed her and let her ransack my pockets. When the last nut was gone and I was about to rise she suddenly jumped up and grabbed my bare forearm, inflicting a four-pronged bite which bled profusely and was extremely painful.

For once I cried out: "You little bitch!" My painting hand which earned me my living had only just healed from her last attack and I was sore in more senses than one. It really wasn't fair! I had groomed her, petted her and fed her, again — and again. I had never lifted a hand against her in anger.

I thought of some of the sentimental books written about raccoons, best-sellers that reached vast numbers of credulous people, especially children. In them the 'coon is invariably portrayed as the most gentle, the most delightful, the most amiable of pets, submitting to all sorts of indignities at the hands of children and their other playful pets. I had been charmed myself until I began some serious research into the real nature of this handsome predator. Intelligent, yes; but once mature, few raccoons are gentle or amiable; they usually become suspicious, mean and vicious unless they are handled daily in captivity.

From these idealized descriptions hundreds of children and adults have been tempted to acquire a raccoon — and there are people who cater to this vile kind of market in wild animals. In the long run it is the raccoons who suffer the most. They are soon rejected after they revert to their wild ways. Then any notion of the owner's responsibliity for having turned a wild creature into a semi-domestic pet is forgotten (if, indeed, there was any awareness of responsibility in the first place), and the poor animal is either turned loose, wholly unprepared, to fend for itself; or else is killed to protect the children, who should never have been allowed to own it in the first place.

Vixen at least would suffer neither fate. She had been reared on the principle that she must be able to live wild. The supplements she received from me were just that — supplements only. She was no longer gastronomically nor emotionally bound to me. All that remained was the problem of where to release her.

I thought of an uninhabited island where I knew that two other raccoons had been released. The shores would abound with small crustaceans and fish beloved of raccoons. So I contacted a wildlife biologist and explained the predicament. He drove over with a live-trap, designed to catch animals without hurting them.

Feeling like Judas, I baited the trap with Vixen's favorite peanuts. She came to my call, trundling past her drainpipe and across the lawn for the last time. She ate unconcernedly from my hand as I sat next to the apparatus. She was curious about the cage and investigated it without fear (it was not yet set). When she seemed to take it for granted I set the trap mechanism.

She walked in and the door slammed shut. The burdened trap was loaded into the truck and a little bit of me went with that wild, caged, desperately distressed raccoon.

I could not accompany Vixen on her lonely journey into exile. But I was told later that it ended well. As soon as she was released the panic left her. She strolled almost casually out of the trap to the shore of her new home. She remained nearby for an hour or so, unhurriedly exploring. When the biologist left she was heading inland, ignoring the tempting food put out for her on the beach.

Although I had hated to part with one of my orphans, I remained convinced that the decision was wise for all concerned. Vixen could live a long life on her island. She could mate, bear other litters, and live out her natural life-span, unmolested. In the meantime my other charges could once more breathe reasonably securely.

So ended the tale of Vixen's life at Ravenshill.

But three years later something happened which brought the memory of her back to haunt me.

One cold night I heard a clang as the lid of our ancient garbage can was knocked to the ground. A scuffling sound came from within. I went to the porch and a shadowy form clambered out and ran off across the lawn. A raccoon.

The next night I set out some pieces of brown bread on the porch, then went inside to see if anything would happen. After a while not one but three raccoons appeared. Tentatively, one ventured up the steps and the others followed, taking the bread avidly. One of them, a male, was crippled. A front leg was paralyzed from the shoulder down and the fingers of his once-beautiful little hand were shrivelled and bent. He walked on three legs and had great difficulty eating because he could not use both hands. Half his tail was missing.

The two females were in good shape. Although one stayed only for a few nights, the injured male and the second female were around for many weeks, taking food from within a foot of where I stood.

It is possible that in spite of all that had happened and all the time that had elapsed, these were Eenie, Meenie and little Mo. How else account for their immediate tameness and familiarity with our back porch if they were not Vixen's offspring?

In time the two left and I saw them no more. But there are still raccoons at Ravenshill. I see them occasionally running in the moonlight. They still try to raid the fat from the bird feeders and I still have to hang the hummingbirds' syrup where they cannot get at it during the night.

*   *   *   *   *

Which brings me last, but by no means least, back to dear old Mr. Bentley himself, who has faithfully followed his way in and out of the pages of this book. He has reached the venerable age of sixteen. His face is snow-white and he is a little gaunt. But his eyes are bright, his step sure and his hearing hardly impaired. He sleeps a lot these days, serene in the knowledge that he is much loved and that all his little comforts will be provided.

On fine days he potters happily about, now and then starting a project as in his younger days — digging up a tree root and literally tearing it with tooth and nail. For hours he hunts rabbits through the bush (they hear him coming and take off, but he hunts just the same). As a result of all this activity he remains in good shape and his teeth are almost as white as a puppy's. Apart from his lapse from grace over Flo, for which he was long ago forgiven, he is tolerant and gentle with all my special creatures. We hope he will remain with us for many happy years.

Meanwhile the seasons come and go, each bringing some new animal to nurse and return to the wild. Ravenshill has taught me many things. Most of all I have come to realize as never before that when humans interfere with nature something always goes wrong, despite good intentions. And once things are out of kilter, we cannot restore the balance. Better to leave them alone and watch and learn, than to meddle. And if, as is constantly happening to me, there arrive on one's doorstep creatures whose lives have already been meddled with — whether they have been trapped; or their mother has been killed, as Vixen's was; or whether they have been found seemingly abandoned, like Cervus — then one must make every effort to do what is best for them, rather than jeopardize their lives for the sake of a momentary, selfish whim.

Whatever sales people or sentimental books may state, WILD ANIMALS DO NOT MAKE GOOD PETS. Captivity, no matter how 'kind', is always cruel.

The pretty squirrel is anxious to move fast; it has no desire to be petted or cuddled, and is endlessly frustrated in a cage — a treadmill is no substitute for a tree.

Fawns grow into big, difficult animals, especially bucks, whose response to the frustrations of captivity during the rutting season I have already referred to.

It is the nature of raccoons to attack anyone entering their territory once they become adult, no matter how much you try to kid yourself they won't bite you.

And birds of types that have not been reared for generations in cages should have all outdoors to fly in.

True, Archimedes seemed contented enough — superficially. He survived for three years, well fed and in good condition apart from his maimed wing; and he had a whole house to move about in. But I wish he could have been free outside.

196

And I am appalled by the abominable traffic in exotic pets, imported under conditions of shameful cruelty which few people are aware of, to satisfy the neurotic desires of lonely or sensation-hungry people. Most of these animals become nuisances to the average person once the novelty has worn off because of the time-consuming amount of care and cleaning required. And captive animals are subject to innumerable ills due to wrong feeding, mental and physical frustration and lack of proper exercise.

It is also essential — and salutary — to realize that wildlings never give anything of themselves to humans. That some may sometimes appear to do so is merely a mark of our own vanity. Wild creatures owe loyalty to no man. Love and tenderness are a one-way affair — from human to animal. For the animal, removed from its natural surroundings, the human is only a means to an end — a source of food and shelter. Nothing more.

I do not believe that zoos, even the most enlightened and the best managed, perform any truly useful function. They cause animals to be captured on their behalf, for gain. Do you really feel that the suffering imposed on these helpless creatures is justified merely to show people what an animal looks like? As to the 'rehabilitation programmes', I question whether these much-publicized happenings are not actually organized as a sop to public opinion and a means by certain zoo-owners to rustle up more donations and bequests from trusting and gullible people.

Through arrogance and greed our planet is being destroyed and unless we act quickly it will very soon be too late to reverse the tide of extinction that threatens about 280 species of mammals, 350 types of birds, and 20,000 varieties of plant life.

The price of survival is education and eternal vigilance. Each of us must do whatever he can.

But what can a single person do to influence politicians, faceless bureaucrats, calculating executives and unthinking shareholders in menacing giant industries?

Rachel Carson was only one person; yet alone she made the whole world aware. Nor was she unique. All progressive legislation has always had its genesis in the mind of one person. In the long run it is the cumulative effect that matters. One can do much. And one and one and one can move mountains.

At Ravenshill — a mere speck on the earth's surface — we have done our best by conserving a place where native wild creatures can continue to live unmolested. Visitors, enchanted by glimpses of animals they do not normally see, are influenced, not by lectures, but by nature herself. She seems to touch hidden springs deep within them.

They see things afresh and gain a new respect for her ways. They realize that dead or dying trees they thought were 'in the way' (of tidiness) become rich stores of food for living things. Woods that are too tidy are barren places. Weeds, too, are precious, for they provide food and housing for multitudes of small creatures. Swampy areas, bane of urban developers, are priceless habitats for all manner of live things and we drain them at our peril. Made aware of this for the first time, people look with new eyes at vacant lots or the untidy areas in their gardens, and leave them alone.

Most rewarding of all are the voluntary vows like Timothy's never again to kill a creature for 'sport'.

Ravenshill exerts a quiet spell over all kinds of people who come to sit and stare at trees and water or the mesmerizing shimmer of hummingbirds. Tensions disappear and voices that were strident with nerves soften. Often we hear people sigh, particularly when a wild animal appears, lending a fairytale quality unknown to people accustomed to city life.

As for us, we experience a second-hand glow. We cannot take the credit since we have done nothing. It is Ravenshill that has worked the miracle.

Notes

CANADA GEESE

Come in several sizes, from the huge 3-foot bird prized by hunters on the Prairies (*Branta canadensis moffitti*) to the smallest (*B. c. minima*) — the 'Cackling Canada', which is not much bigger than a mallard. (Lester, Judy and The Admiral were probably 'Vancouver' birds — *B.c. fulva.*)

GOLDFISH

Indoors: goldfish should be in oblong, open-top tanks. On no account should they be placed in circular glass bowls with in-curved tops. Plants such as duck-weed *Lemna minor* or water milfoil *Myriophyllum spicatum* should be provided; also rocks and sand or soil.

Goldfish detest *new* water, especially water that is chlorinated or contaminated by copper piping. If natural pond water is not available, de-chlorinating tablets are sold.

The fish grow in direct ratio to the surface of the water they live in. Each requires twenty square inches of surface for every inch of its body. Depth is not critical so long as it can immerse itself. The surface area regulates the amount of available oxygen. If it is not correctly calculated the fish will die. They will also die from over-feeding. In both cases they swim to the surface gasping for oxygen.

One fish three inches long, or three one inch long, require a surface area of sixty square inches. A 12'' × 20'' (240 square inches) tank can safely hold four 3-inch or two 6-inch fish.

Outdoors: once built, a concrete pool cannot be moved, so plan it carefully. Make it in an open, sunny location. Trees and shrubs overhanging the water produce too much shade and falling leaves rot and give off toxic gases. One end of the pool should be about six inches deep, graded at the other end to as deep as the land and your pocket will allow. Dump in about two inches of rich topsoil.

Waterlilies in pots can be planted in moderation. Too many leaves give too much shade and deprive the pool of oxygen.

Feeding: Once a day during spring and summer. Taper off in fall from daily to every two or three days to once a week. By November outdoor goldfish go into semi-hibernation and should not be fed, even if they appear at the surface on warmer days. Indoor fish require feeding all year.

Mosquito larvae, frog eggs, small insects, tadpoles, are common natural foods outdoors. Indoors or out excellent foods are freeze-dried worms, brine shrimp; and daphnia (found in shallow ponds). Some packaged meal-type fish-foods have been known to cause the disease salmonella—transmissible to humans, and are best avoided.

HUMMINGBIRDS

The information in these notes is to help you attract hummingbirds to your garden, if you live in one of the areas mentioned in Chapter Ten. I wish to emphasize the fact that it is both illegal and cruel to take a hummingbird from its nest, or to capture one at any time. A stunned bird that has hit a window may be brought indoors and put in a warm dark place, such as a small carton or covered cage, to rest quietly. Put paper towels on the bottom and provide a firm twig about ⅛-inch in diameter, since hummingbirds must perch. No other treatment may be necessary and the bird may be released in an hour or so, providing there is sufficient daylight left for it to take its evening meal. If the bird has to be kept overnight for this reason, offer the food formula given below (make a small phial from a bottle or plastic pill container by drilling a small hole in the centre of the cap). Do not attempt to force-feed.

The recipe is simple to make and is as nearly balanced to a hummingbird's natural food as is possible using artificial ingredients. Commercial humming-bird foods are based on refined sugar. *Do not use them.*

Be prepared for your feeders to become popular. They must be kept filled at all times as the birds become dependent on the supplement to their natural diet. If you are not prepared to do this work, don't please, put out feeders at all — ever.

Make up one cup of feed (see second formula) and hang out a feeder a week or so before the birds' anticipated arrival in your area. Renew the formula after a week if no birds have yet arrived. Increase the number of feeders as the number of birds increases. Place the feeders where they can feed in flight, without obstruction and out of reach of domestic pets.

Nine-ounce glass commercial feeders are well made and fairly easy to clean; they are supplied with red plastic 'flowers' which may be put on until the birds begin to arrive regularly (a week at most). Then remove these 'flowers' because they are angled awkwardly for in-flight feeding.

Feeders are easily made from screw-top glass bottles: drill a 1/16th-inch hole in the centre of the cap and test that the bottle is airtight or it will leak. Do not use plastic bottles which expand and leak in warm weather. Special bee-guards are sold for commercial feeders and are very useful to keep bees and wasps from the syrup in late summer.

Be sure feeders are filled before dusk for the late and very early morning feeds. Nesting birds need it desperately, as do the fledgling babies. In any case, you won't want to get up at four o'clock in the morning, which is about the time hummingbirds begin to feed!

Hummingbirds consume five times their body weight a day (16 hours); 70% of their food is flower nectar (which we approximate with honey); their requirements for protein and fat are low in comparison — 3% each, consisting of some

500-600 fruit and other tiny flies, minute spiders and various insects. Vitamins, minerals and trace elements take up about 1% and the rest is water.

It is important to remember these requirements when formulating artificial feed. If a hummingbird is given syrup containing too much protein or fat, it will still eat (sip) because it must obtain its quota of honey; but in doing so, unavoidably eats too much of the other factors. Unless a correct balance is restored, the little bird will in time sicken from sheer indigestion and constipation and will eventually die.

Many food supplements have been tried by individuals and in zoos around the world, with poor results because mixtures containing raw egg yolk, fruit flies, crushed meal worms, etc. cannot be homogenized. A hummingbird cannot sip liquid which contains ingredients that rise to the surface, or sink. Therefore the diet is immediately unbalanced and a sick bird results; it, too, will eventually die.

The following formula has been found satisfactory for maintenance of health, alertness and aggressiveness; there is no need to alter it for the night feed as recommended by some 'experts'. Proportions in the two recipes are the same, only quantities differ. Do not try to reduce further or you will not be able to calculate amounts small enough (let alone measure them) to produce a balanced ration.

TO MAKE THE FORMULA
  Boil more water than you need for at least two minutes. Unboiled city water may cause cancer in hummingbirds.
  Measure exact amount needed
  Melt honey in a little hot (not boiling) water from measured amount
  Add balance of measured, boiled water when cool
  Add powdered supplement and stir or beat until mixture is completely homogenized
  Add vitamin drops to total quantity, bottle, and store in refrigerator, where it will keep 3 or 4 days.
In warm weather the formula may turn sour and the honey turn syrupy (i.e. drop in 'strings'). If your birds leave your feeders alone this will be the reason. Change the formula after washing the bottle thoroughly.

FORMULA to feed about 40 birds per day
  water (boiled)   800 grams (26-1/2 ounces OR 3-1/3 cups)
  honey (unpasteurized)   121 grams (4 ounces OR 1/2 cup)
  powdered supplement   38 grams (1-1/4 ounces
                               (OR
                               (2 tablespoons + 1-1/2 teaspoons)
  liquid vitamins   10 drops

SAME FORMULA to feed up to 10 birds per day
  water (boiled)   240   grams (8 ounces OR 1 cup)
  honey (unpasteurized)   30.25 grams (1 ounce OR 2 tablespoons)
  powdered supplement   9.5 grams (1/4 ounce
                               (OR
                               (1 tablespoon + 1 teaspoon)
  liquid vitamins   2 drops

POWDERED SUPPLEMENTS

The following powdered supplements are suitable. The author prefers the first two: NEKTAR-MIL II*, SIMILAC, MELLINS BABY FOOD, CASILAN, COMPLAN, SUPER-HYDRAMIN.

WATER-SOLUBLE LIQUID VITAMINS

AVITRON (for birds, at pet stores), ABDEC, MULTIBIONTA*

RACCOONS

Have 12 incisor teeth, 4 canines, 16 premolars and 8 molars. There are 31 species and subspecies under the family name *Procyonidae* plus a subgenus *Euprocyon*. The first named includes the coatimundi and kinkajou, and in China the famous giant panda. You cannot see a raccoon in the wild outside the western hemisphere where their territory covers a range northwards to include parts of Canada, southwards to latitude 10°, Panama and across the United States, except for a small gap. They live on islands off the west coast of Mexico, the Bahamas and Lesser Antilles. The northern limit is Vancouver Island.

There is an interesting difference between Vixen's relatives and the lone subgenus *Euprocyon*. The members of the *Procyon* group (Vixen) have the hair on the napes of their necks lying backwards, an undercoat, and grey forearms like 'Dutch-cut' poodles. *Euprocyon* lacks an undercoat and the hair is reversed on the nape, growing forwards, like the band on the back of a Rhodesian ridgeback dog. The whole coat is shorter and denser, like a short-haired cat.

There are pale biscuit-colored raccoons in the desert regions of the United States and in these the tail rings are hardly visible. The largest sub-species, *Procyon lotor excelsus,* lives in an area which includes southeast Washington, eastern Oregon and southern Idaho. The smallest known comes from Cozumel Island, Yucatan, and is aptly named *Procyon pygmaeus*. Occasionally an albino turns up.

SQUIRRELS

Born naked and blind. Eyes open on or after the 26th day. Young are weaned between 64 and 78 days (9-11 weeks). They leave the nest at 48-57 days, before being weaned, and follow their mother to learn how to feed on adult fare, since she does not take food to them in the nest. They return to the nest of their own free will, probably driven by hunger. The mother returns to suckle them.

---

*NEKTAR-MIL II and MULTIBIONTA are obtainable in West Germany. It is necessary (but worthwhile) to have them sent privately by friends or individual pharmacies. Nektar-Mil II contains ingredients peculiarly suited to hummingbird digestion.

A COMPARISON OF THE MILK OF VARIOUS WILD & DOMESTIC ANIMALS

For the sake of clarity, the table has been abbreviated and shows the major elements only. Reference to the literature will provide more detailed analyses.

Ref.	ANIMAL	FAT	PRO-TEIN	SUGAR	ASH	WATER
1	COW					
	Jersey	4.97	3.66	4.7	0.77	average
	Guernsey	4.55	3.57	4.62	0.77	86.2
	Ayrshire	3.72	3.38	4.57	0.74	
	Shorthorn	3.56	3.32	4.51	0.76	
	Friesian	3.49	3.28	4.46	0.75	
3	Skin milk—fresh	0.07	3.52	5.02	0.78	90.6
	Skim milk—dried	1.5	32.8	47.0	7.5	10.3
4	Evaporated—undiluted, average	7.9	7.0	9.8	1.5	73.8
3	HUMAN	3.75	2.1	6.35	0.3	87.5
	DEER					
2	Columbian Black-Tailed	10.5	8.96	4.67	1.3	74.6
4	White-Tailed	15.06	11.92	3.75	1.51	67.77
2	Reindeer	22.5	10.3	2.5	1.4	63.3
3	DOG	11.8	8.65	3.25	.8	75.5
3	GOAT	7.5	4.4	4.9	.85	82.35
3 & 6	RABBIT	16.71	10.38	1.98	2.2	65.0
5	RACCOON	3.9	4.0	4.7	0.75	88.0
3	RAT	15.0	12.2	2.85	1.6	68.35
5	SEAL (Grey)	53.2	11.2	2.6	0.7	—
5	HORSE	1.6	2.65	6.15	0.5	89.1
5	CHIMPANZEE	3.7	1.2	7.0	0.21	88.1
5	MOUSE (domestic)	12.1	9.0	3.2	1.5	73.1
5	SQUIRREL (Grey)	12.6	9.2	3.4	1.4	72.4
5	CAT (domestic)	4.95	7.15	4.9	0.65	82.35
5	BEAR (Grizzly)	3.0	3.8	4.0	0.3	88.9
7	HEN (egg) — analysis included because much used in animal feeding.					
	Yolk	33.0	17.0	1.0	1.0	48.0
	White	—	11.0	1.0	—	88.0

References

1 McDONALD, P., et al. Animal Nutrition, 1966, p. 272.
2 KITTS, W.D., et al. Journal of Wildlife Management, 1956, Vol. 20, #2, pp. 212-214.
3 LINTON, R.G. Animal Nutrition & Veterinary Dietetics, 1950, pp. 221, 223.

4 SILVER, H. Journal of Wildlife Management, 1961, Vol. 25, pp. 66-70.
5 MILLER-BEN-SHAUL, D. International Zoo Yearbook, 1962, Vol. 4, pp. 334-342.
6 WHITNEY, Leon F. The Complete Book of Dog Care, 1953, p. 185.
7 MAYNARD, L.A. et al. Animal Nutrition, 1969, p. 515.